Newberry County, South Carolina

DEED ABSTRACTS

VOLUME I
Deed Books A-B
1785–1794 [1751–1794]

By

Brent H. Holcomb

SCMAR
1999

HERITAGE BOOKS
2019

HERITAGE BOOKS

AN IMPRINT OF HERITAGE BOOKS, INC.

Books, CDs, and more—Worldwide

For our listing of thousands of titles see our website
at
www.HeritageBooks.com

Published 2019by
HERITAGE BOOKS, INC.
Publishing Division
5810 Ruatan Street
Berwyn Heights, Md. 20740

Copyright © 1999 Brent H. Holcomb
SCMAR
Columbia, South Carolina

Library of Congress Catalog Card Number: 98-75025

International Standard Book Numbers
Paperbound: 978-0-7884-5868-2

INTRODUCTION

Newberry County was formed in 1785 as a county of Ninety Six District. It remained in Ninety Six District through the year 1799 for higher court cases. A small corner of Newberry County (near present-day Chapin) was a part of Orangeburgh District until 1788. In the year 1800 with the end of the county court system, Newberry County became Newberry District. In the colonial period the area of Newberry County was considered part of Craven County or Berkeley (sometimes spelled Barkley) County in South Carolina. Prior to the border surveys of 1764 and 1772, the area was included in the North Carolina counties of Anson, Mecklenburg, and Tryon. For this reason a few grants and deeds from North Carolina are referenced in the Newberry County deeds. Land grants from North Carolina are frequently referred to as "north patents." The South Carolina deeds prior to 1785 were recorded in Charleston and in some cases a few years later. The Charleston deeds have been abstracted and published through the year 1788, those from 1773-1788 by the writer. The deeds of the aforementioned North Carolina counties have also been abstracted and published. The deeds in this volume were recorded 1785-1794. As is common, there are deeds recorded from a much earlier time period. The earliest deed included in this work dates from 6 July 1751 and is found in Deed Book A, page 26. Therefore, with this work, the deed abstracts for the Newberry County area are now in print from the beginning through the year 1794. Researchers should find this work unusually helpful, as the Newberry deed indices contain references only to those instruments which are transfers of real property. Depositions, deeds of gift, and bills of sale for slaves and other personal property are not included in the index available at the Newberry County Court House and on microfilm. For that reason many of these records, containing valuable genealogical information, have gone undetected by most researchers. The instruments in this volume have been abstracted from LDS microfilm and South Carolina Archives microfilm.

The Quaker community in Newberry County is apparent in deeds included in this volume, recognizable by their "affirmations" instead of oaths and in the language such as "the fifth day of the fourth month." Other early settlers in the Newberry County area were German Protestant immigrants, and some were Germans from Pennsylvania. There were also Irish Protestant immigrants, many of whom settled in the area in and around the present town of Prosperity. As indicated in some of the deeds, there were also settlers from North Carolina and other states. Migration from Newberry County to other areas of South Carolina is apparently in deeds as well.

My thanks to Mr. James D. McKain for preparing the excellent index.

Brent H. Holcomb
May 30, 1998

SOUTH CAROLINA COUNTIES & CIRCUIT COURT DISTRICTS A.D. 1785

Compiled by Historical Records Survey, W.P.A. 1938

[at beginning of Deed Book A]: South Carolina. Pursuant to a precept to me directed by John Bremar, Esqr., Surv Genl, Bearing date February 4, 1773, I have admeasured to Samuel Sansom a tract of 100 acres on the north side of Saludy River adj. land of Thomas Eastland, certified 18 April 1773. Granted the 18th of May 1774. John Calwell, Dept. Sur.

A, 1-2: 2 Feb 1776, Robert Mars of Ninety Six District to Samuel Murray, for £150 SC money, 200 acres on a branch of Indian Creek called by the name of jutting fork adj. land of Terance Riley, Jacob Pennington, ____ Anderson. Robert Mars (Seal), Wit: Robt Johnson, William Murray, James Murray (O).

A, 3-4: Lease and release. 22 & 23 March 1785, Joseph Brown & Kezia his wife of Ninety Six District to Aron Cates of district aforesaid, for £50 sterling, tract granted 28 June 1774, recorded in Book QQQ, page 544, to Jacob Felker, 150 acres on the south side of Broad River adj. land of Robert Buzzard, conveyed by Jacob Felker to Joseph Brown by lease & release 1 April 1783. Joseph Brown (LS), Kezia Brown (LS), Wit: W. Malone, John Malone, M. Glazier.

A, 4-5: Lease and release. 30 & 31 Dec 1779, Daniel Johnston, Blacksmith, of Craven County to Wm. Malone for £250 SC money, 100 acres on a small branch of Enoree called Gossets Creek adj. land laid out to Thos Johnston. Daniel Johnston (Seal), Anne Johnston (Seal), Wit: Robt Rutherford, Benjn Hampton, Bartholomew Johnston. Proved 5 Sept 1785 in open court.

A, 6: 18 Aug 1784, Edward Connally and Mary his wife of Ninety Six District, to John Malone of same, for £100 old S'o Currency, 100 acres on a small branch of Broad River called Second Creek adj. Michael Elivine, John Souter, Daniel Johnson, Samuel Wilson, Alexander Davison, by grant dated 30 Sept 1774. Ed. Connally (Seal), Mary Connally (X) (Seal), Wit: W. Malone Sen'r, W. Malone Jnr, Benj'n Hamton.

A, 7-8: Lease and release. 8 & 9 May 1774, George Montgomery and Ann his wife of Ninety Six District, to John Knox of same, for £90 currency, 100 acres on south side Broad River part of tract surveyed for said George Montgomery, certified by John Win, Deputy Surveyor, 15 Dec 1773. George Montgomery (O) (Seal), Ann Montgomery (X) (Seal), Wit: William Johnston, Robert Johnston, Mary Johnston.

A, 9-10: 25 June 1785, Samuel Sansom, planter, to William Anderson., planter, for £30 sterling, 100 acres on north side Saludy River in Craven County formerly, adj. land of John Lang, Sansom, James Dyson, Thomas East, granted to said Samuel Sansom 18 May 1773. Samuel Sansom (S) (Seal), Wit: Mich'l McKie, Thomas Norrel, John Jackson.

A, 11-12: 17 Sept 1785, Maria Cathrina Lang, Michal Gromer her husband & George Lever her son of Ninety Six District, Newberry County, planter, to James Young of District aforesaid, wheelrite, by grant dated 6 April 1768 to Maria Cathrena Lang, 150 acres, in the fork of Broad and Saludy River on a branch of Bush River, recorded in Book DDD, page 10, now for £42 s17 sterling. Michal Gromer (Seal), George Level (Seal), Maria Cathrena Lang (mark) (Seal), Wit: John Hair (mark), Joachim Bulow, William Blair.

A, 12: 13 Nov 1785. Edmond Martin, Esqr., Sheriff of Ninety Six District, to Joachim Bulow of same, whereas Peter Karr of Savannah Town in Georgia, planter, was seized of a tract of 350 acres, and said Peter Karr became indebted to Joachim Bulow in the sum of £299 s6 d3, and at April Court held at Ninety Six last, by writ of fieri facias, sheriff sells said tract for £10 s5 sterling. Edmond Martin (Seal), Wit: Rob't Rutherford, James Creswell, Aron Cates.

A, 13-14: Lease and release. 5 Dec 1785, Robert Rutherford, sheriff of Ninety Six District, to Joachim Bulow, planter, of same, whereas Peter Karr of Savannah Town in Georgia, planter, was seized of a tract of land adj. Matthias Elmore, Wm Elmore, Rob't Bull, John Embre, 105 acres by a resurvey, part of two different tracts, and said Peter Karr became indebted to Joachim Bulow in the sum of £299 s6 d3, and at April Court held at Ninety Six last, by writ of fieri facias, sheriff sells said tract for £10 s5 sterling. Robert Rutherford (Seal), Wit: A. Robison, Henry Sumer, Thomas Boyd.

A, 15: 15 Nov 1785, Stephen Rogers & Frances his wife of Chatham County, North Carolina, to Aron Cates of Newberry County, SC, for £2 s7 sterling SC money, 100 acres on a branch on the south side of Enoree River adj. land of Joseph Fish, John Evans, Collins. Stephen Rodgers (Seal), Frances Rodgers (X) (Seal), Wit: Thos Cates Snr, Robt Cates, Thos Cates Junr.

A, 16-17: Lease and release. 27 & 28 March 1783, Jacob Furger alias Falker of Ninety Six District, planter, to Thomas Wood of same place, by grant dated 21 May 1772 to Jacob Furger alias Falker, 350 acres in the fork between Broad & Saludy Rivers adj. Wm[?] Kallor, Jacob Oxner, Uldraugh Eaynes, now conveys 200 acres, part of said 350 acres for £250. Jacob Falker (IF) (Seal), Wit: George Buckhannon, Mich'l Dickert, Chatherina Sharp (X).

A, 18-19: 23 Nov 1775, Van Davis of Ninety Six District to William Tanney of same, by grant dated 17 May 1774 to said Van Davis, 150 acres on a branch of Davies Creek between Broad & Saludy Rivers adj. Van Davis, Wm Willcocks, recorded in Book QQ, page 289, now for £300 SC money conveys to Wm Tanney. Van Davis (Seal), Wit: Robert Brooks, James Burns (X), William Willcocks.

A, 20-21: Lease and release. 2 & 3 Aug 1775, Benjamin Norwood & Mary his wife of Indian Creek in Ninety Six District, yeoman, to James Burns of same creek and district, by grant dated 23 June 1774 to said Benjamin Norwood,

150 acres on a small branch of Indian Creek adj. James Wilson, Wm. Blackburn, now for £150 SC money. Benjamin Norwood (B) (Seal), Mary Norwood (X) (Seal), Wit: Robert Brooks, William Arther, Richard Brooks.

A, 22-23: Lease and release. 27 & 28 Oct 1777, Peter Richardson of Ninety Six District and Martha his wife to David Edwards of Camden District, planter, by grant dated 12 Dec 1768 to Arthur McQueenling 100 acres in Craven County on waters of Broad River, recorded in Book CCC, page 164, and by lease and release 26 & 27 April 1771 said Arther McQueenling sold to s'd Peter Richardson, now for £450 SC money, conveyed to David Edwards. Peter Richardson (P) (Seal), Martha Richardson (Seal), Wit: John Pearson, Michal Kennamore (M).

A, 24-25: Lease and release. 26 & 27 April 1771, Arthur McQueenling of Craven County, planter, to Peter Richardson of same, planter, by grant dated 12 Dec 1776 [sic, for 1768] to Arthur McQueenling 100 acres in Craven County on waters of Broad River, now for £55 SC money. Arthur McQueenling (Seal), Elizabeth McQueenling (X) (Seal), Wit: John Gant, Joseph Smith, Thomas Cargill.

A, 26: 6 July 1751, Nicholas Durr of Berkley County, carpenter, to Frederick Arnold of same, planter, for £100 SC money, tract of 150 acres in Berkley County on Wateree Creek in Saludie fork. Nicholas Durr (Seal), Wit: Christopher Rowe, John Abram SchwerdFeger.

A, 27: State of South Carolina, Orangeburgh District. Personally appeared Jacob Vanset before me and declared on his oath that about three weeks ago he and Jacob Son being about bargain'g for a tract of land on the Wateree Creek and the s'd Jacob Son sheweth this Depon't the titles saying here is from Nicholas Farr leases to Arnold and from him to Grim this depon't asketh him where is Grim to you says Jacob Son I have them but after some time the s'd Son sayeth to this depon't he had no titles of Grim for s'd land & further this depon't sayeth not. Sworn 9 Nov 1781 before Michl Leitner, J.P. Jacob Vanset (X).

State of South Carolina, Orangeburgh District. Personally appeared Wm Newman before me and declared on this oath that about the year 1757 this depon't lived about five years in this settlement with Mr. Peter Grim and Benjamin Gregory Sen'r deceased this Deponant further sayeth that he never heard the above mentioned Grim deceased make any Bargain with a certain Jacob Son on account of a tract of land which s'd Grim had bought of one John Pearson Esq're for a Mill seat on Broad River neither did this depon't ever hear or help to divide the s'd land but to the best of his knowledge says that he heard the s'd Grim say he would have nothing to do with s'd Jacob Son and further sayeth on his oath that to the best of his knowledge this depon't was evidence to a set of titles signed over to the s'd Peter Grim by one Frederick Arnold to a certain tract of land on Wateree Creek and did see the titles delivered to s'd Grim and the s'd Grim as the deponant sayeth rented the s'd plantation to one John Cocks and after s'd Cocks left the plantation one Fight Ketinger came to live on the s'd plantation. April 5th 1783. Wm. Newman before Michl. Leitner, J.P.

A, 28: State of South Carolina, Ninety Six District. Receivd of Mr. John Folmar full satisfaction for a certain piece of land upon the Wateree Creek between Saluda & Broad Rivers which was some time ago in Dispute between me and Peter Crim and will have from this day foreward no further claim, 4th Feb 1784. Geo Jacob Son. Wit: Joachim Bulow.

A, 29-30: 28 March 1780. Joseph White of Ninety Six District to Nicholas Eveleigh of same, by conveyance dated 20 Feb 1767 by Patrick Reiley to s'd Joseph White, 200 acres on Saludy River adj. s'd river and land since surveyed by Elizabeth Jones, and grant to Distree Miller, recorded in Book OO, page 213, also by another conveyance by Joseph Cruse to Joseph White 20 May 1773, 79 acres, part of 100 acres granted to John McDugal 30 May 1768, recorded in Book DDD, page 228, also a memorial entered in Book I No. 9, page 87, 7 Sept 1768, adj. land of Joseph White, William Furlow, Joseph Freeman, now for £60,000 SC money. Joseph White (Seal), Wit: Wm Freeman, William Sergeant.

A, 31-33: 18 Nov 1785, James Mason of Ninety Six District to Nicholas Eveleigh of same, for ten shillings sterling, 50 acres on north side of Saludy River, grant recorded in Book EEEE, page 273. Jas Mason (Seal), Wit: W. Swift, Hugh Henry.

A, 34-35: 12 Nov 1785, John Turner of Ninety Six District to Nicholas Eveleigh of same, for 28,00 weight of neat inspected merchantable tobacco, five negroes Carolina, Madeira, Nanny, Cinda, and June. John Turner (X) (Seal), Wit: Jas Mason, Wm. Swift.

A, 36-37: 30 Nov 1785, Edmond Martin, Esq'r, Sheriff of Ninety Six District, to Joseph Kennerly, planter, of same, whereas the administrator of Fredrick Dubbert of Ninety Six District, planter, was seized of a tract adj. lands of Adam Setzler & Bundrick, 325 acres, and said Dubert became indebted unto Richard Strother in the sum of £55 SC money, payable on or before April Court last held at Orangeburgh, and said Richard Strother in April Term did implead s'd Jones and Catarna admrs. in the court of common pleas, by write of fieri facias, sheriff sells to Joseph Kennerly for £38 sterling. Edmond Martin (Seal), Wit: Robert Rutherford, Joachim Bulow, A. Cates.

A, 38-39: 10 Dec 1773, Conrad Gallman of Nobles Creek, Granvil County, planter, to Fredrick Dubber, Min'r of the Gospel, for £200 SC money, 125 acres, being the middle part of a tract of 450 acres granted to Henry Gallman deceased, in Berkley County on Cannons Creek in the fork of Broad & Saludy Rivers adj. land of Adam Setzler, John Fredrick Dubbert, George Hughes, Gosper Gallman. John Conrad Gallman (Seal), Wit: John Gallman, Johannas Murff[?] (X).

A, 40-41: 10 Dec 1773, Herman Gallman of Nobles Creek, Granvil County, miller and planter, to Fredrick Dubbert, Min'r of the Gospel, in Craven County, for £400 SC money, 200 acres, being the north east part of 450 acres granted to Henry Gallman deceased in Berkley County on Cannons Creek in the fork of Broad River adj. Adam Setzler, Nicholas Bundrick, Conrad Gallman (sold to Revd. John Frederick Dubbert). Herman Gallman (Seal), Henry Gallman, George Stroub Jr.

A, 42-43: South Carolina, Ninety Six District. 8 Nov 1785, Thomas Eastland of district aforesaid to William Stripling of same, for £500 sterling, 150 acres granted to Thomas Eastland 27 Nov 1770 adj. Coleman Brown. Thomas Eastland (Seal), Wit: George Goggans, William Irby, William Blandon.

A, 44-45: 18 Oct 1785, John Holman & Christian his wife to John Lester of same, for £22 s16 d9 sterling, 50 acres, taken off a tract of 250 acres in Newberry County, Ninety Six District, on waters of Big Saluda on north side in the fork between Broad & Saluda Rivers, adj. James Lester Sen'r, granted to said John Holman 3 Feb 1767. John Holman (X) (Seal), Christian Holman (mark) (Seal), Wit: James Williams, Ellis Pugh, Timothy Thomas.

A, 46: 17 March 1785, Richard Strother of Camden District to James Hord of Ninety Six District, for £50 sterling, 350 acres between Saludy & Broad Rivers adj. land laid out to Johannes Keller, granted to Johannes Trayer 27 Aug 1751. Richard Strother (Seal), Wit: Wm Hutchison, John Buckhanan.

A, 47-48: 20 April 1786, John Mackleduff & Fenter Mackleduff his wife, William Mackleduff & Daniel Mackleduff of Union County, SC, to David Sims of the State of Virginia, for £300 sterling, 200 acres in Newberry County in the fork of Broad & Saludy Rivers on south side Tyger River, granted to Thomas Mckelduff 12 Oct 1755, the said John Mackleduff being heir at law to his grandfather Thos McKleduff. John McKleduff (Seal), Fenter McKleduff (Seal), William McKleduff (Seal), Wit: Thos Gordon, Reubin Sims, W. Hardwick.

A, 49-50: 26 Oct 1785, Moses Embree, farmer, of State of North Carolina, to James Wadlington, planter, of Newberry County, for £108 s15 sterling, 150 acres on a branch of Bush River, land formerly granted to Benjamin Busby. Moses Embree (Seal), Margaret Embree (Seal), Wit: Enos Elleman, John Elleman, John Embree.

[pages 51-52 blank]

A, 53-54: 17 Jan 1786, John Embree of State of Georgia, planter, and Mary his wife, to Samuel Pearson & Mercer Babb in company or fellowship, of Newberry County, planter, of Newberry County, for £10 sterling, 5 acres in the fork of Broad & Saludy Rivers in Newberry County on Bush River, land formerly granted to Stephen Elmore 2 April 1762 and conveyed by him to

John Embree. John Embree (Seal), Mary Embree (M) (Seal), Wit: Enoch Pearson, Jesse Toland, Jesse Embree.

A, 55-56: 31 May 1786, Mathew Brooks of Ninety Six District, Newberry County, planter, to Henry Stedham of same, planter, for £40 sterling, 200 acres on a branch of Saludy River called Beaver Dam, 200 acres granted to said Mathew Brooks 29 April 1768. Mathew Brooks (Seal), Agness Brooks (X) (Seal), Wit: Enos Elleman, Mercer Babb, Samuel Pearson.

A, 57-58: 2 June 1786, Mathew Brooks of Ninety Six District, Newberry County, planter, to Jonathan Taylor of same, planter, for £40 sterling, 100 acres in Berkley County at the time of surveying now Newberry County on waters Beaver Dam a small branch of Saludy River, adj. William Nelson, James Brooks, granted to said Mathew Brooks. Mathew Brooks (Seal), Agness Brooks (X) (Seal), Wit: Enos Elleman, Mercer Babb, Samuel Pearson.

A, 59-60: 3 May 1786, Samuel Pearson & Mary his Newberry County to Henry Steddam of same, for £10 sterling, tract on a small branch of Little River, waters of Saludy River, called the Mill Creek, tract formerly granted 29 April 1768 to Mary Stiddem now Pearson. Samuel Pearson (Seal), Mary Pearson (mark) (Seal), Wit: Enos Elleman, Mercer Babb, Joshua Inman.

A, 61-62: 3 Feb 1786, Joachim Bulow of Charleston, merchant, to Samuel Pearson & Mercer Babb in Company or fellowship, both of Newberry County, for £300 sterling, 104 acres formerly granted to Moses Embree by John Embree, part of two tracts formerly granted the one to Conrad Imick[?] 20 Jan 1771 and conveyed to Stephen Elmore to John Embree & John Embreee to Moses Embree then to Joachim Bulow & Peter Karr, the said Karr became possessed of the whole tract but s'd Joachim Bulow having obtained a judgment the other to Stephen Elmore 2 April 1762, on both side of Bush River adj. Matthias Elmore, including the meeting house land. Joachim Bulow (Seal), Aemelia Bulow (X) (Seal), Wit: Joshua Inman, Jacob Toland, Burr Johnston warden of the city.

A, 63-64: 2 March 1787, William Gillum, farmer, of Newberry County, for £7 s3 sterling, to James Wadlington, planter, of same, 10 acres, part of tract he now lives on, in the fork between Broad & Saludy Rivers & on a branch of Bush River adj. land formerly granted to Benjamin Busby, Mary Taylor. William Gillum (X) (Seal), Wit: Mercer Babb, Jacob Toland, Jane Wadlington (X).

A, 65: ____ Sept 1785, Joseph Caldwell of Newberry County to Nathan Fike of same, for £30 sterling, 100 acres on a small branch of Indian Creek, granted to John Caldwell Junr, plat dated 20 Sept 1774, grant dated 8 Dec 1774, recorded in Book TTT, page 510. Joseph Caldwel (Seal), Wit: Rob't Rutherford, Tho's B. Rutherford, James Dawkins.

A, 66-68: Lease and release. 15 & 16 Sept 1774, Michael Livistone of Ninety Six District, planter, to John William Houseal of same place, planter, by grant dated 4 July 1754 to Hans Peter Veyman [sic, for Weyman?], 250 acres in the fork of Broad & Saludy Rivers on Cannons Creek one of the south branches of Broad River, properly transferred unto the s'd Mich'l Livistone 2 & 3 July 1773, now for £200 SC money conveyed to Jno Wm Houseal. Mich ____ [German signature] (LS), Rosina Livistone (X) (LS), Wit: Martin Single, Phillipp Metz [German signature]. Proved 28 Jan 1775 by the oath of Martin Single before Mich'l Dickert, J.P. Recorded 12 March 1792.

A, 69-70: 21 Dec 1774, Jonathan Taylor of Ninety Six District, planter, to William Taylor, son of said Jonathan Taylor, of same, planter, by grant dated 15 Feb 1769 to William Gillem, tract of 500 acres in the fork between Broad & Saludy Rivers on a small branch of Bush Creek, and said William Gillum for £150 conveyed to Jonathan Taylor, 14 July 1774, 250 acres, part of said tract of 500 acres, now for £250 to William Taylor. Jonathan Taylor (Seal), Mary Taylor (Seal), Wit: Richard Taylor, "Dutch Name," Eleanor Taylor.

A, 71-72: 4 Jan 1772, Benjamin Inman & Jemima his wife of Berkley County, SC, to Mercer Babb of same, by grant of 250 acres adj. land of William Gillum, now for £150 SC money. Benjamin Inman (Seal), Jemima Inman (mark) (Seal), Wit: Samuel Nelson, Joshua Inman, George Nicols (mark).

A, 73-74: 3 July 1783, George Jacob Son, of Ninety Six District, doctor, to Nimrod Morries of same, planter, by grant to Frederick Scrader dated 8 March 1755, 200 acres in the fork of Broad & Saludy Rivers adj. land laid out to John George Resinger, Herman Geiger deceased, John George Infinger, recorded in Book PP, page 409, and conveyed 11 & 12 Oct 1756 by said Frederick Scrader to Jacob Cooner and from said Jacob Cooner and Sarah his wife to William Harris 5 & 6 Nov 1756 and by said William Harris to said Jacob Sons, now to Nimrod Morris for £72 sterling. Geo. Jacob Son (Seal), Wit: John Buchannan Sen'r, Michl Dickert, "Dutch Name."

A, 75: 9 Dec 1784, Daniel Gaurtman of Ninety Six District, planter, to Richard Strother of same, planter, for two shillings, 300 acres including three separate tracts, the first of 50 acres between Saludy & Broad Rivers, the second of 100 acres adj. land of Adam George Keller, John George Infinger, estate of Hermand Geiger deceased, Hans Jacob Morff, and the third 150 acres in Craven County on Second Creek adj. land granted to Maryann Smitten, John Murff, estate of Hermond Geiger, Charles Maty. Daniel Gartman (Seal), Cateran Gartman (X) (Seal), Wit: Jno Buchannan Sen'r, Joseph Swindler, W. Hancock. Recorded 5 March 1787.

[Page 76 is blank.]

A, 77-78: 26 Sept 1785, Philip Grober of Ninety Six District, planter, to James Grayham of same, planter, by grant dated 24 Jan 1759 to Philip Grober 100 acres in the forks of Broad & Saludy, recorded in Book TT, page 200, now conveyed for £150. Philip Gruber (Seal), Wit: Wm. Cauldwell, Henry Anderson, Jeremiah Williams.

A, 79: 27 Dec 1784, Samuel Wilson of Richmond Co., Georgia, to John Hampton of Ninety Six District, SC, for £42 17/2 sterling 200 acres between Broad & Saludy Rivers on a small branch of Broad River called Second Creek, bounded then by vacant lands on al sides but since joyn'd by Edw'd Connally, Daniel Johnson, Alexander Johnson & Joseph Hogg, grant recorded in Book WW, page 106, entered in the Auditor Gen'r office in Book F. No. 6, page 251, 4 April 1764. Samuel Wilson (X) (Seal), Wit: W. Malone Sen'r, George Johnson, Alexander Johnston.

A, 80: Adam Summer Sen'r of Orangeburgh District, planter, for love, good will & effection to my loving son Adam Summer Jun'r of same, planter, 50 acres, part of tract granted to Elizabeth Cabler in Craven county on waters of Broad River adj. line of Adam Summer, Amigh, to the land whereon William Summer now lives, dated 2 Dec 1784. Adam Summer Sen'r (A) (Seal), Wit: Mich'l Dickert, John Follmer, Henry Amigh (HE).

A, 81: 30 May 1786. Catharene Edwards & Benjamin Ketchener her son for £5 sterling to Thos Gordon, both of Newberry County, 100 acres on south side Enoree River adj. Joshua Anderson. Benjamin Ketchener (mark) (Seal), Catharene Edwards (mark) (Seal), Wit: John Follmer, John Sweightenburgh, Isaiah Shirer.

A, 82: 31 Dec 1785, Mary Wicker of Newberry County, widow of Mathias Wicker decd., to Gabriel Anderson of same, for £100 lawful money, 100 acres granted to Mary Rittlehover maiden on the Bounty, 25 May 1774, recorded in Book GGG, 1701 [sic], and a memorial entered in Book No. No. 13, page 29, 12 Oct 1774, adj. John Hogg. Mary Wicker (X) (Seal), Wit: Mich'l Dickert, Jas Lindsey, Margaret Dickert (MD).

A, 83: Newberry County. Personally appeared James Clear and saith that he did hear Col. David Glyn (decd) say in his life time that a Negro woman then in his possession was not his property and that he had no manner of claim to s'd negro named Lucy, and further sayeth that he heard the mother of Mrs. Rosannah Glenn say that the s'd Negro named Lucy came into the family through & by the means of her, 5 May 1786. James Blair. John Lindsay, J.P.

Similar deposition by William Sparks 29 May 1786 before John Lindsay, J.P.

A, 84: South Carolina. August the 7th day 1771. Then received of John Green my father £50 being my part or full satisfaction for my part of his estate. Edward Green. Test: William Dukesson.

State of So Carolina, Ninety Six Dist. Before me George Ruff, J. P., appeared Miltret Liles formerly the wife of William Green deceased & declared that the will her husband had which as she believes it being the last will & testament of John Green deceas'd, she declares she does not know what has become of the s'd will but as the Brittish has Destroyed a good many of their effects & papers, possible the will was destroyed at that time. 6 July 1782 before George Ruff, J.P. Miltret Liles (X).

A, 84: State of So Carolina, Ninety Six Dist. Personally appeared Mich'l Dickert before George Ruff and sayeth that in the year 1779 by virtue of a dedimus to him directed by the honor William Bowers Esq'r then Ordinary of South Carolina, this deponant was authorised to qualify the evidences that subscribed their names to the will of John green deceased & accordingly he qualifyed Elizer Mobley being one of the witnesses & write his provment on the back of the will and that to the best of his Knowledge John Green left heir at law in this will to his father John Green Estates now deceased as also it specifyed in s'd that another son of the name of William Green was cut off with a shilling sterling. Mich'l Dickert, 6 July 1786 before George Ruff, J.P.

A, 85: State of So Carolina, Ninety Six Dist. Before George Ruff, J.P., Daniel Gore declared that he saw & wrote a certain will which he believes was the last will & testament of John Green deceased wherein it was mentioned & specifyed that John Green & Thomas Green was left heirs at law to their Father's estate & all the rest of the other three was cut off with one shilling sterling each. Daniel Gorre, 6 July 1782 before George Ruff, J.P.

State of So Carolina, Newberry County. Before George Ruff, J.P., appeared Mich'l Dickert who saith that five or six years ago a certain will was proved before him by a witness to the best of his knowledged by the name of Eliz'r Mobbley, the will of John Green deceased, authorised & empowered by a detimus from the Ordinary of Charleston. Mich'l Dickert, 7 Dec 1785 before George Ruff, J.P.

Personally appeared Eleazir Mobley and saith that John Green Sen'r made a will and he willed his whole estate to his two sons namely John & Thomas Green (except one shilling to his eldest son Edward Green) which was proved before Michael Dickert, and Eleaz'r Mobley & William Hill subscribed their names as witnesses, dated 4 Sept 1786 before John Lindsey, J.P.

A, 86: 19 May 1784, William Webster of Ninety Six District, to Gabriel Anderson of the settlement of Indian Creek, black smith, by grant dated 23 June 1774, recorded in Book RRR, page 54, to William Webster, 100 acres in Barkley County in the fork between Broad and Saludy Rivers on a branch of Fairforest Creek called Morrises Branch adj. land laid out to George Earnest, William Holliday, now conveyed for £200 SC money, said 100 acres. Wm Webster (Seal), Wit: John Speaks, John Connell, Richard Speake.

A, 87: South Carolina, Ninety Six District. 5 Dec 1778, Isaac Morgan & ann his wife of Ninety Six District to Robert Rutherford of Chatham County, North Carolina, for £900 SC currency, 250 acres in the fork between Broad & Saludy Rivers on a fork of Second Creek called horses branch, adj. Wm

Dawkins, Daniel Horsey & "New Irish." Isaac Morgan (Seal), Wit: Thomas Smith, Thomas Mathis, George Linam.

A, 88: South Carolina, Ninety Six District. 5 Dec 1778, Isaac Morgan & Ann his wife of Ninety Six District to Robert Rutherford of Chatham County, North Carolina, for £900 SC currency, 150 acres in the fork between Broad & Saludy Rivers on a fork of Second Creek called horses branch, granted 1 Dec 1769. Isaac Morgan (Seal), Wit: Thomas Smith, Thomas Mathis, George Linam.

A, 89: Wm Boyles sells to Robt Rutherford, three negroes Tom, Tenah & HAnnah for £151 s10 d5, 2 June 1786. William boyles (Seal), Wit: George Gartman, A. Cates.

Nancy Norman of Ninety Six District for £120 SC money to William Dawkins, one negro wench Winney which was bequeathed to me by George Dawkins deceased, 12 Oct 1782. Nancy Norman (X) (Seal), Wit: Anthony Elton, James Dawkings.

A, 90-92: 29 Sept 1774, John Mills & Mary his wife & Rebecca Mills, mother, of Barkley County, Ninety Six District, SC, to Joseph Scott of s'd province, for £60 SC money, 300 acres on Youngs Fork between Broad & Saludy Rivers the north side of a survey granted to William Mills Senior deceased, adj. John Mills, certifyed by me 31 Nov 1773 John Armstrong, D. S., the old tract of 300 acres granted to sd William Mills Senr deceased 20 Aug 1767. Rebeccah Mills (X) (Seal), John Mills (I), Mary Mills (mark) (Seal), William Mills (mark) (Seal), Wit: Danl Clary Jun'r, Jeremiah Ham, Daniel Clary Snr.

A, 93-94: 20 Oct 1783, Benjamin Chitty of Sate of North Carolina to James Sherer of Ninety Six District, SC, planter, by grant dated 12 Dec 1768 for 100 acres to Jacob Gilder and conveyed by s'd Gilder to Benjamin Chitty on a small creek called Gilders Creek, a small branch of Indian Creek in the fork between Broad & Saludy Rivers adj. Andrew Bowers, now conveyed for £275. Benjamin Chitty (mark) (Seal), Wit: Thomas Dugan, Anthony Parks, John Speake.

A, 95: 22 Oct 1785, James Sherer of Newberry County to John Blalock, late of the North State but now of county aforesaid, for £100 sterling, 100 acres granted 12 Dec 1768 to Jacob Gilder, recorded in Book 3 D, page 16, on a small creek called Gilders Creek, a small branch of Indian Creek in the fork between Broad & Saludy Rivers. James Shearer (Seal), Wit: John Lindsey, John Speake, John Thomas S. M.

A, 96-98: 12 March 1786, Edward Wadlington, planter, of Newberry County to David Lake & Daniel Lake of same, black smith, for £40 sterling, 150 acres between Broad & Saludy Rivers on a branch of Broad River commonly called Enoree on a branch called Camp branch, adj. land laid out to James Caldwell, Govin Gordon, Thos Gordon, Isaac Perklin. Edward Wadlington (Seal),

Frances Wadlington (X), Wit: W. Wadlington, Mecheck Chandler (M) Thomas Lake.

A, 99-100: ____ 1766, Ferdinand Fither [sic, for Fisher?] of Charleston, Joiner, to Christophel Satser for £8 SC money, 50 acres in the limits of Saxagotha on Warteree Creek, granted 15 May 1752 to said Ferdinand Fither, adj. land of Tobias Walthareres. "I do hereby certify that the Remaining part of this above Release was never given into our office June 4th 1786. W. Malone, Clk. Ct.

A, 101-102: 15 Feb 1777, William Dawkins of Ninety Six District to Maximilian Haynie of same, by grant dated 23 June 1774 to William Dawkins, 200 acres adj. Henry Richards, recorded in Book M No. 13, Page 107, now conveyed for £250. William Dawkins (Seal), Jane Dawkins (mark) (Seal), Wit: John Buchanan, George Montgomery, George S[?] Montgomery.

A, 103-104: 16 Dec 1773, Adam Mack of Ninety Six District to Matthias Wickard of same, planter, by grant dated 21 May 1772 to Michael Wingard 100 acres in Craven County on the head of Kelleys Creek, waters of Enoree River adj. Joseph Killard, recorded in Book LLL, page 291, now conveyed for £100 SC money. Adam Mack (X) (Seal), Mary Mack (O) (Seal), Wit: Mich'l Dickert, George Mich'l Rildehoober, "& Dutch Name."

A, 105-106: 21 Jan 1779, William Herring & his wife Delilah of Berkley County, Ninety Six District, SC, to John Baggs of same, by grant dated 21 April 1774 to William Herring, 300 acres in Barkley County in the fork between Broad & Saludy Rivers on a small branch of Cannons Creek called Roofs branch adj. land of Thomas Hamilton, Jeremiah Williams, now conveyed for £300. William Herring (Seal), Delilah Herring (Seal), Wit: Nathan Brown, William Bean, Wm Hamilton.

A, 107-108: 9 Aug 1774, Joseph Thomas, planter, & Elizabeth his wife, to Nathan Brown, all of Ninety Six District, for £250 SC money, 300 acres in Barkley County between Broad & Saludy Rivers on a branch of Kings Creek, waters of Enoree River adj. Thomas Crosson, William Wadlington, Simon Polson, surveyed by Enoch Pearson, D. S., 5 Nov 1771. Joseph Thomas (Seal), Elizabeth Thomas (mark) (Seal), Wit: Robert Dugan Jun'r, Charles Frew, Thomas Johnston.

A, 109-110: State of South Carolina, Newberry County. 1 March 1786, William Beard of state & county aforesaid to Jeremiah Dial, planter, of same, for £5 sterling, 50 acres on waters of the hunting fork adj. land laid out for Jeremiah Dial, John Hope, part of tract to Thomas Beard surveyed by Enoch Pearson, D. S., the east end of said survey. William Baird (Seal), Elinor Baird (mark) (Seal), Wit: Jeremiah Dial, James McCrecken.

A, 111-112: 7 July 1785, Isaack Lindsey, planter, of Newberry County to Benjamin Hampton of same, farmer, for £5 s14 sterling, 150 acres on the south side of Enoree River on a branch of said River called Fosters branch, adj. land formerly laid out to Jacob Pennington. Isaac Lindsey (Seal), Wit: William Calmes, Betsy Calmes, Benjamin Hampton.

A, 113-114: 30 Dec 1772, John Cargill Sen'r of Craven County, SC, planter, to Jeremiah Williams Jn'r of same, planter, by grant dated 28 Nov 1772 to John Cargill Sen'r, 200 acres in Craven County on south side of Broad River adj. Thomas Hammilton's land, now conveyed for £30 SC money. John Cargill (Seal), Rachel Cargill (Seal), Wit: George Graham, Sherwood Allin, Cornelius Cargill.

A, 115: 30 May 1786, Bartholomew Johnson & Jean his wife of Newberry County to George Johnson of same, for one shilling, 76 acres in the fork between Broad & Saludy Rivers on a small branch of Enoree River adj. Bartholomew Johnson, part of surveyed granted to Bartholomew Johnson, adj. W. Malone Sen'r land, Levi Johnson's land, George Johnson's land. Bartholomew Johnson (Seal), Jean Johnson (X) (Seal), Wit: Thomas B. Rutherford, Benjamin Gordon.

A, 116: State of South Carolina, Ninety Six District. Jacob Miller, son of Barnard Miller, with consent of his brother George Miller of same place, apprentice to George Cromer of same place, to serve him during the full term of eight years, 24 Jan 1785. Jacob Miller (m) (Seal), George Miller (X) (Seal), George Crommer (C) (Seal), Wit: George Glyn (X), Michael Dickert.

A, 117-118: 2 May 1786, Casper Gallman of Edgefield County, SC, to Philip Sligh, planter, of Newberry County, by grant dated 29 Nov 1750 to Henry Gallman Sen'r, 450 acres in the fork of Saludy & Broad Rivers on Cannons Creek, recorded in Grant Book MM, now for £50 sterling, conveyed 125 acres, being that northwest part of the above s'd 450 acres on both sides Cannons Creek, adj. Casper Gallman, Frederick Dowber. Gosper Gallman (Seal), Wit: John Levinston (IL).

A, 119-120: 4 July 1773, Captain Charles King & Charity his wife of Craven County, to John Lindsey of same, for £675 SC money, 300 acres, tract granted 8 Aug 1751 to George Wildlifes [sic] and Elizabeth his wife, conveyed to Isaac Pennington and bequeathed to his oldest daughter Charity, wife of Captain Charles King in the fork between Broad and Saludy river on a branch of Broad River, Pennington Creek, now called Kings Creek, adj. Joseph Hampton, John Lindsey Jun'r. Charles King (Seal), Charity King (Seal), Wit: Abel Pennington, James Lindsey, John Lindsey Sen'r.

A, 121: 4 July 1785, John Lindsey and Elizabeth his wife of Newberry County, to Edward Finch of same, for £200 sterling SC money, 157 acres in the fork between Broad & Saludy Rivers on a branch of Enoree River called Kings Creek, part of tract granted 27 Aug 1751 to George Wiles and conveyed by him to Isaac Pennington and willed to his daughter Charity, wife of Captain Charles King, and conveyed to John Lindsey Junr. John Lindsey (Seal), Elizabeth Lindsey (Seal), Wit: Blalock, John Anderson, John Speake.

A, 122-123: 25 Nov 1774, Thomas Morgan and Isobel his wife of Craven County, Ninety Six District, to Abel Anderson of same, by grant dated 17 Feb 1766 to Thomas Morgan, tract in Barkley County on a small branch of Enoree River called Kings Creek adj. John Brown, recorded in Book AAA, page 399, memorial entered in Book H. No. 8, page 182, now conveyed for £135 SC money, 100 acres, part of said tract. Thomas Morgin (X) (Seal), Isabell Morgin (X) (Seal), Wit: George Anderson, Joseph Thomas, James Ford.

A, 124: James Willingham of Hanover County, Virginia for £51 s15 d7 sterling to George Montgomery of Newberry County, one negro fellow named Jo about 24 years of age, dated 20 Jan 1786. James Winningham (I) (Seal), Wit: John Means, John Hampton.

A, 125-126: 21 Oct 1771, John Clark, carpenter, of the settlement of Enoree, Craven County, SC, to John Hogg of same, by grant dated 1 Dec 1769 to said John Clark, 150 acres on south side of Enoree River, a branch of Broad River now for £200 SC money conveyed to John Hogg. John Clark (Seal), Mary Clark (Seal), Wit: John Lindsey Jun'r, Joseph Hogg, Jeremiah Chandler.

A, 127: South Carolina. Thomas Gibson do discharge a negro man named Sam and another named Frank & a wench named Bett and her two children Press & Hanner from the service of s'd Thomas Gibson Sen'r or any person laying any claim, Sam Frank & Bett & her two children they having all been free born in my family, dated 29 Oct 1785. Thomas Gibson (T) (Seal), Wit: George Ruff J. P., Levi Casey, J.P.

South Carolina, Chester County. Thomas Geril declared that he knew the within name free wench Betty to be purchased by Rob't Turner in Virginia with her two sons Bash & Buck that he purchased them as free negroes to serve only till thirty one years of age & no longer, that he likewise knew the other children of the s'd Betty within mentioned which was born in the possession f the s'd Turner, that Sill was left to this deponant & Mary his wife to serve them till thirty one years of age & Buck, Bash, Genny & Priss was left to Thomas Gibson, dated 25 Oct 1785. Thomas Geril (C), before Jo Brown, J.P.

South Carolina, Chester County. Mrs. Sarah Travers declares that she knew the above mentioned negro Sam who was lately in the possession of Thomas Gibson and that he always past for a free born negro, and s'd to be the son of the above mentioned free wench Priss, dated 25 Oct 1785. Sarah Travers (mark), before Jo Brown, J.P.

A, 128: South Carolina, Chester County. Mrs. Mary Geril declares that negro man Sam now present which was born & raised in the possession of Thomas Gibson now of Newberry County in this state was born of a free negro woman named Priss who was bound to s'd Gibson in her infancy to serve him till she should arrive to the age of thirty one & that she the deponant was present at his birth & Was the Midwife who Delivered his mother of him, and that the s'd free Negro woman Priss likewise born in the possession of s'd Gibson a son named Frank & daughter named Betty all free born, 25 October 1785. Mary Geril (M), before Jo Brown, J.P.

A, 129-130: Lease and release. 7 Dec 1785, James Daughty of Ninety Six District, planter, to William Speckman of same, planter, for £21 s8, 100 acres granted to Charles McBride and conveyed to said James Daughty. James Daugharty (Seal), Agness Daugharty (X) (Seal), Wit: George Daugharty, Thomas Speakman (O), Wm. Speckman (W). Proved in open court 4 Sept 1786.

A, 131-133: Lease and release. 3 Aug 1786, Michal Long of Newberry County, sadler & planter, to James Young of same, for 100 acres and a young mare, tract of 202 acres on a small branch of Campling Creek now Newberry County formerly Craven adj. William Houseal, Michal Cromer, granted 19 Nov 1772 to Jacob Long. Michal Long (Seal), Wit: George Long (X), Jacob Long (X). Isaiah Quartermus. Acknowledged in open court 4 Sept 1786.

A, 134-136: Lease and release. 1 & 2 Aug 1786, Robert Wiseman of Ninety Six District, planter, to Alexander Cross of same, by grant dated 21 March 1768, 250 acres in the fork between Broad & Saluda Rivers on a small branch of Second Creek, recorded in Book CCC, page 425, now conveyed for £300 SC money. Robert Wiseman (Seal), Wit: George Montgomery (O), Thomas Crossan, Andrew Russel. Acknowledged in open court 4 Sept 1786.

A, 137-139: Lease and release. 21 & 22 May 1775, Abraham Wright of Berkley County, SC, weaver, to Thomas Campbell of said province, planter, for £150 SC money, 200 acres on Indian Creek granted 5 Oct 1756 to John Evans, adj. Henry Hendrickson, conveyed by s'd Evans to William Cannon 13 Jan 1768, and from William Cannon to William Turner, then from William Turner to John Ree Sen'r 18 May 1773, and James Ree being heir at law of his father John Ree Sen'r conveyed to Abraham Wright 6 Sept 1774. Abraham Wright (Seal), Wit: William Wilson, William Campbell (X), George Campbell (G). Proved in open court 4 Sept 1786.

A, 140-142: Lease and release. 16 & 17 Jan 1785. Margaret Godfrey, John Stone, Mary Godfrey, Hannah Godfrey & Sarah Godfrey, of Fairfield County, SC, to Sanford Cockerill of Newberry County, for £--- sterling, 200 acres in the fork of Broad & Saludy Rivers adj. Matthias Wicker, John Hallor, Mich'l Suber, Jacob Felker, tract of 200 acres to Benjamin Shettlesworth recorded in Book OOO, page 639, and conveyed 9 & 10 Aug 1774 to John Godfrey (now deceas'd) who in his will did devise to his wife Margaret Godfrey and to her heirs and assigns & the s'd John Stone being son in law & the said Mary Godfrey, Hannah Godfrey & Sarah Godfrey, daughters of said John Godfrey deceased. Margaret Godfrey (Seal), John Stone (X) (Seal), Mary Godfrey (X) (Seal), Hannah Godfrey (Seal), Sarah Godfrey (X) (Seal), Wit: James Liles (mark), Mathew Day, Edward Day (X). Proved in open court 4 Sept 1786.

A, 143: _____ 1785, Thomas Horsey of Charles Town to James Kelly of Newberry County, for £30, 150 acres in Newberry County adj. land of John Green, Adam Mock. Thomas Horsey (Seal), Wit: Thomas Parrott, Joseph Dawkins. Proved in open Court 4 Sept 1786.

A, 144-146: Lease and release. 9 & 10 Jan 1784, George Sligh of Ninety Six District, planter, to Henry Matts of same place, planter, for £15, by grant of 200 acres to John George Infinger 8 March 1755 on Second Creek adj. Michael Crommer, "Ann Brigitta hard Cockin," Adam George Keller [Hiller?], estate of Herman Geiger deceased, recorded in Book PP, page 410, and transferred by said Infinger to Charles Matts 9 & 10 Oct 1765, and said Charles Matts conveyed to John Stockman, and said Stockman transferred 200 acres to Fallentine Virtress 26 & 27 Jan 1779, and by him to George Sligh 23 & 24 Feb 1786 [sic]. George Sligh (X) (Seal), Wit: Martin Souter (S), Mich'l Dickart Sen'r, Michael Dickart. Proved in open Court 4 Sept 1786.

A, 147-149: Lease and release. 30 & 31 March 1786, Nancy Wiseman, widow, of Newberry County, to John Knox Steel for £20 sterling, 75 acres in Newberry County on a branch of Second Creek, part of 150 acres granted to s'd Nancy Wiseman 6 Feb 1786, recorded in Book FFFF, page 491. Nancy Wiseman (O) (Seal), Wit: Adam Glazier, John Baggs, John Riley. Proved in open Court 4 Sept 1786.

A, 150-152: Lease and release. State of So Carolina. 9 December 1784, John Sigler of Ninety Six District, Planter, to Martin Souter of same place, planter, by a grant bearing date 2 January 1754 to Carolus Sigler, a plantation of 250 acres in the fork between Broad & Saludy Rivers on a branch of Cannons Creek called Cattail Branch, adj. Uldrick Sligh, recorded in Book OO, page 397, and whereas said Carolus Sigler died intested [sic for intestate] and the said 250 acres devolved into the possession of the sd. John Sigler, land adj. Ulrick Sligh and lands not granted, now for £50 lawfull current money. John Sigler (S) (Seal), Wit: Henry Matts (mark), Michal Dickert. Proved in open Court 4 Sept 1786.

A, 153: 20 May 1786, Agness Wiseman of Newberry County, spinster, for natural love and affection and for ten shillings to Hugh Wiseman, 75 acres on waters of Second Creek, granted 6 Feb 1786, recorded in Book FFFF, page 491. Agness Wiseman (O) (Seal), Wit: Adam Glazier, Ephraim Cannon. Proved in open Court 4 Sept 1786.

A, 154: 10 Jan 1786, Samuel McConall of Newberry County, planter, for love, good will and affection, to Jenn Crossen of same, all my lands, tenements, goods, household furniture, and all my estate, excepting 50 ares, part of 200 acres on waters of Cannons Creek adj. lands of Matthias Kinard, John Stone & Grey. Samuel McConall (S) (Seal), Wit: Mich'l Dickart Sen'r, Thomas Crossen. Proved in open Court 4 Sept 1786.

A, 155: John Dalrymple, blacksmith, of Newberry County, to love & good will & affection to my loving nephew Samuel Dalrymple of same, "olfant," tract of land of 160 acres on south side Bush River adj. land of John Dalrymple, Providence Williams, Ephraim Cannon, dated 24 Dec 1785. Jno Dalrymple (Seal), Wit: David Ruff, Elizabeth Ruff (ER), Ephraim Cannon. N. B. If the above Samuel Dalrymple should died without heir, then the above tract shall be sold & equally divided amongst four of his sisters Margaret, Ruth, Ellenor, and Rachel. Jno Dalrymple. Acknowledged in open Court 4 Sept 1786.

A, 156-158: Lease and release. 7 & 8 June 1786, John Reed of Ninety Six District, Taylor, to Hugh Boyd of same, for 230 SC money, 150 acres, part of 250 acres granted to John Reed 1 Sept 1768 on Gilders Creek. John Reed (Seal), Wit: John Blalock Sen'r, John Blalock Jun'r, Simon Keary. Proved in open Court 4 Sept 1786.

A, 159: 22 Feb 1786, George Gibson and Jane his wife to Joseph Scott, for £70 sterling, tract in Ninety Six District on waters of Bush River granted to said George Gibson 4 Nov 1772, memorial entered in Book M. No. 12, page 87, 29 Jan 1773, grant recorded in Book MMM, page 554. George Gibson (G) (Seal), Jane Gibson (X) (Seal), Wit: Nathl Abney D. S., James Johnson, Cynthia Johnson. Proved in open Court 4 Sept 1786.

A, 160: 15 April 1786, John Taylor of Newberry County to George Bowl of same, for £17 s17 d1 sterling, 100 acres adj. land of Joseph Chatman, half of 200 acres granted to James Neil (the SE part of said tract). John Taylor (Seal), Wit: Robt Rutherford, Aron Cates, Thos Rutherford. Proved in open Court 4 Sept 1786.

A, 161-163: Lease and release. 29 & 30 Aug 1785, James Brown of Ninety Six District, planter, to Adam Taylor of same, planter, by grant of 350 acres ion waters of Kings & Cannons Creek adj. Francis Wilson, James Neail, David Tennent, recorded in Book M. No. 13, page 281 15 Feb 1775, now conveyed for £50 SC money. James Brown (Seal), Wit: John Howell (X), Wm Young. Proved in open Court 5 Sept 1786.

A, 164-166: Lease and release. 18 & 19 July 1786, Frederick Gray of Ninety Six District, planter, to John Howell of same, planter, for £20 sterling, 160 acres granted to Frederick Gray in Newberry County adj. William Elmore, recorded in Book DDD, page 313. Frederick Gray (Seal), Wit: Adam Daylor (A), William Golden (mark), William Howell (X). Proved in open Court 4 Sept 1786.

A, 167-168: 8 Dec 1785, John Mitchell, Robert Campbell & Elizabeth Campbell of St. John's Parish, SC, to Major Thomas Gordon of said state, for £71 s8 d6 sterling, 310 acres, being the original land of John Mitchel granted 1 March 1775 on south side of Broad River including Peters cabin adj. Thomas Gordon, John Gordon. John Mitchel (Seal), Robert Campbell (Seal),

Elizabeth Campbell (Seal), Wit: John Cook, Jehu Wilson, John McNeail. Proved in open Court 4 Sept 1786.

A, 169-171: Lease and release. 8 & 9 Jan 1784, John & Tho's Green of Ninety Six District, planters, to James Kelley of same place, planter, for £25 SC money, 200 acres, part of 550 acres granted to John Green in Berkley County, in the fork between Broad & Saludy Rivers on Enoree River adj. land formerly held by Richard Kelley, Aubrey Nolan, Allen, So'l Aubry, Cromer's corner, Wadlington's line, Stephen Boyer's, recorded in Book GGG, page 167. John Green (X) (Seal), Sarah Green (mark) (Seal), Thomas Green (mark) (Seal), Wit: Daniel Goree, John Dickey, John Kelley (mark). Proved in open Court 4 Sept 1786.

A, 172: 22 April 1786, Robert Leverett & Mary Leverett of Union County, to John Stewart of Newberry County, for £20 sterling, 100 acres in Newberry County on south side Tyger River adj. John Morris. Rob't Leverett (R) (Seal), Mary Leverett (mark) (Seal), Wit: Rob't Leveret Jun'r, Reuben Jones, Susanah Hawkins (mark). Proved in open Court 5 Sept 1786.

A, 173-175: Lease and release. 16 Oct 1782, George Montgomery of Berkley County, SC, planter, to Alexander Johnston, for £250 SC money, 150 acres in the fork of Broad & Saludy Rivers on Second Creek granted 17 Oct 1782 [sic], adj. Alexander Johnston, Alexander Davison, John Knox, John Johnston. George Montgomery (mark) (Seal), Wit: Jos. Caldwell, William Johnston, Anthony Elton. Proved in open Court 5 Sept 1786.

A, 176-178: Lease and release. 3 & 4 Oct 1782, John Sigler of Ninety Six District, planter, to William Hutchison, planter, of same place, by a grant bearing date 2 January 1754 to Carolus Sigler, recorded in Book OO, page 397, a plantation of 250 acres in the fork between Broad & Saludy Rivers on a branch of Cannons Creek called Cattail Branch, and whereas said Carolus Sigler died intested [sic for intestate] and the said 250 acres devolved unto his elder son John Sigler, land adj. Ulrick Sligh and lands not granted, now for £50 lawful current money, now conveys 25 acres, part of said 250 acres. John Seigler (mark) (Seal), Barbara Seigler (mark) (Seal), Wit: Joseph Dawkins, Michl Dickert. Proved in open Court 6 Sept 1786.

A, 179-181: Lease and release. 22 & 23 March 1785, William Dudgeon of the State of Virginia, planter, to Samuel Hanes, Brick layer of Newberry County, for £40, 150 acres, half of 300 acres on waters of Mudlick Creek adj. at the time of survey to Nathaniel Fooshee, Oliver Towles, granted to William Caldwell 12 Aug 1768, and sold to s'd William Dudgeon one half of said tract 8 (8 May 1772. William Dudgeon (Seal), Wit: Wm Caldwell, Samuel Goodman, Harris Gillam. Proved in open Court 5 Sept 1786.

A, 182-183: Lease and release. 16 & 17 July 1786, Peter Crim, planter, of Fairfield County to George Freshley, planter, for £50 sterling, 250 acres in the fork between Saluda & Broad Rivers adj. land laid out for John Ulrick Mayer, granted to Nicholas Durr 6 Nov 1761, recorded in Book NN, page 153. Peter Crim (Seal), Wit: John Hampton, William Dawkins. Proved in open Court 5 Sept 1786.

A, 184: 14 Dec 1784, Richard Brooks of Ninety Six District to John Gary Jun'r of same, for £200 SC money, 200 acres in Berkley County on waters of Indian Creek adj. land said to belong to Charles McBride, James Wilson, granted to Richard Brooks 31 Aug 1774. Richard Brooks (Seal) & Lucreasy his wife (Seal), Wit: John Loften, Daniel Walter. John Walter. Proved in open Court 5 Sept 1786.

A, 185: 5 Sept 1786, Bartholomew Johnson & Jane his wife of Newberry County to Levi Johnston of same, for £200 SC money, 71 acres on the branch of Enoree formerly called Gossets Creek adj. George Johnson, Levi Johnson. Bartholomew Johnson (Seal), Jane Johnson (X) (Seal), Wit: Lewis Hogg, David Cannon, Robert Rutherford. Proved in open Court 5 Sept 1786.

A, 186: 5 Sept 1786, indenture between Thomas Willoughby Waters, Sadler, of Newberry County, and Stephen Elmore, son of Stephen Elmore and Sarah his wife, both deceased, of same, Stephen Elmore puts himself apprentice to Thomas W. Waters to learn the act or mistery of a sadler to live with after the manner of an apprentice for eight years from 25 December next, and said Waters is to find s'd apprentice sufficient meat, drink, washing, lodging, and apparel and to give said apprentice eighteen months schooling, twelve of which is to be at the said Waters' pleasure, the remaining six months in the two last years of his servitude, and at the expiration of said term to give said apprentice one suit of god decent clothes, one pair of pinchers, one small hammer, marking irons, knife, thimble and needles. Thos W. Waters (Seal), Stephen Elmore (X) (Seal), Wit: W. Malone, C. Ct. Acknowledged in open Court 5 Sept 1786.

A, 187-188: Lease and release. 30 Sept & 1 Oct 1785, John Wright of Ninety Six District to Joseph Thomson of same, for £10 sterling, 200 acres on a branch on north side of Saludy called Beaver Dam Creek, adj. Stephen Holson, part of 300 acres granted to John Wright 27 Sept 1769, 100 acres conveyed to John Cote. John Wright (Seal), Wit: William Oneall, Jos Wright (mark), Isaac Cook (I). Permitted on a former proof to record 6 Sept 1786.

A, 189-191: Lease and release. 20 & 21 Sept 1770, David Mote of Berkly County, SC, to Thomas Pugh of same, for £200 SC money, 100 acres on north side of Saludy River on a branch thereof called Beaverdam Creek, part of tract granted to Stephen Holson 20 June 1754, conveyed by him to Henry Havard 15 June 1759, and to said David Mote 21 Aug 1764. David Mote (Seal), Wit: Jos Wright, William Wright, John Wright (W). Acknowledged in open Court 6 Sept 1786.

A, 192-193: Lease and release. 30 Sept & 1 Oct 1785, Thomas Pugh of State of Virginia to Joseph Thomson of 96 District, SC, for £10 sterling, 100 acres in Ninety Six District on north side Saludy River on Beaverdam Creek, an equal half of tract granted to Stephen Holson 20 June 1754, conveyed to Henry Havard 10 June 1759, then to David Mote 21 Aug 1764, and then to Thomas Pugh 20 Sept 1770. Thomas Pugh (Seal), Ann Pugh (Seal), Wit: Jos Wright, Isaac Cook (I), William Oneall. Permitted on a former proof 5 Sept 1786.

A, 194: 15 Aug 1786. Col. Thomas Sabb of St. Matthews Parish, SC, gent., appoints Martin Armstrong of Spartanburgh County, my true & Lawful attorney to recover a certain negro woman about fourteen years old feloniously taken in the year 1782 from the estate of Mrs. Robt Swanston near Monks Corner in this state, and supposed to be in the possession of Mrs. Anderson in this state. Thomas Sabb admr. of the estate of Robert Swanston (Seal), Wit: James ___, J. P. Acknowledged in open Court 6 Sept 1786.

A, 195-197: Lease and release. 19 & 20 Nov 1785, James Johnston, planter, of Ninety Six District, Newberry County, to Hugh Boyd, waggoner, of same, for £50 sterling, 144 acres on waters of Indian Creek, granted 3 Oct 1785 to said James Johnston, recorded in Book 4F, page 91. James Johnston (Seal), Wit: Wm Woodall, George Ekins, William Gray. Proved in open Court 5 Sept 1786.

A, 198: 5 Sept 1786, indenture between John Steel of Newberry County, planter, and Thomas Medill, said Thomas Medill does put himself apprentice to John Steel to learn the art or mistery of a weaver from 5 Sept 1786. John Steel (Seal), Thomas Medell (X) (Seal). Acknowledged by both parties in open Court 5 Sept 1786.

A, 199-201: Lease and release. 30 Dec 1785, William Killpatrick Sen'r of Ninety Six District, Newberry County, to Hugh Boyd, waggoner, of same, for £100 sterling, 300 acres on a branch of Indian Creek, granted 6 Feb 1773 to said Killpatrick, recorded in Book 3T, page 212. William Killpatrick (P) (Seal), Wit: John Blalock, Jno Blalock Jun'r, Wm Woodall. Proved in open Court 5 Sept 1786.

A, 202-204: Lease and release. 19 & 20 July 1785, William Kilpatrick & his wife Marthew of Indian Creek, Ninety Six District, planter, to John Glasgow of Gilders Creek, Ninety Six District, by grant dated 5 Feb 1773, recorded in Auditor's office Book M No. 12, page 318, 300 acres, now for £14 SC money, conveys 150 acres, part of said tract adj. William Kilpatrick, Jane Kilpatrick. William Kilpatrick (mark) (Seal), Marthew Kilpatrick (mark) (Seal), Wit: Robert Glasgow, Patrick Lowry. Proved in open Court 5 Sept 1786.

A, 205-207: Lease and release. 22 & 23 Apr 1784, William Largen & Ann his wife on Indian Creek, Ninety Six District, to Robert Brooks of same creek and district, for £500 lawful currency, 350 acres on Indian Creek in the District & state aforesaid, granted 18 Oct 1757 to said Largen. William Largen (M)

(Seal), Wit Ann Largen (mark) (Seal), Wit: Benjamin Stone (mark), Charles Allen, Reuben Roberts. Proved in open Court 6 Sept 1786.

A, 208-210: Lease and release. 9 Aug 1785, Robert Brooks on Indian Creek, Newberry County, to William Conner & Uriah Conner Jun'r, each of same, by grant dated 18 Oct 1757 to William Largen, 350 acres, recorded in Book SS, page 144, and conveyed by William Largen and wife Ann to said Robert Brooks, now conveyed for £200 sterling. Robert Brooks, Mary Brooks (S), Wit: John Johnston, Michael Johnston. Acknowledged in open Court 6 Sept 1786.

A, 211-213: Lease and release. 2 & 3 Jan 1786, Robert Moore of Newberry County, planter, to Rosanah Glyn of same, by grant dated 6 Sept 1772 to George Gray, 200 acres on waters of Cannons Creek adj. lands of Mr. Gray, Barnet Mountz, David Martin, Roper, William More, James Shepherd, recorded in Book MMM, page 175, now for £28 s11 d4 conveys 100 acres, part of said tract, conveyed to said Robert More by George Gray 17 & 18 March 1776. Robert Moore (Seal), Wit: Sims Brown, John Baggs, Robert Brown. Proved in open Court 6 Sept 1786.

A, 214-215: Lease and release. 25 & 26 Dec 1785, John Garrot & Susannah his wife of Indian Creek, Ninety Six District, SC, to John Johnston Sen'r of Gilders Creek, Ninety Six District, for £100 SC money, 250 acres on Indian Creek in Newberry County granted to John Garrot 24 March 1756 then adj. land of Jacob Pennington. John Garrot (mark) (Seal), Susannah Garrot (S) (Seal), Wit: Uriah Conner, Pk. Lowry. Proved in open Court 6 Sept 1786.

A, 216-218: Lease and release. 15 March 1786, Robert Brooks and Mary his wife of Newberry County to Michael Johnston, late of county & state aforementioned, by grant dated 31 Aug 1774, 100 acres on Indian Creek called Joshua's branch, adj. land of Joshua Anderson, recorded in Book SSS, page 31, now conveyed for £43 sterling. Robert Brooks (Seal), Mary Brooks (X) (Seal), Wit: William Tinney, Jas Lindsey. Acknowledged in open Court 6 Sept 1786.

A, 219-220: Lease and release. 10 & 11 July 1786, Jas Daugharty of Ninety Six District, planter, to Frederick Cromer of same, planter, for £75 sterling, 25 acres on waters of Second Creek adj. Geo. Agness, Matthias Wicker, Wm Taggart, Frederick Cromer, part of 63 acres granted to said James Daugharty 3 April 1786, recorded in Book JJJJ, page 184. James Daugharty (Seal), Wit: Jas Daugharty, Henry Mets (H). Proved in open Court 6 Sept 1786.

A, 221-222: Lease and release. 9 May 1786, Joachim Bulow of Charles Town, SC, to John Mills of Ninety Six District, for £10 sterling, 182 acres on waters of Bush River adj. Azeriah Pugh, Enoch Pearson, Joseph Summers, John Mills, by a resurvey of the same, seized from Peter Harr by order of court of common pleas in April 1785 and sold at publick outcry, purchased by said Joachim Bulow from Robert Rutherford, sheriff 5 Dec 1785. Joachim Bulow

(Seal), Amelia Bulow (Seal), Wit: Reason Reagan, Wm Jackson (mark), Timothy Thomas. Proved in open Court 6 Sept 1786.

A, 223-224: Lease and release. 20 Nov 1785, John Mills of Ninety Six District to Thomas Mills of same, for £10 sterling, 150 acres on waters of Bush River adj. Matthias Elmore, Joseph Scott, Israel Gaunt, Isaac Mills, part of tract granted to William Mills Sen'r deceased for 300 acres 20 Aug 1767. John Mills (I) (Seal), Mary Mills (mark) (Seal), Wit: Reason Reagan, Robert Mills (R), Isaac Mills (I). Proved in open Court 6 Sept 1786.

A, 225-227: Lease and release. 6 June 1784, John Mills of Berkley County, Ninety Six District, and Mary his wife, to Isaac Mills of same, for one shilling sterling, 100 acres on Youngs fork, waters of Bush River part of tract granted to William Mills Sen'r deceased for 300 acres 20 Aug 1767, adj. Joseph Scott. John Mills (I) (Seal), Mary Mills (mark) (Seal), William Mills (W) (Seal), Wit: William Aspenell (O), William Ham, Jeremiah Ham. Proved in open Court 6 Sept 1786.

A, 228: 4 July 1785, John Lindsey of Newberry County for £50 to Edward Finch, 49 acres on Kings Creek, part of tract granted to John Lindsey 30 Sept 1774, adj. Joseph Davies, Wiles's old corner, William Hamilton. John Lindsey (Seal), Wit: Jno Blalock Jr., Jno Anderson, John Speake. Proved in open Court 6 Sept 1786.

A, 229-231: 10 Dec 1784, Daniel Gartman of Ninety Six District, to Richard Strother of same, for £350 SC money, 300 acres being in three separate tracts, the first of 50 acres granted to George Adam Keller plat dated 12 March 1752, the second tract 100 acres granted to Margaret Smitten adj. Adam George Keller, John George Infinger, estate of Herman Geiger decd, Hans Jacob Morff, granted 8 March 1755, the third tract of 150 acres granted to said Daniel Gartman on Second Creek adj. land granted to Margaret Smitten, John Murff, estate of Hermond Geiger decd, granted 1 April 1773. Daniel Gartman (Seal), Cateran Gartman (X) (Seal), Wit: Joseph Swingler, Wm Hancock. Proved in open court 5 March 1787.

A, 232: South Carolina, Newberry County, Ninety Six District. 15 Nov 1786, William Hancock to Elijah Parrott, for ten shillings, 315 acres on north side Enoree River adj. Rich'd Kelly, Williamson Liles. William Hancock (Seal), Elizabeth Hancock (X), Wit: Ep. Liles, Eman Rice (mark). Proved in open court 5 March 1787.

A, 233-235: Lease and release. 7 & 8 Nov 1786, Bartholomew Brooks & Elizabeth Brooks his wife of Newberry County, Ninety Six District, planter, to Isaac Grant of same, gentleman, for £30 sterling, 140 acres granted to said Bartholomew Brooks granted 12 Oct 1785, recorded in Book 4, page 466. Bartholomew Brooks (X) (Seal), Elizabeth Brooks (X) (Seal), Wit: Rob't Gillam, Jno Satterwhite, Elisha Brooks. Proved in open court 5 March 1787.

A, 236-238: Lease and release. 13 Dec 1786, Thomas Pitts, planter, of Ninety Six District, to Berry Harris, carpenter, of same, for £35 sterling, tract on waters of Little River, one half of 200 acres granted to Elizabeth Johnston 19 June 1772 and conveyed by Elizabeth Johnston to Joseph Hays 23 & 24 Feb 1773, then conveyed by Joseph Hays to Thos Pitts 8 & 9 Dec 1777, on north side of the mane country road from Rabuns Creek to Charleston, adj. Jas Waldrop, John Monk, William Gilliland, William Anderson. Thos Pitts (X) (Seal), Sally Pitts (X) (Seal), Wit: Samuel Harris, Reuben Golding, Harris Gillam. Proved in open court 5 March 1787.

A, 239-241: Lease and release. 19 Dec 1786, David Edwards of Newberry County, planter, to John Wheatingman of same, planter, for £100 sterling, tract of 100 acres in Craven County on waters of Broad River granted 12 Dec 1768 to Arthur McQueenling, conveyed by him to Peter Richardson 26 & 27 Apr 1771, and by him to David Edwards 27 & 28 Oct 1777. David Edwards (Seal), Jane Edwards (Seal), Wit: Michl Dickert Senr, Christopher Wheatingman (W), Christian Wheatingman (mark). Proved in open court 5 March 1787.

A, 242: 9 Nov 1786. Thomas Gordon & Elizabeth Gordon his wife of Newberry County to Thomas Hardy of Luningsburgh County, Virginia, for £194 s9 sterling, 204 acres, part of a larger tract granted to George Robison 13 Oct 1756, since purchased by John Mitchell, conveyed to Thomas Gordon 28 Dec 1785 by John Mitchel Jun'r, Robert Campbell & Elizabeth Campbell, heirs at law to the estate of John Mitchell Sen'r deceased, adj. land granted to William Cureton Senr 4 July 1786, on south side Tyger River on Peter's Creek including Peters old Cabin. Thos Gordon (Seal), Wit: Saml Otterson, Jas Beuford, William Mays. Proved in open court 5 March 1787.

A, 243: 5 March 1787. Thomas Gordon of Newberry County to James Murfey of same, for £5, 330 acres on north side Enoree River adj. Littleton's land. Thos Gordon (Seal), Wit: Thos Hill, Ephraim Liles, John Sparks. Proved in open court 5 March 1787.

A, 244: State of So Carolina, Newberry County, 96 District. 5 March 1787, Francis Wafer Sen'r to Wm Wadlington, planter, for £50, tract on north side of Enoree River originally granted to s'd Wafer 5 Sept 1785, memorial entered in Grant Book 4F, page 15, 140 acres, part of tract of 300 acres adj. Adam Stephens, on Clark's old line. Francis Wafer (Seal), Wit: Abednego Chandler, Marcus Littleton, George Wadlington. Proved in open court 5 March 1787.

A, 245-248: Lease and release. 9 & 10 Jan 1787, Francis Wafer Sen'r of Newberry County to John Chandler of same, planter, for £80 SC money, 200 acres between Broad & Saludy Rivers on a branch of Enoree called Collenses Creek adj. Wadlington. Francis Wafer (Seal), Mary Wafer (X) (Seal), Wit: William Sparks, Abednego Chandler, Claudes Gorree (+). Proved in open court 5 March 1787. Recorded 17 May 1787.

A, 249-251: Lease and release. 3 & 4 Jan 1787, Jacob Falker of Newberry County, planter, to Richard Strother of same, planter, by grant dated 21 May 1772 to Jacob Furger (alias Jacob Falker), 350 acres between Broad & Saludy Rivers adj. Mr. Kaller, Jacob Oxner, recorded in Book LLL, page 219, and said Jacob Falker Sen'r did properly transfer said 350 acres to his son Jacob Falker Jun'r 8 & 9 Sept 1775, now conveyed for £50 SC money, conveys 150 acres of said tract. Jacob Falker (X) (Seal), Barbara Falker (BF) (Seal), Wit: Thos Wood, James Hord. Proved in open court 5 March 1787. Recorded 17 May 1787.

A, 252-254: Lease and release. 11 & 12 Oct 1770, George Smith of Craven County, South Carolina, Gun Smith, to Joseph Smith of same, for £20, land granted to said George Smith 12 Jan 1769, 150 acres on waters of Second Creek adj. Robt Weir, grant recorded in Book 3D, page 59. George Smith (Seal), Agness Smith (Seal), Wit: John Lum, Jeremiah Williams, John Grayham. Proved in open court 5 March 1787. Recorded 18 May 1787.

A, 255: 3 April 1783, Jacob Falker of Ninety six District, planter, bound to Thomas Wood of same, planter, in the sum of £5000 SC money, not to lay any claim to 200 acres conveyed to Thomas Wood 27 & 28 March 1783. Jacob Falker (IF) (Seal), Catherine Sharp (mark (Seal), Wit: George Buckhannon, Mich'l Dickert. Proved in open court 5 March 1787. Recorded 18 May 1787.

A, 256-258: Lease and release. State of So Carolina, Laurence [sic, for Laurens] County, 96 D't. 18 & 19 Jan 1787, John Dickey & Jane his wife of said county, to John Boyes of same, for £10 sterling, 100 acres granted to Jane Hood wife of s'd John Dickey on a small branch of Bullocks Creek, fork of Thicketty, recorded in Book 3T, page 606, 8 Dec 1774. John Dickey (Seal), Jane Dickey (D) (Seal), Wit: Alexander Dickey, Ann Dickey (A), Jean Dickey (mark). Proved in open court 5 March 1787. Recorded 18 May 1787.

A, 259-260: Lease and release. 10 & 11 Jan 1787, Tobias Putteet & Elizabeth his wife of Greenville County, SC, to Josiah Fish of Newberry County, for £50 sterling, tract of 200 acres on south side of Broad River. Tobias Putteet (T) (Seal), Elizabeth Putteet (mark) (Seal), Wit: Matthias Seleer[?], Jonathan Holcomb, John Putteet. Proved in open court 5 March 1787. Recorded 20 May 1787.

A, 261-263: Lease and release. 22 & 23 Nov 1786, Thomas Hamilton of Abbeville County, Tanner, to Casper Piester, planter, of Newberry County, for £70 sterling, 150 acres granted to Nicholas Weiss 20 June 1754 in the fork between Broad & Saluda adj. George Pfiester, Casper Gray, conveyed by s'd Weiss & Mary his wife 1 & 2 Oct 1765 to Thomas Hamilton. Tho's Hamilton (Seal), Wit: Wm Hamilton, James Hamilton. Proved in open court 5 March 1787. Recorded 21 May 1787.

A, 264: 11 Nov 1786, John Grasty of Ninety Six District, Newberry County, to Menoah Bonds of same, planter, for ten shillings, 50 acres in the fork between

Broad & Saludy Rivers on a small branch of Enoree called Beaver Creek adj. John Anderson, Marshall Grasty, John Robinson, memorial entered in Book M No. 13, page 109, 17 Nov 1774. John Grasty (Seal), Wit: Barber Hancock, James Chandler (X), Thomas Lake. Proved in open court 5 March 1787. Recorded 21 May 1787.

A, 265-267: Lease and release. 14 & 15 Oct 1786, Michael Dickert of Newberry County, planter, to Mathias Quatlebaum of same, planter, by grant dated 22 Aug 1766 to Peter Dickert, 300 acres on south side Broad River on a branch of Crims Creek adj. land surv'd for one Cock, Francis Huet, grant recorded in the secretary's office Book YY, page 116, and said Peter Dickert died intested the above 300 acres devolved to s'd Michael Dickert he being heir at law, now for £50 sterling conveyed to Matthias Quattlebaum. Michael Dickert Sen'r (Seal), Wit: Henry Snelgrove (H), John Shealy (X), F. Jos. Wallern, V. D. M. Proved in open court 5 March 1787. Recorded 22 May 1787.

A, 268: 2 Dec 1786, 2 Dec 1786, George Johnson & Elizabeth his wife of Newberry County to William Malone Jun'r of same, for £28 10/6 sterling, 36 acres on the waters of Enoree River adj. Bartholomew Johnson. George Johnson (Seal), Elizabeth Johnson (X) (Seal), Wit: W. Malone Sen'r, Bartholomew Johnson, Ann Johnson. Proved in open court 5 March 1787. Recorded 22 May 1787.

A, 269: 3 March 1787, Samuel Proctor of Fairfield County to Micajah Bennet of Newberry County, for £40 sterling, 100 acres on both sides Pattersons Creek, a branch of Indian Creek. S. Proctor (Seal), Wit: W. Wadlington, John McCutchen, Wm McCrackin. Proved in open court 5 March 1787. Recorded 22 May 1787.

A, 270-272: Lease and release. 6 & 7 Aug 1786, Rudolph Buzzard of Ninety Six District, planter, to Andrew Russell of same, for £500, 60 acres granted to Henry Oxner 25 May 1774 on south side Broad River adj. Jacob Falker, Rudolph Buzzard, Richard Clark, recorded in Book GGG, page 44, conveyed by said Henry Oxner & his wife Eliz'th 3 & 4 Nov 1777, transferred to Rudolph Buzzard by John Person. Rudolph Buzzard (R) (Seal), Wit: John Riley, Mathias Eagner, Edward Kelley. Proved in open court 5 March 1787. Recorded 24 May 1787.

A, 273-275: Lease and release. 26 July 1784, Rudolph Buzzard of Ninety Six District, planter, to Andrew Russell of same, planter, for £200, 150 acres in Craven County on south side Broad River, granted to Rudolph Buzzard 2 April 1773, recorded in Book OOO, page 250. Rudolph Buzzard (RB) (Seal), Wit: John Riley, David Ruff, Henry Graff. Presented in open court 5 March 1787 and permitted on a former proof. Recorded 24 May 1787.

A, 276-278: Lease and release. 3 & 4 Nov 1777, Henry Oxner of Ninety Six District, planter, to John Pearson of same, for £300, 60 acres granted to Henry Oxner 25 May 1774 on south side Broad River adj. Jacob Falker, Rudolph Buzzard, Richard Clark, recorded in Book 3G, page 44. Henry Oxner (OH) (Seal), Eliz'th Oxner (X) (Seal), Wit: David Edwards, Mich'l Kenemore (M). Presented in open court and permitted on a former proof 5 March 1787. Recorded 25 May 1787.

A, 279-281: Lease and release. 1 & 2 April 1777, John Pearson of Ninety Six District, planter, to Rudolph Buzzard of same, for £500, 60 acres granted to Henry Oxner 25 May 1774 on south side Broad River adj. Jacob Falker, Rudolph Buzzard, Richard Clark, recorded in Book 3G, page 44, conveyed by said Henry Oxner and his wife Eliz'th 3 & 4 Nov 1777 to John Pearson. John Pearson (Seal), Elis Pearson (E) (Seal), Wit: Peter Reece, John Badner (I), Conrad Zuber. Presented in open court and permitted on a former proof 5 March 1787. Recorded 25 May 1787.

A, 282: 8 Feb 1787, Marthey Awbrey of Richmon County, Georgia, for £60 sterling to Thomas Gordon of Newberry County, SC, negro man named Frank. Marthey Awbrey (O) (Seal), Wit: Jonathan Downs, Thos Gordon. Proved in open court 6 March 1787 and recorded on May "the last day" 1787.

A, 283-285: Lease and release. 18 & 19 Nov 1785, James Shepherd of Newberry County, planter, to William Shepherd, taylor, of same, for £5 sterling, 300 acres in the fork between Broad & Saludy Rivers on a small branch of Cannons Creek adj. James Shepherd, Robert More, granted to said James Shepherd 19 June 1772. James Shepherd (JS) (Seal), Wit: M. Glazier, John Riley, Josiah Edwards. Proved in open court 6 March 1787 and recorded 31 May 1787.

A, 286-287: Lease and release. 8 & 9 Nov 1786, Joseph Thompson of Ninety Six District to David Pugh of same, for £80 sterling, 188 acres on waters of Scotch creek of Bush River adj. David Jenkins, Thomas Lewis, Cornelius Cockran, John Williamson, 200 acres granted to Stephen Elmore 18 May 1771 conveyed to said Joseph Thompson 30 & 31 Dec 1773. Joseph Thompson (Seal), Wit: Benjamin Vanhorn, John Coppock, Wm. Jinkins. Proved in open court 6 March 1787 and recorded 1 June 1787.

A, 288-290: Lease and release. 16 & 17 March 1772, James Proctor of Berkley County, planter, to Edward Gore of same, for £75 SC money, 100 acres in the fork between Broad and Saludy River on a small branch of Patterson's Creek, a fork of Indian Creek, granted 1 Sept 1768 to Edward Gore, recorded in Book DDD, page 193, memorial in Book I No. 9, page 187. James Proctor (Seal), Mary Proctor (X), Wit: Abraham Gray, Martha Boyes, Rob't Proctor (mark). Proved in open court 6 March 1787 and recorded 1 June 1787.

A, 291: 7 May 1786, Charles King of Newberry County to Andrew Yeargain of same, for £100 sterling, 200 acres in the fork of Broad and Saludy Rivers on the north fork of Kings Creek, granted to said Charles King 13 Aug 1766, entered in the Auditor's office in Book H, No. 8, page 88, 12 Sept 1766, recorded in Book AAA, page 83. Charles King (Seal), Wit: Edw'd Finch, Levi Casey, Garrett Smith. Acknowledged in open court 6 March 1787 and recorded 1 June 1787.

A, 292: 5 March 1787, George Boulware of Edgefield County to Thomas B. Rutherford of Newberry County for £12 s11 sterling, 100 acres adj. land of Joseph Chapman, half of a tract of 200 acres granted to James Neill. George Boulware (Seal), Wit: James Kelley, Rob't Rutherford, Elizabeth Rutherford. Proved in open court 6 March 1787 and recorded 1 June 1787.

A, 293-294: South Carolina, Newberry County. Before Phil'n Waters, J.P., appeared Timothy Griffin and saith that he the s'd Griffin bought a tract of 100 acres of Jacob Jones on the waters of Little River for the consideration of one cow & calf & £5 old currency sometime in the year 1772, and that the s'd Jacob Jones made him titles by way of lease & Release and the s'd Griffin sold the tract to Christopher Hardy by lease and release, sworn 6 April 1787. Timothy Griffin (O), before P. Waters, J.P.

This day came Jean Hardy before Robert Gillam, J.P., and saith that the above mentioned 100 acres on the waters of Little River that her husband Christopher Hardy bought it from Timothy Griffin & sold the same to George Ellet & made title by lease and release, sworn 9 April 1787. Jean Hardy (I), before Robert Gillam, J.P.

This day came Wm Pitts before Robt Gillam, J.P., and saith that some years past the s'd Pitts was present at the signing & Sealing of the lease and release from Christopher Hardy to George Ellet, sworn 9 April 1787. William Pitts before Robert Gillam, J.P.

This day came William Ellett & Rebecah Ellett and says that about 8 years ago last winter that George Ellett was in the possession of the lease & release from Jacob Jones to Timothy Griffin & from Griffin to Christopher Hardy & From Hardy to George Ellet and that the afores'd George Ellet's house was burn near that time and they believe that the s'd lease & Release was burnt and also the original grant of Jacob Jones, sworn 9 April 1787. William Ellit (X), Rebeccah Ellit (X) before Robert Gillam, J.P.

This day George Ellet came before Robert Gillam, J.P., and saith that about 8 years ago the s'd Ellet had in his possession the leases & Releases of the 100 acres granted to Jacob Jones on the waters of Little River and by the misfortune of his house being was burnt.... 9 April 1787. George Ellit (X) before Robert Gillam, J.P.

Plat: Pursuant to a precept directed by John Bremar Esquire, Deputy Surveyor General, bearing date 3 April 1770, I have admeasured & laid out to Jacob Jones 100 acres in Craven County on waters of Little River adj. Charles Pitts and all other sides bounds on vacant land, certifyed 15 August 1770. Pr Jno Caldwell, Dept. Sur. Sur Genls office, 3 April 1787, A True Copy from the original plat. Memorial entered in Book M. No. 12, page 3, 26 Sept 1772.

A, 295-297: Lease and release. 18 March 1776, George Gray of Charleston, Tavern keeper, to Robert More of Craven County, planter, for £125 SC money, 200 acres between Broad & Saludy Rivers on waters of Cannons Creek adj. Wm Gray, Barnett Mountz, David Martin, Mr. Roper, Wm. Moore, James Shepherd, granted 26 Sept 1772 to George Gray. George Gray (Seal), Wit: James Shepherd, James Craig, William Moore. Presented in open court and permitted on a former proof 5 June 1787. Recorded 18 June 1787.

A, 298-300: Lease and release. 27 & 28 Nov 1782. George Smith, planter, of Ninety Six District, planter, to John Windle of same, planter, for £300 SC money, 100 acres on waters of Cannons Creek in Craven County, grant recorded in Book FFF, page 290, granted to Adam Black 25 May 1774 and conveyed by him to William Taylor 20 & 21 Dec 1776, and by s'd Taylor to John Edwards 9 & 10 Dec 1777, and by s'd Edwards to George Smith 11 & 12 Aug 1778. George Smith (GS) (Seal), Wit: William Taylor (T), Jacob Sengle (X). Permitted on a former proof 5 June 1787 and recorded 12 June 1787.

A, 301-303: _____ 1787, James Lester Sen'r of Ninety Six District to James Lester Jun'r of same, for £10 sterling, 105 acres on waters of Saludy adj. Summers land, James Lester Sen'r, Godfrey Tryer, part of 350 acres granted to s'd James Lester Sen'r 6 June 1785. James Lester Senr (Seal), Caterina Lester (X) (Seal), Wit: John Lester, Charles Lester (X), Samuel Duncan. Plat included for 105-acre tract dated 20 April 1786. Proved in open court 5 June 1787 and recorded 19 June 1787.

A, 304: State of South Carolina, Newberry County. William Malone Sen'r of county aforesaid for love, good will & affection to my son William Malone Jun'r of same, 100 acres on the waters of Enoree River, part of tract granted to Daniel Johnson, 31 May 1787. W Malone (Seal), Wit: Thomas Mathis, Gilbert Gilder, Thomas B. Rutherford. Acknowledged in open court 5 June 1787 and recorded 19 June 1787.

A, 305-307: Lease and release. 30 & 31 May 1787, Jacob Rogers, planter, of the state of North Carolina, to John Wilson of Newberry County, for £41 SC money, 100 acres on a branch called Beaverdam Creek adj. land of Saml Lonam, granted to Jacob Rogers 28 July 1769, recorded in Book DDD, page 316. Jacob Rogers Jun'r (Seal), Wit: Samuel Pearson, Mercer Babb, Joseph Coppock. Proved in open court 5 June 1787 and recorded 19 June 1787.

A, 308-310: Lease and release. 17 & 18 May 1787, Jesse Brooks of Newberry County & Anne his wife, of Newberry County, to Samuel Pearson, of same, for £100 SC money, 100 acres adj. said Brooks, Mercer Babb, said Samuel Pearson. Jesse Brooks (Seal), Ann Brooks (mark) (Seal), Wit: Thomas Brooks,

Mercer Babb, William Pearson. Proved in open court 5 June 1787 and recorded 21 June 1787.

A, 311-313: Lease and release. 13 & 14 April 1774, James Williams of Ninety Six District, to Samuel Pearson of same, for £200 SC money, 200 acres in the fork of Broad & Saludy Rivers on a branch of Bush River called Beaverdam, recorded in Book 3B, page 176, granted to Providence Williams 20 Aug 1767, the said Providence Williams being deceased intested, the above named James Williams being the eldest son & heir at law. James Williams (Seal), Wit: Elijah Teague, Samuel Crumton (X), John Furnas. Permitted to be recorded on a former proof 5 June 1787 and recorded 27 June 1787.

A, 314-316: Lease and release. 9 & 10 May 1787, Samuel Pearson, farmer, of the settlement of Bush River, to Jesse Spray of the settlement of Beaverdam branch, both of Newberry County, for £500 old currency, 200 acres granted to Providence Williams 28 Aug 1767 and conveyed to Samuel Pearson 13 & 14 Apr 1774 by James Williams, eldest son and heir to Providence Williams deceased, on the beaverdam near Bush River in Craven County, memorial entered in Book H. No. 8, page 276, 12 Sept 1767. Samuel Pearson (Seal), Wit: Mercer Babb, Thomas Brooks, William Pearson. Acknowledged in open court 5 June 1767.

A, 317-319: Lease and release. 30 & 31 May 1787, Charles Gary of Newberry County to Nathan Williams of same, for £50 sterling, 150 acres granted to Charles Gary 6 March 1786 adj. Charles Gary, Samuel Newman, John Gary. Charles Gary (C) (Seal), Wit: Charles Griffin, John Pitts, William Gary. Acknowledged in open court 5 June 1787 and recorded 3 July 1787.

A, 320-322: Lease and release. 19 & 20 April 1787, Michael Johnston of Gilders Creek, Ninety Six District, planter, to Rose Glynn of Enoree, Newberry County, Ninety Six District, planter, for £7 SC money, 90 acres on south side Enoree adj. John Johnson, Mary Frost, granted to Michael Johnson 9 Feb 1787, recorded in Book 3Z, page 226. Michael Johnston (Seal), Wit: William Murray, James Johnston, Christopher Krausse. Acknowledged in open court 6 June 1787 and recorded 3 July 1787.

A, 323-326: Lease and release. 3 & 4 May 1775, Peter Ruble of Craven County, to William Aspinell of same, for £40 SC money, 200 acres in Berkley County granted to said Peter Ruble 8 July 1774. Peter Ruble (Seal), Wit: William Elmore, John Elmore, John Aspinell. Permitted to go on record on a former proof 6 June 1787 and recorded 6 July 1787.

A, 326-328: Lease and release. 7 & 8 Dec 1786, Joseph Cannon of Newberry County, settlement of Indian Creek, for £50 sterling, 100 acres granted to Joseph Cannon granted 13 Sept 1774 in Berkley County on a small branch of Indian Creek, recorded in Book TTT, 16 Oct. Joseph Cannon (IC) (Seal), Rosanah Cannon (R) (Seal), Wit: William Simpson (mark), Elizabeth Cannon

(X), James Lindsey. Proved 6 June 1787 in open court and recorded 6 July 1787.

A, 329-331: Lease and release. 4 & 21 Aug 1785, William Young of Ninety Six District & Elizabeth his wife to John Riser of same, planter, for £50 SC money, 50 acres, part of 200 acres in Berkley County in the fork between Broad & Saludy Rivers on a small branch of Canons Creek adj. land laid out to Abraham Norsdick, Matthias Brittle, Michael Sapport, Mary Gray, Doris Feltmet, granted to Abraham Taylor 21 May 1772 conveyed to William Young 7 Dec 1772. William Young (Seal), Elizabeth Young (X) (Seal), Wit: Jacob Bozsart, John Eigleberger. Acknowledged in open court 6 June 1787 and recorded 6 July 1787.

A, 332-334: Lease and release. 28 & 29 July 1785, William Young of Ninety Six District, yeoman, & Elizabeth his wife to John Riser of same, planter, for £50 SC money, 75 acres, part of 200 acres in Berkley County in the fork between Broad & Saludy Rivers on a small branch of Canons Creek adj. land laid out to Abraham Norsdick, Matthias Brittle, Michael Sapport, Mary Gray, Doris Feltmet, granted to Abraham Taylor 21 May 1772 conveyed to William Young 7 Dec 1772. William Young (Seal), Elizabeth Young (X) (Seal), Wit: Jacob Bozsart, John Eigleberger. Acknowledged in open court 6 June 1787 and recorded 6 July 1787.

A, 335-337: Lease and release. State of So Carolina, Newberry County. 2 & 3 Feb 1787, Jacob Braight of Newberry County, Planter, to Jacob Hovacre, for £ 50 sterling, 100 acres originally granted unto Mathias Bresh (alias Braight), on a branch of Broad River called Cannons Creek in Berkley County adj. Michael Seaboolls, Elizabeth Lecrowns, Jacob Metts, Laurence Lecrownes, recorded in Book VV, page 207. Jacob Braight (X) (Seal), Barbara Braight (X) (Seal), Wit: Jacob Boszart, Andreas Thomas (X), Adam Schwank (X). Proved in open court 6 June 1787 and recorded 7 July 1787.

A, 338: Catharine Jones, widow, for love, good will U& affection to my loving sons Joseph Jones, John Little Jones & Thomas Jones, son of Thomas Jones deceased, tract of land of 294 acres granted to Catherine Jones 7 Nov 1785 on a branch of Broad River on the north side of Saludy River, dated 6 June 1787. Catherine Jones (Seal), Wit: Thos B. Rutherford, Thos Hill, John Cox. Acknowledged in open court 6 June 1787 and recorded 9 July 1787.

A, 339-341: Lease and release. 16 & 17 Sept 1782, John Ferdress of Ninety Six District, planter, and Catherine his wife, to William Hutchison of same, for £200 SC money, tract granted to Michael Earlybush, 50 acres in Craven County, now Ninety Six District., on a branch of Second Creek adj. Conrad Fulk, Adam Setzler, Charles Seigler, recorded in Book FFF, page 99, and said Mich'l Earlybush has conveyed to Michael Leitner Esq'r 16 & 17 Jan 1775 and said Michael Leitner transferred to John Ferdress 5 & 6 April 1779. John Ferdrees (Seal), Cathrine Ferdrees (X) (Seal), Wit: John Buchannan Senr,

William Sower, Mary Leitner (X). Proved in open court 7 June 1787 and recorded 10 July 1787.

A, 342: State of South Carolina, Newberry County. 18 April 1787, Maximillian Haynie of county aforesaid for love & good will to my daughter Nancy Rutherford, wife of Thomas B. Rutherford, negro boy named Charles about 16 years of age. Maximilian Haynie (Seal), Wit: Thomas Mathis, William Amburgey, Robert Rutherford. Proved in open court by the oaths of Thomas Mathis & William Amburgey 7 June 1787 and recorded 10 July 1787.

A, 343-345: Lease and release. 4 Dec 1786, Francis Sommers & his wife Christiana Sommers of Newberry County to Nathan Busby of same, for £10 sterling, 100 acres, part of 300 acres in the district of Orangeburgh on Pennys Creek, a branch of Broad River, granted 5 June 1786, recorded in Book NNNN, page 139. Francis Sommers (Seal), Wit: Geo Ruff, David Edwards, Michael Mintz. Proved in open court 7 June 1787 and recorded 11 July 1787. "Memorials transmited."

A, 346: John Reid, taylor, of Newberry County, Ninety Six District, for £10 sterling to Thomas Stark Senior of same, planter, 50 acres on a branch of Gilders Creek, dated 13 Aug 1787, right retained for redemption until 1 Jan 1788. John Reid (Seal), Wit: Josiah Elliot, William Stark. Acknowledged in open court by John Reid 3 Sept 1787 and recorded 17 Sept 1787.

A, 347: State of South Carolina, Newberry County, 96 Dist. 29 March 1787, Joel Chandler of county aforesaid, planter, to Charles Littleton, planter, of same, for £100 sterling, tract on north side Enoree River granted to said Chandler 15 May ___, memorial entered in Book L., No. 11, Page 289, 150 acres adj. John Clark, James Murfey, Charles Littleton. Joel Chandler (X) (Seal), Wit: W. Wadlington, John Clark, John Chandler (mark). Proved by the oaths of John Chandler and John Clark 3 Sept 1787.

A, 348-350: Lease and release. 27 & 28 Oct 1786, Samuel Brown of Newberry County, Ninety Six District, farmer & Ann his wife, to Walter Herbert of same, for £12 SC money, 225 acres on waters of little River adj. John Copack, Wilson, Jane McKewn, Peter Tuton, William Miles, granted to Samuel Brown 2 May 1785. Samuel Brown (Seal), Ann Brown (Seal), Wit: Daniel Smith, Isaac Jenkins. Acknowledged in open court by Samuel Brown 3 Sept 1787 and recorded 18 Sept 1787.

A, 351-353: Lease and release. 13 Dec 1786, Hugh Gregg of Newberry County, and Elizabeth his wife, to Seth Hatcher of same, for £7 sterling, 67½ acres on north side Saludy River adj. John Krand[?], granted to Rosena Kraud[?], now wife of Adam Black, 100 acres 25 May 1774. Hugh Gregg (Seal), Elizabeth Gregg (mark) (Seal), Wit: Daniel Clary, John Boyd (B). Proved by the oath of Daniel Clary and John Boyd 3 Sept 1787 and recorded 19 Sept 1787.

A, 354: Newberry County, Ninety Six District, 11 Aug 1787. Amry Day to William Swift of Abbeville County for £35 sterling, negro wench about 11 years of age named Venes, 11 Aug 1787. Amry Day (X) (Seal), Wit: James Mayson, James Goodman. Proved by the oaths of James Mayson Esq'r and James Goodman 3 Sept 1787.

A, 355: 3 March 1787. William Hancock of Newberry County, planter, to Henry Mills of same, for ten shillings, tract on north side Enoree, part of tract laid out to John Anderson, 174 acres adj. Elijah Parott, William Liles, Thomas Lake. William Hancock (Seal), Betsey Hancock (X) (Seal), Wit: Thoroughgood Chambers, James Kelly, Richard Hancock. Proved 3 Sept 1787 by the oath of James Kelly and Richard Hancock. Recorded 20 Sept 1787.

A, 356-357: Lease and release. 1 & 22 Apr 1787, Charles Jones of Newberry County to John Gary of same, for £50 sterling, 100 acres granted to Charles Jones 5 June 1786 adj. Wm Johnston, Moses Kirkland, John Dalrymple. Charles Jones (Seal), Martha Jones (mark) (Seal), Wit: Thomas Gary, James Smith (mark), Mary Jones. Acknowledged in open court 3 Sept 1787 by said Charles Jones and recorded 20 Sept 1787.

A, 358-360: Lease and release. 11 & 12 May 1786, Jeremiah Chandler of Ninety Six District to Thomas Perry of Newberry County for £30 sterling, 52 acres in the fork between Broad and Saludy on a branch called Enoree adj. William Gordon, Thomas Perry, John Caldwell. Jeremiah Chandler (Seal), Susannah Chandler (mark) (Seal), Wit: Eli Langford, Joel Chandler (X). Acknowledged in open court 3 Sept 1787 by said Charles Jones and recorded 20 Sept 1787.

A, 361: 18 July 1787, John Duncan of Newberry County and Jean his wife to William Adington of same, for £17 s17 sterling, 136 acres, part of 200 acres granted to said John Duncan on the lick branch of Duncans Creek in the fork between Broad and Saludy Rivers, granted 11 Aug 1774, recorded in Book RRR, page 574. John Duncan (I) (Seal), Jean Duncan (mark) (Seal), Wit: James Duncan, Moses Duncan (mark), Ringnall Odell. Acknowledged in open court 3 Sept 1787.

A, 362-363: Lease and release. 1 Sept 1787, John Johnston and Margret his wife of Indian Creek, Ninety Six District, blacksmith, to Andrew McLees of Gilders Creek, district aforesaid, planter, by £250 SC money, 150 acres on Kings Creek branch called Rocky Branch, waters of Enoree, adj. Thos Wadlington, Reubin Gilder, Charles King, granted 15 Feb 1772 to said Johnston. John Johnston (Seal), Margret Johnston (mark) (Seal), Wit: Josiah Elliott, S. M; Patrick Lowry. Proved by the oaths of Josiah Elliott and Patrick Lowry 3 Sept 1787.

A, 364: 31 Aug 1787, Charles Littleton of Newberry County, planter, to Edw'd Wadlington of same, for £5 sterling, 30 acres on north side Enoree River adj. Thos Perry. Charles Littleton (Seal), Wit: John Clark, William Henson (X),

Stephen Clark. Proved by the oaths of John Clark and William Henson 3 Sept 1787.

A, 365: John Grasty of Newberry County for love, good will & affection to my loving brother Thomas Grasty of same, tract of 150 acres in the fork of Broad & Enoree River about two miles from Liles ford, on a branch called Beaverdam, adj. Sarshel Grasty, Bond's land, 27 Aug 1787. John Grasty (Seal), Wit: Thos Gordon Senr, Thos Gordon Junr, Jesse Gordon. Acknowledged in open court 3 Sept 1787.

A, 366-368: Lease and release. 19 & 20 July 1787, Charles King of Newberry County to James Campbell of same, for £50 sterling, 125 acres on Patterson's Creek, being the east end of a 230-acre tract granted 6 March 1786 to Charles King, grant recorded in Book HHHH, page 280. Charles King (Seal), Wit: Thomas Lindsey, Penington King, James Lindsey. Acknowledged in open court 3 Sept 1787.

A, 369-371: Lease and release. 2 & 3 June 1787, William Aspinell of Ninety Six District, to William Jackson of same, for £25 sterling, 100 acres in the fork between Broad & Saludy Rivers on a branch of Cannons Creek, part of 200 acres granted to s'd Aspinell 1 Jan 1785. William Aspinell (O) (Seal), Wit: Peter Julian Jun'r, Moses Smith (X), Thos W. Waters. Acknowledged in open court 3 Sept 1787.

A, 372-373: Lease and release. 9 Sept 1785, William Aspinell of Ninety Six District, to Moses Smith of same, for £20 sterling, 100 acres in the fork between Broad & Saludy Rivers on a branch of Cannons Creek, part of 200 acres granted to s'd Aspinell 1 Jan 1785. William Aspinell (O) (Seal), Wit: Reason Reagan, Tho's Reagen, Thos W. Waters. Acknowledged in open court 3 Sept 1787.

A, 374-375: Lease and release. 3 Sept 1787, Philemon Waters of Newberry County, Colonel of the Ridgment and Quorom of the Peace, to Charles Thompson of same, planter, for £6 s10 d6 sterling, 150 acres on south branch of Broad River adj. said Charles Thompson, Absalom Thompson, Robert Moore plat certified 16 July 1785, granted 5 June 1786, recorded in Book NNNN, page 161. P Waters (Seal), Wit: John Means, Geo Ruff. Acknowledged in open court 3 Sept 1787.

A, 376: 3 Sept 1787, Joseph Goodman of Newberry County to Philip Fagans of same, for £20 sterling, 88 acres on a small branch of Bush River granted to said Joseph Goodman 6 Nov 1786. Jos. Goodman (Seal), Wit: Thos W Waters, Peter Buffington. Acknowledged in open court 4 Sept 1787.

A, 377-379: Lease and release. 7 & 8 Sept 1785, Terrel Riley of Ninety Six District, planter, to Christopher Weateman of same, planter, for £100 sterling, 250 acres granted to Terrence Riley and he died intestate, descended unto Terrel Riley, in two separate grants, one dated 1775 recorded in Book CC, page 329, 100 acres on the waters of Cannons Creek, and one (plat dated 3 June 1769) recorded in Book K No. 10, page 155, 50 acres adj. land of Terrence Riley. Terrel Riley (Seal), Wit: Lewis Coursey, David Weedingman (X), Christian Weedingman (X). Proved in open court 4 Sept 1787.

A, 380: 13 June 1787, Jeremiah Stark of Newberry County to Samuel Ward of same, for £50 sterling, 100 acres in the fork of Saludy and Enoree Rivers, granted to said Jeremiah Stark 21 May 1772, entered in the Aud'r Genls office in Book L, No. 11, page 350, 15 Aug 1772, recorded in Secretary's Office in Book LLL, page 316. Jeremiah Stark (Seal), Wit: Charles King, Thomas Lindsey, William Tinney. Acknowledged in open court 4 Sept 1787 by said Jeremiah Stark.

A, 381: 31 Aug 1787, John Lindsey of Newberry County for £50 sterling to Edward Finch of same, 110 acres in Newberry County on waters of Kings Creek, part of tract granted to said John Lindsey in 1774, recorded in Book TTT, page 233, at Davises old mark, Hamilton's corner, Joseph Hampton's line. John Lindsey (Seal), Wit: Charles Kink, Thos Stark, Saml Lindsey. Acknowledged in open court 4 Sept 1787.

A, 382: South Carolina, Newberry County. Personally appeared Peter Hawkins and made oath that in the month of January 1770 that he saw John Adkins and Sarah his wife sign a deed unto Joseph Scott, lease & release, tract of 200 acres on waters of Bush River, and was proved before John Caldwell Esquire now deceased and that he was the person that proved them, 3 March 1787. Peter Hawkins before Robt Rutherford, J.P.

Also Diana Cambell saith that she was a subscribing evidence to the above, 3 March 1787. Diana Cambell (X) before Robt Rutherford, J.P.

Also appeared Joseph Scot & saith that the within lease and release was burnt in his house and other effects on 25 Dec 1786, 3 March 1787 Joseph Scot before Robt Rutherford, J.P.

The above were presented in open court 4 Sept 1787.

A, 383-385: Lease and release. 25 Apr 1776, John Cobbs of Craven County, planter, and Judith his wife to William Johnson of same, for £100 SC money, 200 acres in Craven County on waters of Bush Creek, adj. William Geary, one Dalrymple, granted 12 Apr 1771. John Cobbs (Seal), Judith Cobbs (X) (Seal), Wit: Joseph Atkins, Thomas Atkins, Mary Atkins. Presented in open court 5 Sept 1787 and recorded on a proof made before John Hunter in the year 1783.

A, 386-388: Lease and release. 9 & 10 March 1787, William Johnston of Newberry County to Benjamin Willson, planter, of Laurence County, SC, for £156 SC money, 200 acres on waters of Bush Creek adj. William Geary, one Dalrymple, granted 12 Apr 1771 to John Cobbs, and conveyed to said

Johnston 25 Apr 1776. William Johnston (Seal), Wit: Thomas Johnston Jun'r, Jehu Johnston (X), James Goggans. Acknowledged in open court 5 Sept 1787.

A, 389-391: Lease and release. 10 & 11 Aug 1787, Christian Shubert & Mary Shubert his wife of Orangeburgh District to Maryann Lane of same, for £100 sterling, 200 acres in Craven County on south side Broad River adj. Peter Crim, Benjamin Busby, granted 18 May 1771 to Charles Leobolt Shubert, recorded in Book HHH, page 340, and said Christian Shubert being son & heir at law of said Charles Leobolt Shubert. Christian Shubert (Seal), Mary Shubert (X) (Seal), Wit: Daniel Beem, William Strickland, Maryann Lightsey (X). Proved in open court 5 Sept 1787 by the oath of Daniel Beem & Mary Lightsey.

A, 392: Martin Dye of Newberry County to John Gary of same, one cow, one plow, one pot, one chest, one little spinning wheel, one pail 2 working tubs & chairs, a quantity of bacon, a quantity of cotton, a quantity of pewter, and one feather bed and furniture, 30 May 1787. Martin Dye (mark), Wit: Robert Hayes. Charles Neal. Proved by the oaths of Robert Hayes and Charles Neal in open court 5 Sept 1787.

4 Sept 1787, George Bridges of Newberry County, planter, to William Adkins, son f Wm. Adkins deceased, with the approbation of his mother Margaret Adkins doth put himself apprentice to said George Bridges to learn the art or mistery of a blacksmith for 3 years. George Bridges (Seal), William Atkins (mark) (Seal), Wit: Test W. Malone Clk, Ct. Acknowledged in open court 5 Sept 1787.

A, 393-395: Lease and release. 18 & 19 Aug 1777, John Fish of Craven County, SC, and Ann his wife, to Daniel Horsey Jun'r of same, for £100 SC money, tract granted 3 April 1775 to Joseph Fish, 100 acres on south side Enoree River adj. Daniel Johnston, John Souter, Isaac Horsey. Joseph Fish (Seal), Ann Fish (X) (Seal), Wit: Thomas Jones, Charles Coats, Thomas Johnston. Acknowledged in open court 5 Sept 1787.

A, 396: 17 May 1787, William Johnson of Newberry County to Robt Rutherford & Joseph Hampton, both of same place, for £100 sterling, 182 acres on a branch of Second Creek adj. Thomas Jones. Wm Johnston (Seal), Wit: Jas Strother, William Amburgey, John Goodwin (mark). Proved in open court 6 June 1787 by the oath of James Strother and ordered to lie for further proof and proved 5 Sept 1787 by the oath of Wm Amburgey.

A, 397-399: Lease and release. 30 & 31 March 1787. Jacob Wern (Warn) of Orangeburgh District, now Newberry County, planter, to John Wern of same, planter, for £50 SC money, tract of 350 acres granted to Felix Frederick Warren (otherwise Vernn), in Craven County on Beaver Creek (otherwise Bear Creek) grant says on waters of Broad River, but actually on waters of Saludy River, recorded in Book NN, page 157, and said Felix Frederick Warren (otherwise Wernn) died intestate whereby his eldest son Jacob Wernn became heir at law. Jacob Warn (Seal), Mary Warn (X) (Seal), Wit: John Follmore, George Setzler, Michl Leitner. Proved at a court for Newberry County 5 June 1787 by the oath of John Follmer & ordered to lie for further proof and at a court 5 Sept 1787 proved by the oath of George Setsler.

A, 400-401: Lease and release. 13 & 14 Apr 1787, William Burton & & Phebe his wife of Newberry County, to Daniel Mackey of same, for £200 sterling, 523 acres, being two tracts of land: one of 400 acres in the fork between Broad & Saludy Rivers on a small branch of Saludy called Little Creek granted to said William Burton 25 Aug 1769; the other part of 300 acres on Little River adj. David Emery, Hamilton Murdock, Robert Goudey, Thomas Green, Wm Burton, granted to William Dogeon 12 Apr 1771 conveyed to said Wm Dogeon to Wm Burton 5 Aug 1773 and recorded in Book Q No 5, page 103. William Burton (Seal), Phebe Burton (X) (Seal), Wit: John Saterwhite Jun'r, Gideon Jones (mark), Alexander McKie. Acknowledged in open court 6 Sept 1787.

A, 402-404: Lease and release. 15 & 16 July 1783, John Lindsey Jun'r of Ninety Six District to John Lindsey Sen'r of same, for £500 SC money, 193 acres on Pennington's Creek, a branch of Collins or Enoree River, part of 350 acres granted to George Wiles and conveyed to Isaac Pennington and said Isaac Pennington did bequeath the said land to his eldest daughter Charity King, wife of Charles King, and said Charles King & Charity his wife conveyed to John Lindsey Junr. John Lindsey Jun'r (Seal), Wit: Jno Blalock Junr, John Speak, Benj'n Taylor (R). Acknowledged in open court 6 Sept 1787.

A, 405-407: Lease and release. 12 & 13 Apr 1785, John Griffin, son and heir at law of Jones Griffin deceased, to Horatio Griffin, both of District of Ninety Six, for £10 sterling, 100 acres, part of 200 acres granted to Edward Brown 12 June 1751 and conveyed by said Edward Brown in his will to Gabriel Clemons and conveyed by said Clemons to John Bates and from thence conveyed to Jones Griffin, father of the above John Griffin, 30 Apr & 1 May 1778, on north side of Saluda River on Bigg Creek adj. John Musgrove, Walles Jones. John Griffin (Seal), Wit: Phil Waters, Isaac Mills. Plat included dated 12 April 1785 by P. Waters, D. S. Proved in open court by the oath of Isaac Mills 6 Sept 1787.

A, 408: 29 Aug 1787. John Hampton, planter, of Newberry County, SC, to John McCoy of state aforesaid, carpenter, for £10 sterling, tract on south side of Enoree River, 100 acres, part of tract laid out to John Hampton and granted 4 Sept 1786, adj. Hampton's old corner. John Hampton (Seal), Wit: W. Malone, Thos B. Rutherford, Henry Slappy. Acknowledged in open court 7 Sept 1787 by said John Hampton.

A, 409-411: Lease and release. South Carolina, Ninety Six District. 1 & 2 May 1784, Mathew Brooks of district aforesaid to William Burton of same, for £2000 SC money, 200 acres, part of 300 acres granted to said Mathew Brooks 10 Jan 1771 on a branch of Saludy River called the beaver Dam adj. Gibeon

Jones, James Johnston, Thomas Brooks. Mathew Brooks (Seal), Agatha Brooks (X) (Seal), Wit: David Terrel Riley, William Burton, Gibeon Burton. At a court 7 Sept 1787 admitted on a former proof which was made before Bartlet Saterwhite, Esqr.

A, 412-414: Lease and release. 10 Feb 1786, Gibeon Jones of Berkley County to William Burton of same, for £100 sterling, 200 acres, part of tract of 300 acres granted to Gibson Jones 1 Oct 1769 adj. James Cleland. Gibeon Jones (mark) (Seal), Catharine Jones (X) (Seal), Wit: George Goggans, Sintha Burton (X), William Burton, Gibeon Burton. Proved in open court 7 Sept 1787 by the oaths of William Burton & Gibeon Burton.

A, 415-417: Lease and release. 1 June 1787, John Neelly of the City of Charleston, SC, to John Cunningham of same, shopkeeper, for £60 sterling, 200 acres in Berkley County on north side of Saludy River on a small branch thereof, granted 29 Apr 1768. John Neelly (Seal), Wit: Robt Tate, Richard Speake, John Murray, John Lindsey. Proved in open court 7 Sept 1787 by the oaths of Richard Speake and John Lindsey.

A, 418-420: Lease and release. 15 & 16 March 1773, John Miller & Anes his wife of Craven County, to John Johnston of same, for £155 SC money, tract of 150 acres in the fork between Broad & Saludy Rivers in Craven County adj. Jacob Cromer, granted 13 May 1768 to John Miller grant recorded in Book DDD, page 198. John Miller (Seal), Annes Miller (mark) (Seal), Wit: William Johnston, Hugh Wiseman, Alexander Johnston. Proved in open court 7 Sept 1787 by the oaths of William Johnston & Alexander Johnston.

A, 421: 10 May 1788, Thos Johnston Jun'r of Newberry County to James Goggans of same, one sorrel hose about 8 years old, four hands high, paces & trots, a small streek in his face, no brand to be seen, one rone mair 14 hands high about 13 years old, natural pacer, branded on the rump 13, also one black cow marked with tow half crops in his forehead, and one black cow marked with two half crops the uper side of the left ear, and the underside of the right, and one black yearling calf, one dun pided cow copped off left ear, one bed, pided calf, one feather bed & furniture, two pewter dishes, one pewter bason, four pewter plates, one earthen dish, six earthen plates, three punch bowls, 1 small spinning wheel, one frame table, one pail one small piggin, one iron pot, two chairs. Thomas Johnston Jun'r (Seal), Wit: Thomas Johnston Sen'r, David Johnston. Proved in Newberry County by the oath of Thomas Johnston & David Johnston 4 June 1788 before John Hampton, J.P. Recorded 7 June 1788.

A, 422-424: Lease and release. 5 & 6 Dec 1787, Moses Embree of Washington County, North Carolina, planter, to Henry Steedam of Newberry County, SC, for £10 sterling, two tracts of land containing 200 acres: 150 acres on south side of Bush River adj. Jacob Brooks, part of 200 acres granted to John Jones 13 June 1770 and conveyed to Moses Embree 9 March 1771; the other of 50 acres adj. said 150 acres adj. Jacob Brooks, Benjamin Buzbee, John Ridgell, granted to James Daugharty 10 April 1771 and conveyed to Moses Embree 8 Oct 1771. Moses Embree (Seal), Margret Embree (Seal), Wit: Joshua Inman, Jehu Inman, Evan Embree. Proved 2 June 1788 in open court.

A, 425-427: Lease and release. 3 & 4 March 1788, George Gray Sen'r of Newberry County, to George Gray Jun'r of same, miller, for £100 sterling, 250 acres in the fork between Broad and Saludy Rivers on a branch of Cannons Creek granted 7 Nov 1752 to Adam Roop, adj. Nicholas Wise, Casper Gray, conveyed by said Roop to George Gray 4 & 5 Oct 1768. George Greh[?] (German signature) Seal, Wit: David Ruff, Casper Pfister (German signature). Proved in Newberry County by the oath of Casper Piester 3 June 1788 before Geo Ruff, J.P. Recorded 18 June 1788.

A, 428: 14 Jan 1788, Susanna Windel of Newberry County to George Gray Sen'r of same, for £100 sterling, tract on Cannon's Creek granted to Barnard Livingston 13 March 1752 and conveyed to his son John Livingston by heirship and from said John Livingston to Daniel Dewalt by impowering John Martin to make sufficient title 5 & 6 Oct 1769, which the said Susannah Windel was the s'd Daniel Dawalt's deceased lawful wife, this tract being the third part of said tract, 116 acres. Susanna Windle (X) (Seal), Wit: David Ruff, Casper Pfister. Proved in Newberry County by the oath of Casper Piester 4 June 1788 before Geo Ruff, J.P. Recorded 18 June 1788.

A, 429-430: 31 Dec 1782, William Caldwell of Ninety Six District, planter, to James Caldwell of same, for the better maintenance of the said James Caldwell, 450 acres on a branch called Mill Creek adj. John Neely, James Martin, Oliver Towles (decd), Christopher Neely, Nathaniel Foshee, John Phillips (decd). Wm Caldwell (Seal), Wit: John Saterwhite Sen'r, John Saterwhite Jun'r. Proved in Ninety Six District by the oath of John Saterwhite Jun'r 2 Jan 1783 before J. W. ____, J.P. Recorded 10 July 1788.

A, 431-433: Lease and release. 27 & 28 May 1788, Wm Turner, planter, of Newberry County, 96 District, admr. of the estate of Bartholomew Flanagan deceased, to Michael Burtz, planter, for £10 SC money, 200 acres on waters of Beaver Dam adj. Mathew Brooks, Nathaniel Hayworth, recorded in Book RRR, page 582. William Turner (Seal), Wit: Jehu Inman, Robert Russel, Frederick Burtz. Proved in Newberry Court in open court 2 June 1788 by Jehu Inman.

A, 434: 8 Jan 1788, Thomas Gordon and his wife Elizabeth to Barbery Hancock, all of Newberry County, for £82 sterling money of SC, 36 acres on waters of Peters Creek, part of tract of 310 acres granted by North Carolina to George Robinson 13 Oct 1756 and purchased by John Mitchel and since purchased by Thomas Gordon of the said John Mitchel (deceased) and conveyed to Thomas Gordon 28 Dec 1785, between Enoree and Tigar River adj. Croll, Thomas Hill, Thomas Gordon. Acknowledged in open court by Thomas and Elizabeth Gordon 2 June 1788.

A, 435: State of South Carolina, Orangeburg District. Thomas Turner and Mary Turner have rece'd of Thomas Gibson Jun'r and Ann Gibson, one negro boy named Jack and sundry other articles, as their full portion of her deceased Father's William Umphreys estate, 25 Aug 1785. Thomas Turner (X), Mary Turner (X), Wit: Levi Manning, John Watkins. Proved by the oath of Levi Manning 4 June 1788.

A, 435: Arraminta Wilson of Ninety Six District, Newberry County, to John Musgrove, son of William Musgrove, of Newberry County, one bay gelding seven years old, no brand, having a white streak on the right side of neck, and a snip on his under lip, also having a long tail, dated 25 Jan 1788. Araminta Wilson (Seal), Wit: Mary Musgrove (mark), Carolina Musgrove (X). Acknowledged in open court by Arraminta Willson 4 June 1788.

A, 436: 17 July 1784, Solomon Nicholls of Ninety Six District, to Elizabeth Nicholls and William Miller, her son, of same, after my decease to occupy all my said personal estate, two cows and calves marked 2 crop and hole in each ear & under keal in the left ear & a bay mare and colt, one negro wench named Bett, remainder of s'd personal estate to be divided amongst the children of Elizabeth Nicholls. Solomon Nicholls (mark) (Seal), Wit: Charles Willson, Saml Kelley. Acknowledged in open court 4 June 1788.

A, 437-438: 17 July 1784, Solomon Nicholls of Ninety Six District, to Mary Anne Renwick of same, 187 acres on a small branch of Indian Creek in the fork between Broad & Saludy Rivers, adj. Thomas Wadlington, Thomas Dugan, Jacob Ducket, Eve Catherine Keysirin, granted 19 Sept 1770 to Margaret Herbison. Solomon Nicholls (mark) (Seal), Wit: Charles Willson, Saml Kelley. Acknowledged in open court 4 June 1788.

A, 439-440: 17 July 1784, Solomon Nicholls of Ninety Six District, to Agness Renwick of same, 150 on Gilders Creek in the fork between Broad & Saludy Rivers, adj. Daniel Gullen, Margaret Herbison, Robert Dugan, in three separate tracts of 50 acres each granted to Andrew Powers 17 Nov 17--, 50 acres granted to Michael Callerson[?] 17 July 17--, adj. land of Margaret Herbison, Robert Dugan. Solomon Nicholls (mark) (Seal), Wit: Charles Willson, Saml Kelley. Acknowledged in open court 4 June 1788.

A, 441-442: 17 July 1784, Solomon Nicholls of Ninety Six District, to Elizabeth Nicholls and William Miller, her son, of same, 250 on Gilders Creek in the fork between Broad & Saludy Rivers, granted 17 Feb 1767 to Daniel Gullick. Solomon Nicholls (mark) (Seal), Wit: Charles Willson, Saml Kelley. Acknowledged in open court 4 June 1788.

A, 443-435: Lease and release. 14 & 15 Aug 1774, Nathaniel Hillin & Kesiah his wife of Edisto in the Province of SC, planter, to William Tanney, planter, of Ninety Six District, for £150 SC money, tract granted 3 June 1765 to Nathaniel Hillin, 100 acres on a branch of Gilders Creek called Jackson[?] branch. Natt Hillin (Seal), Keziah Hillin (X), Wit: James Hillin, John Cannon (mark), Keziah Cannon (mark). Proved in Orangeburgh District by the oath of James Hillin 16 Aug 1774 before Samuel Rowe, J.P. Recorded 18 July 1788.

A, 446-449: Lease and release. 26 & 27 Feb 1788, William Tinney, of Ninety Six District, to John Huston Jun'r of same, for £100 sterling, tract granted 3 June 1765 to Nathaniel Hillin, 100 acres on a branch of Gilders Creek, recorded in Book YY, page 533, memorial entered in Book G No 7, page 378, and conveyed by said Nathaniel Hillin to William Tinney 15 Aug 1774. William Tinney (Seal), Wit: Robert Turner, Joseph Brown, William Tinney (X). Proved in Newberry County by the oath of William Tinney Jun'r 3 June 1788. Recorded 20 July 1788.

A, 450-452: Lease and release. 7 & 8 Oct 1771, James Daugherty of Berkley County, SC, planter, to Moses Embree of same, planter, for £20 SC money, 50 acres granted to James Daugherty 10 Apr 1771, in Berkley County on waters of Bush River adj. John Ridgdall, Benjamin Busby, Jacob Brooks, James Hogg. James Daugherty (Seal), Jeane Daugherty (mark) (Seal), Wit: Henry Coats (mark), John Coats, Enos Elleman. Proved in Craven County by the oath of Enos Elleman before Saml Cannon, J. P., 22 Nov 1771. Recorded 20 July 1788.

A, 453-455: Lease and release. 11 & 13 Dec 1787. William Simpson, farmer, of the settlement of Indian Creek, to James Brooks, planter, of Newberry County, for £50 sterling, 115 acres on a small branch of Indian Creek adj. land laid out to & claim by Rich'd Broks, John Loften, Wm Speakman, Ansel Bearden, granted 2 Nov 1785, recorded in Book FFFF, page 306. William Simpson (Seal), Mary Simpson (X) (Seal), Wit: Clement Gore, Ja's Lindsey, John Loften. Proved 3 June 1788 by the oath of James Lindsey & Clement Gore before Rob't Rutherford, J.P. Recorded 21 June 1788.

A, 456-458: Lease and release. 12 & 13 May 1787, Arthur Barrett, planter, of Ninety Six District, Newberry County, to Robert Russell, planter, of same, for £--, 51 acres on north side Saludy River on waters of said River, grant recorded in Book LLLL, page 90, dated 5 June 1786. Arthur Barrott (Seal), Sarah Barrott (X) (Seal), Wit: James Cleland, Martin Chester. Proved in Newberry County by the oath of James Cleland 2 June 1788 before Geo Ruff, J.P. Recorded 20 June 1788.

A, 459-461: Lease and release. 25 & 26 Feb 1788, John North, planter, of the State of Georgia, to Joshua Inman of Newberry County, SC, for ten shillings, 100 acres on waters of Beaver Dam Cree a branch of Saludy River surveyed for said John North 15 Nov 1771 adj. Thos Yates, Jonathan Gilbert, William Turner. John North (Seal), Wit: Jacob Barrett, James Barrett, John Spann (I). Proved in Newberry County by the oath of James Barrott 2 June 1788 before Geo Ruff, J.P. Recorded 21 June 1788.

A, 462-464: Lease and release. 28 & 29 Oct 1787, John Ridgdal of Ninety Six District, to Thomas Haskett of same, for £10 sterling, 150 acres on waters of

Bush Creek adj. said John Ridgdal, part of tract granted to said John Ridgdal 22 March 1767. John Ridgdall (Seal), Wit: Robt Speer, John Maxwell, John Wilson. Plat included. Proved by the oath of Robert Speer 2 June 1788 before Geo Ruff, J.P. Recorded 22 June 1788.

A, 465-467: Lease and release. 14 & 15 April 1788, Jacob Hoffman of Ninety Six District, to Reason Reagan of same, for £500 sterling, tract on waters of Bush River, on a branch called Palmeto and granted to Jacob Hoffman (deceased) 1 Feb 1758, recorded in Book SS, page 215, adj. Azariah Pugh, Thos Jenkins, John Riley, Enoch Pearson, and fell to the present Hoffman as heir to said Jacob Hoffman deceased. Jacob Hoffman (mark) (Seal), Wit: Azariah Pugh, Jesse Pugh, Thos Reagan. Proved in Newberry County by the oath of Jesse Pugh 2 June 1788 before Geo Ruff, J.P. Recorded 22 June 1788.

A, 468-470: Lease and release. 15 & 16 Jan 1788, Samuel Rall of Lexington County, SC, yeoman, to Israel Gaunt of Newberry County, for £35 s15 d3 sterling, 100 acres on waters of Edisto River, on a branch thereof called Chinkapin Creek between Black Creek and Lightwood not Bridge Creek. Saml Rall (Seal), Wit: John McClelland, John Vanlew, Jacob Neets. Proved in Newberry County by the oath of John McCleland 2 June 1788 before Geo Ruff, J.P. Recorded 23 June 1788.

A, 471-473: Lease and release. 5 Feb 1788, Isum Wiott and Nelly his wife, and Susannah Lisenba of Ninety Six District, to Samuel Harris, bricklayer, of same, for £30 sterling, 100 acres on waters of Pages Creek adj. Charles Gilliam, Samuel Proctor, granted to Solomon Wiott 6 Sept 1772, and the above Isum Wiott & Susannah Lisenba became possessed of said tract by virtue of being heirs at Law to said Solomon Wiott deceased. Susannah Lisenba (S) (Seal), Isum Wiott (Seal), Elender Wiott (X), Wit: John Rodgers, Little B. Harris, Harris Gillam. Proved in Newberry County by the oath of Little Berry Harris 2 June 1788 before William Caldwell, J.P. Recorded 24 June 1788.

A, 474: 9 Nov 1787, William Taylor of Newberry County for love & good will to my loving daughter Sarah Taylor, 50 acres of land whereon I now live, four cows & their increase, one black mare & her increase, and all my household furniture to be her own right after my death, by the course of nature that my wife Mary Less[?] Taylor have any other children by me, then the articles to be equally divided amongst the aforesaid Sarah Taylor & others that I should have. William Taylor (Seal), Wit: Thomas Rutherford, Nancy Rutherford (X). Proved in Newberry County by the oath of Thomas Rutherford 9 June 1788 before Robt Rutherford, J.P. Recorded 28 June 1788.

A, 475-477: Lease and release. 20 & 21 June 1787, James Willson of Newberry County, Ninety Six District, and wife Jane, to Adam Glazier, planter & School Master of same, for £35 sterling, tract granted 6 Feb 1773 to Jane Williams, 100 acres in Craven County on Williams Creek, a branch of Broad River, recorded in Book FFF, page 190. James Willson (Seal), Jane Willson (X) (Seal), Wit: Thos B. Rutherford, Jeremiah Williams, Joseph Caldwell. Proved in Newberry County by the oath of Thomas Rutherford 9 June 1788 before Robt Rutherford, J.P. Recorded 28 June 1788.

A, 478-480: Lease and release. 25 & 26 Jan 1775, George Strawther of Orangeburgh District, SC, to Isaac Morgan of same place, planter, for £200 SC money, 250 acres in Berkley County in the fork Between Broad & Saludy Rivers on a fork of Second Creek called Horses branch, waters of Broad River, granted 7 May 1774, adj. Daniel Horsey & New Irish. George Strother (Seal), Wit: John Minck, Jacob Lindner [Sen'r], Jacob Lindner [Jun'r]. Proved 6 Nov 1777 before Wm Houseal, J.P. for Ninety Six District, by the oath of John Minck. Recorded 28 June 1788.

A, 481-483: Lease and release. 31 Aug & 1 Sept 1787, Frederick Gray of 96 Dist, Newberry District, planter, to Jeremiah Williams, of same, planter, for £30 sterling, 61 acres on Williams Creek waters of Broad River below the Lane, adj. Wm Hamilton, Thomas Hamilton, Crosson, Jeremiah Williams, recorded in Book DDDD, page 317, granted to Frederick Gray 6 June 1765. Frederick Gray (Seal), Wit: Wm. Young, James Graham, Henry Anderson. Proved in Newberry County by the oath of Henry Anderson 3 June 1788 before Geo Ruff, J.P. Recorded 29 June 1788.

A, 484: Barbery Barns of Saludy in the District of Ninety Six, for natural love and affection to my grand daughter Elizabeth Barns, daughter of Barnet Barns of same, one feather bed and furniture, three head of sheep marked with a crop in the right ear & a slit & under bit in the left ear, also three head of cattle marked with a crop in the right ear and slip and under bit in the left ear, one cow & heifer calf, & speckled bull calf; to my grandson James Barns, son of Barnett Barnes, twenty head of neat cattle marked with a crop in the right ear & a slit and under bit in the left ear, also 13 head of sheep, one feather bed & Furniture, one rifle gun, two iron potts, a frying pan, one small black mare, one mouse coloured horse branded AS, one black horse branded IB, one yearling colt, neither marked nor branded, dated 14 June 1787. Barbery Brans (mark) (Seal), Wit: George Goggans, John Edwards, Barney Barnes (B). Proved by the oath of Barney Barnes before George Ruff, Esq., 3 June 1788. Recorded 28 June 1788.

A, 485: State of South Carolina, Newberry County. 11 Feb 1788, John Robison of Newberry County to Thomas Hill of same, planter, for £53 Virginia currency, 53 acres adj. Gordon's line, Thomas Willson. John Robison (X) (Seal), Wit: John Hill, William Hill, Beth [Elizabeth] Barrot (X). Proved 4 June 1788 by the oath of William Hill before Robt Rutherford, J.P.

A, 486: 31 May 1788. Joe Chandler and Haggeth his wife, of Greenville County, to John Maxidon of Newberry County, for £100 sterling, 200 acres in the fork between Broad and Saludy Rivers adj. Farguson, Tedson, Clark, Nathl Davis, granted to said Joel Chandler in 1771. Joel Chandler (X) (Seal), Wit: John Robison (X), James Waters, W. Wadlington. Proved 4 June 1788 by the oath of John <u>Robertson</u> before Robt Rutherford, J.P. Recorded 29 June 1788.

A, 487: 3 June 1788, Rebeca McNeel of Newberry County to my beloved son Abel Anderson McNeel of same, give one molatto boy named Joseph, provided the said Abel Anderson McNeel shall pay unto his brother Edward McNeel £20. Rebeckah McNeel (X) (Seal), Wit: Henry Anderson, Abm. Anderson. Proved 4 June 1788 by the oath of Abraham Anderson before Robt Rutherford. Recorded 29 June 1788.

A, 488-490: Lease and release. 17 & 18 Sept 1785, Gibeon Jones of Ninety Six District for £150 SC money, to James Cleland of same, 100 acres, part of 300 acres granted to Gibeon Jones 31 Oct 1769 in Berkley County on north side of the Beaverdam upon a small branch. Gibeon Jones (mark) (Seal), Wit: George Goggans, Moses Anderson. Proved in Newberry County by the oath of George Goggans 3 June 1788 before Geo Ruff, J.,P. Recorded "last day of August" 1788.

A, 491: Richard Strother of State & Colony of South Carolina and Newberry County hath agreed to settle Elizabeth McCray on the land & premises calld Bunkers Hill, during her life and her child after her & the said Richard Strother doth give her Liberty to use water from a fountain without the bounds of the above land which is computed two acres, dated 19 March 1788. R. Strother (Seal), Wit: Sanford Cockrill, Wm. Hutchison. Proved in Newberry County by the oath of Sanford Cockrill 6 June 1788 before John Hampton, J.P. Recorded 5 Oct 1788.

A, 492-494: Lease and release. 8 & 9 March 1771, John Jones of Berkley County, SC, planter, and Mary his wife, to Moses Embree of same, weaver, for 15 shillings, 200 acres in the fork of Broad & Saludy River, adj. Jacob Brooks, granted to John Jones 13 July 1770, grant recorded in Book FFF, page 6. John Jones (Seal), Mary Jones (X) (Seal), Wit: Enos Ellimon, John Duncan (mark), John Jones Jun'r. Proved by the oath of John Duncan 12 July 1771 before John Caldwell, J. P. for Craven County.

A, 495-497: Lease and release. 16 & 17 May 1788, Thomas Stark Sen'r of Newberry County and settlement of Gilders Creek, to Robert Anderson & John Turner, late from the Kingdom of Ireland but now of county aforesaid, for £200 Virginia money, 300 acres on Gilders Creek, a small branch of Enoree, granted to Thomas Stark. Tho's Stark (Seal), Rachel Stark (X) (Seal), Wit: Michael Johnston, John Huston Jun'r, Robert Turner. Proved 3 June 1788 by the oath of John Huston Junior before George Ruff, J.P. Recorded 8 Oct 1788.

A, 498-499: 11 Feb 1788, John Clark of Union County, SC, and Mary his wife, to Rignall Odell of Newberry County, for £70 sterling, 250 acres in Newberry County on a small branch of Enoree River called Duncans Creek, recorded in Book FFF, page 3. John Clark (Seal), Mary Clark (X) (Seal), Wit: Ralph

Hunt, Henry Clark, John Pearson. Proved in Newberry County by the affirmation of John Pearson 1 Sept 1788 before Robert Rutherford, J.P. Recorded 10 Oct 1788.

A, 500-502: Lease and release. South Carolina, Laurance County. 20 & 25 April 1788, James Johnson & Peggy his wife of Winton County, SC, to John Williams Junior of County aforesaid, for £400 sterling, 395 acres in Newberry County on north side Saluda River on Mudlick Creek, in two different tracts, both granted to James Johnson, one of 100 acres 2 Oct 1768 and other 296 acres 11 May 1771. James Johnson (Seal), Peggy Johnson (mark) (Seal), Wit: John Saterwhite Jr., Beveley Holt (mark). Proved 2 June 1788 by the oath of Beveley Holt before William Caldwell, J.P. Recorded 10 Oct 1788.

A, 503: South Carolina, Ninety Six District. 27 Sept 1787, William Davis of County of Laurance, Senior, to Mary Morriss, widow, of Roan County, North Carolina, but now of county aforesaid, for £10 sterling, 30 acres, part of 200 acres granted to s'd William Davis 22 Sept 1769 in Berkley County in the fork between Broad & Saluda Rivers on a branch of Indian Creek called Hedlys Creek. William Davis (Seal), Wit: James Lindsey, Joseph Davis. Proved 2 July 1788 by the oath of John Lindsey before Levi Casey, J. P. Recorded 11 Oct 1788.

A, 504-506: Lease and release. 28 & 29 March 1788, John Roberts of Ninety Six District, planter, to Joshua Reeder, planter, of Gilders Creek, district aforesaid, for £100 SC money, tract granted to John Roberts 1 April 1786, recorded in Book KKKK, page 44, adj. Joshua Reeder, Herman Davis, Volentine, William Wilson. John Roberts (Seal), Wit: P'tk Lowry, Josiah Elliott, William Tinney. Proved 3 June 1788 by the oath of William Tinney & Isiah Elliott before James Mayson, J.P. Recorded 11 Oct 1788.

A, 507-510: Lease and release. 26 & 27 Feb 1788, Benjamin Cobb and Ann his wife of Newberry County for £30 sterling to Isaac Grant, Shoemaker, of same, 198 acres on north side Saluda River and waters of Mudlick Creek adj. Oliver Towles, Graham, Henry Wilson, James Caldwell, Nathl Fooshee, granted to said Benjamin Cobb 7 Nov 1785. Benjamin Cobb (Seal), Ann Cobb (An) (Seal), Wit: William Satterwhite, Little B. Harris. Proved by the oath of John Satterwhite 2 June 1788 before George Ruff, J. P.

A, 510-513: Lease and release. 30 & 31 May 1788, James Ballinger of Newberry County, Ninety Six District, farmer, and Liddia his wife, to David Jenkins of same, for £57 s2 d10 sterling, 200 acres on north side of Bush River on a little branch thereof, surveyed 10 March 1767 for Cornelius Cockran, granted to James Ballinger 10 Apr 1771, and another tract of 100 acres adj. said James Ballinger, granted 11 Feb 1773. James Ballinger (Seal), Lydia Ballinger (+) (Seal), wit: Enoch Pearson, David Pugh, Walter Harbert (H). Proved in Newberry County by the attestation of David Pugh 3 June 1788 before George Ruff, J.P. Recorded 19 Oct 1788.

A, 514-515: 4 Jan 1788, Richard Speake of Newberry County, SC, to William Finch of same, for £100 Virginia currency, 150 acres on south side Broad River on both sides Second Creek, tract granted to Robert More 7 May 1774, recorded in Book QQQ, page 211, conveyed to Fight Risinger, then to George Dawkins and will by George Dawkins to his son Joseph Dawkins and conveyed by Joseph Dawkins to Rich'd Speake, adj. land of Daniel Johnson, Peter Collins, Samuel Willson. Richard Speake (Seal), Wit: John Dawson, James Lindsey, Charles Crenshaw. Proved in Newberry County by the oath of Charles Crenshaw 12 July 1788 before John Lindsey, J.P.

A, 515-517: 17 Oct 1786, Daniel Blackburn of Effingham County, Georgia, to Ansel Beardin of Newberry County, SC, for £50 sterling, tract granted 11 Aug 1774 to Daniel Blackburn, 150 acres in Berkley County now Newberry County adj. land of William Loften, Mr. Kennada. Danl Blackburn (Seal), Wit: William Tinney, Daniel Winchester, William Bearden (X). Proved 2 Sept 1788 by the oath of Daniel Winchester before John Lindsey, J.P. Recorded 5 Nov 1788.

A, 518-520: Lease and release. 16 & 17 March 1772, William Gilliland, constable of St. Marks Parish, to John Waldroup of said parish, for £50 SC money, 200 acres in Berkley County in the fork between Broad and Saludy Rivers on a branch of Little River called Sandy Run adj. Oliver Towles, granted 15 March 1771 to said William Gilliland, recorded in Book GGG, page 346. William Gilliland (Seal), Wit: Wm. Thos Caldwell, Jean Caldwell. Proved before John Caldwell, J.P. for Craven County by the oath of Wm Thos Caldwell 22 July 1772. Recorded 12 Nov 1788.

A, 521-523: Lease and release. 27 & 28 Dec 1773, Joseph King Sen'r on Saluda River, District of Ninety Six, planter, to Caleb Gilbert on the Beaver Dam branch of Bush Creek, same district, for £250 SC money, 150 acres on a branch call'd the Beaverdam, granted 28 Aug 1767 to said Joseph King Senr, recorded in Book BBB, page 240. Jo's King (Seal), Elizabeth King (X) (Seal), Wit: John Bates (B), Peter Russell. Proved before John Caldwell, J. P. for Ninety Six District, by the oath of Peter Russell 1 Jan 1774. Recorded 8 Dec 1788.

A, 524-526: Lease and release. 7 & 8 Oct 1783, James Neill of Ninety Six District, planter, to John Taylor of same place, planter, for £20 sterling, 200 acres on north fork of Cannons Creek in Craven County, three feet wide & six inches deep, adj. land of Joseph Chapman, recorded in Book 3Q, page 80. James Neill (J) (Seal), Catrin Neill (O), Wit: Georg Miller, Georg Crim, Martin Taylor. Proved in Newberry County by the oath of Martin Taylor 2 Sept 1788 before Robert Rutherford, J.P. Recorded 10 Dec 1788.

A, 527-529: Lease and release. 21 & 22 May 1787, Joseph Thompson of Ninety Six District, to Robert McClure of same, for £30 sterling, 96½ acres on waters of Bush Creek, 84 acres of said land granted to Joth'n Downs, Esqr., recorded in Book NNN, page 376, and transferred to Joseph Thompson, recorded in

Book O-4, page 18, the remaining 12½ acres part of tract granted to Stephen Elmore and conveyed to Joseph Thompson and recorded in Book N-4, page 87. Joseph Thompson (Seal), Wit: David Pugh, William Jenkins, Frances Atkins. Proved in Newberry County by the attestation of David Pugh 1 Sept 1788 before George Ruff, J.,P. Recorded 9 Dec 1788.

A, 530-532: Lease and release. 30 & 31 Oct 1786, John Goodin of Newberry County, to Clement Gore of same, for £20 sterling, 36 acres, part of tract of 250 acres granted to said John Goodin 5 March 1785 on Guilders Creek or a small branch of it, adj. Joshua Reader. John Goodin (mark) (Seal), Wit: Abraham Goodin (A), James Lindsey. Proved in Newberry County 21 July 1788 by the oath of James Lindsey before John Lindsey, J.P. Recorded 11 Dec 1788.

A, 533-535: Lease and release. 30 & 31 Dec 1787, James Cassells of Newberry County, Ninety Six District, planter, to Euclidus Longshore of same, planter, for £40 SC money, 170 acres on a small branch of Saluda called Beaver Dam Creek adj. Jehu Inman, Benjamin Pearson, Mathew Brooks, Willm Turner, Joshua Inman, grant recorded in Book HHHH, page 1, granted 2 Jan 1786 to James Cassells. James Cassells (X) (Seal), Wit: Mercer Babb, Wm Turner, Levi Chester. Proved 1 Sept 1788 by the oath of Mercer Babb before James Mayson, J.P. Recorded 12 Dec 1788.

A, 536-538: Lease and release. 26 & 27 Nov 1787, Michael Shaver, planter, of Ninety Six District, to William Powell, planter, of same, for £80 sterling, 100 acres on waters of Cannons Creek, granted to s'd Shaver 1 Feb 1787, recorded in Book BBBB, page 428. Mich'l Sheffer (German signature) (Seal), Wit: Thomas Harbert, S[aml]. Farrow, John Lindsey. Proved 2 Sept 1788 by the oath of John Lindsey Esq'r before W. Wadlington, J.P. Recorded 13 Dec 1788.

A, 539-541: Lease and release. 11 & 12 Sept 1787, James Johnson of Ninety Six District to Robert Johnston of same, for £100 sterling, 133 acres, part of tract granted to James Johnson of 400 acres 14 Aug 1770 in Berkley County on a small branch of Little River called Davis's branch adj. George Goggans, Daniel Goggans, the rock spring branch. James Johnson (Seal), Rachel Johnson (+) (Seal), Wit: George Goggans, Robert Russell. Proved in Ninety Six District by the oath of Rob't Russell 2 Sept 1788 before George Ruff, J.P. Recorded 14 Dec 1788.

A, 542-543: 26 Feb 1783, John Roberson Sen'r of District of Ninety Six & Elizabeth his wife to Randolph Robinson of same, for £1000 SC money, 225 acres in Berkley County on the fork between Broad & Saluda Rivers on the north side of Enoree River on a small branch called Beaver Dam Creek adj. James Stewart, granted to s'd John Robinson. John Robinson (mark), Elizabeth Robinson (mark), Wit: Thomas Hill, John Hill, John Robinson Jr. Proved in Newberry County 8 Nov 1788 by the oath of John Hill (X) before W. Wadlington, J.P. Recorded 10 Nov 1788.

A, 544-546: Lease and release. 29 & 30 Jan 1787, William Dial of Newberry County, settlement of Indian Creek, to William Guy, late from Virginia, for £20 SC money, 100 acres adj. land of James Willson, Elizabeth Brown, granted 8 Dec 1774 to Wm Dial, recorded in Book FFF, page 539. William Dial (Seal), Wit: Susanah Eatcherson (W), Ann Atcherson (mark), James Lindsey. Proved 30 Jan 1787 by the oath of James lindsey before Levi Casey, J.P. Recorded 5 Jan 1789.

A, 547: James Cook of Edgefield County, SC, for 8,000 weight of merchantable tobacco delivered at the house of William Irby, sells to said William Irby, one negro wench named Jean about 50 years of age, one negro girl about ten years of age named Rhoda, dated 18 July 178. James Cook (Seal), Wit: Wm Anderson, Zachariah Sinquefield. Proved in Newberry County by the oath of William Anderson Esq'r before John Lindsey, J.p., 4 Sept 1788. Recorded 12 Jan 1789.

A, 548-549: 1 May 1786, Col. Thos Brandon of Union County to James Campbell of Newberry County, for £33 sterling, 65 acres to William Hendricks adj. land of John Speak, Robert Willson, Obadiah Edwards, Richard Towles, including the wagon road call'd the Ninetysix Road on Duncans Creek, by power of attorney from William Hendricks dated 7 May 1785, recorded in Union County Book 1, page 96, said 65 acres being part of 200 acres. Tho's Brandon (Seal), Wit: Elizabeth Brandon, James Lindsey. Proved in Newberry County by the oath of James Lindsey 26 Aug 1788 before John Lindsey, J.P. Recorded 12 Jan 1789.

A, 550-552: Lease and release. 4 Aug 1787, John Duncan of Newberry County, 96 District, farmer, & Elizabeth his wife, to George Watson of same, shoemaker, for £17 sterling, £33 in Ninety Six District on north side of Saluda River below the antient boundary on waters of Bush River, granted to said John Duncan 4 Dec 1786. John Duncan (mark) (Seal), Elizabeth Duncan (X) (Seal), Wit: George Bridges, Miles Duncan (mark). Proved in Newberry County by the oath of George Bridges 4 Sept 1788 before John Lindsey, J.P. Recorded 13 Jan 1789.

A, 553-556: Lease and release. 27 July 1775, John Brooks, Blacksmith of Georgia, to Thomas Brooks, planter, of South Carolina, for £350 SC money, 125 acres between Broad & Saluda Rivers in Ninety Six District on a branch of Bush River call'd Scotch Creek adj. Benjamin Pearson, Hugh Craton, John Brooks, one Wiley, Francis Davis, Jean Wiley. John Broks (Seal), Wit: Elijah Teague, James Daugherty. Proved 3 Sept 1788 by the oath of James Daugherty before Robt Rutherford, J.P. Recorded 19 Jan 1789.

A, 557-559: Lease and release. 20 & 21 Apr 1783, Jacob Felker Senior of Ninety Six District, to Joseph Brown of same, for £250 SC money, tract granted to Jacob Felker 23 June 1774 recorded in Book QQQ, page 544, on south side Broad River adj. Robert Buzard. Jacob Felker (IF) (Seal), Wit:

James Lindsey, William Sharp, Ephraim Liles. Proved 5 Aug 1785 by the oath of James Lindsey before Robert Rutherford, J.P. Recorded 20 Jan 1789.

A, 560-562: Lease and release. 24 & 25 April 1786, Aaron Cates of Ninety Six District to Henry Liles of same, for £50 sterling, 150 acres on south side Broad River adj. land of Robert Buzard, granted to Jacob Felker 28 June 1775 and transferred by him to Joseph Brown 1 April 1783 and from said Brown to Aaron Cates 23 March 1785. Aaron Cates (Seal), Wit: Ephraim Liles, Leonard Zuber, Mich'l Zuber (X). Proved in Ninety Six District by the oath of Michael Zuber 13 Dec 1788 before George Ruff, J.P. Recorded 22 Jan 1789.

A, 563-564: 19 Sept 1787, Joseph Brown and Kiza his wife of Fairfield County, SC, to Henry Liles of same, for £85 sterling, 150 acres in Newberry County on south side Broad River adj. land of Robert Buzzard, granted to Jacob Felker 28 June 1775 and transferred by him to Joseph Brown. Joseph Brown (Seal), Wit: Andrew Russell, Michael Ashford. Proved in Ninety Six District by the oath of Andrew Russell 15 Dec 1788 before George Ruff, J.P. Recorded 23 Jan 1789.

A, 564-568: Lease and release. 8 & 9 March 1768, Hans Peter Boyers of Province of SC, to Patrick Reily of same, for £25 SC money, part of a tract of land between Broad & Saludy Rivers on a small branch that runeth into a creek called Cannons adj. Tarons Reily, granted 3 June 1757, recorded 5 March 1761 in Book E page 40. Hans Peter Boyers (mark) (Seal), Christiana Boyers (mark) (Seal), Wit: Cha's Mason, Isaac Morgan, Abel Anderson. Proved by the oath of Abel Anderson 8 Oct 1788 before Rob't Rutherford, J.P. Recorded 26 Jan 1789.

A, 569-571: Lease and release. 19 & 20 Oct 1782, Patrick Reily of Ninety Six District, SC, mason, to John Reily of same, for £500 SC money, part of a tract of 100 acres between Broad & Saludy Rivers on Cannons Creek, granted 3 June 1757 to Hans Peter Boyers, grant recorded in Book FF, page 164, conveyed to Patrick Reily 8 & 9 March 1758 [sic]. Patrick Reily (P) (Seal), Wit: Michael Dickert, John Seigler (I), Michael Dickert Jun'r. Proved in Ninety Six District by the oath of Michael Dickert 26 Oct 1782 before Geo Ruff, J.P. Recorded 30 Jan 1789.

A, 572-574: Lease and release. 16 & 17 April 1788, William Stark, planter, of Ninety Six District, to Thos Stark of same, yeoman, for £300 sterling, tract granted to Wm Stark of 293 acres on a branch of Bush River called Dry Creek adj. Robert McAdams, William Crow, Jonathan Neil, Jonathan Taylor. William Stark (Seal), Ann Stark (mark) (Seal), Wit: Robert Anderson, Andrew Turner (mark), Hugh Boyd (mark). Proved in Newberry County by the oath of Hugh Boyd 2 Sept 1788 before Levi Casey, J.P. Recorded 2 Feb 1789.

A, 575-578: Lease and release. 4 & 5 Apr 1770, Awbry Noland, Gent., of Berkley County, SC, to W. Wadlington of same, farmer, for £200 SC money,

100 acres between Broad and Saludy Rivers on a branch of Broad Creek called Enoree River. Awbry Noland (Seal), Wit: Charles Littleton, Shadrack Vassels (X), Elizabeth Awbry (EA). Proved in Ninety Six District 2 Sept 1774 by the oath of Cha's Littleton before Thos Wadlington, J.P. Recorded 3 Feb 1789.

A, 579-582: Lease and release. 8 & 9 May 1775, Zachariah Sparks, planter, of craven County, SC, to William Wadlington, farmer of same, for £225 SC money, 100 acres on a branch of Broad River called Enoree River adj. John Clark, Awbry Noland. Zachariah Sparks (Seal), Mary Sparks (+) (Seal), Wit: Daniel Johnson, Joel Chandler (+), John Hogg (J). Proved 11 May 1785 in Ninety Six District by the oath of Joel Chandler before Edw'd Wadlington, J.P. Recorded 4 Feb 1789.

A, 583-585: Lease and release. 10 & 11 Sept 1787, Ansel Bearden, hatter, of Edgefield County, Ninety Six District, to Samuel Beaks, farmer, of Newberry County, same district, for £50 sterling, 150 acres in Berkley County but now in Newberry County in the fork between Broad & Saluda Rivers, on a small branch called George's branch on waters of Indian Creek, adj. Wm Lofton, Mr. Kennedy, now held by John Lindsey and others, granted to Daniel Blackburn 11 Aug 1775, recorded in Book RRR, page 558, entered in the Auditors office in Book M. No. 13, page 233, 9 Jan 1775, and conveyed to Ansel Bearden 17 Oct 1786. Ansel Bearden (A) (Seal), Wit: James Lindsey, John Garratt (mark). Proved 2 Sept 1788 by the oath of James Lindsey before John Lindsey, J.P. Recorded 5 Feb 1789.

A, 586-589: Lease and release. 10 & 11 Aug 1788, James Brooks of Newberry County, Ninety Six District, and Sarah his wife, to Abijah ONeal of same, for £100 SC money, 100 acres in the fork between Broad & Saludy Rivers on the head spring branch, waters of Bush Creek, granted to Benj. Heaton 5 July 1769, and conveyed to said James Brooks 23 & 24 May 1781, also a tract of 100 acres on north side of a branch of Saluda called Bush Creek granted to James Patty 30 Oct 1770, conveyed by James Patty and Margaret his wife 2 & 3 Nov 1781 to James Brooks. James Brooks (Seal), Sarah Brooks (X) (Seal), Wit: Elisha Ford, Hugh ONeall. Proved in Newberry County by the oath of Elisha Ford 2 Sept 1788 before Levi Casey, J.P. Recorded 5 Feb 1789.

A, 589-592: Lease and release. 7 & 8 July 1788, William Powell Riddell of Newberry County, SC, planter, to John Wheatingman Sen'r of same, planter, for £50 sterling, 100 acres on waters of Cannons Creek, granted to Michael Shaver (alias Shearer) 5 Feb 1787 and conveyed 6 & 7 Nov 1787 to said Wm Powell Riddell, recorded in Book BBBB, page 428. Will'm Powell Riddell (Seal), Wit: Ephraim Cannon, Joseph Caldwell. Proved in Ninety Six District by the oath of Joseph Caldwell 14 July 1788 before Geo. Ruff, J. P. Recorded 6 Feb 1789.

A, 592-595: Lease and release. 29 & 30 Aug 178, John Wilkeson Sen'r of Newberry County, farmer, and Mary his wife, to David Pugh, taylor, of same, for £90 SC money, 200 acres granted to said John Wilkison 30 Oct 1767 in Berkley County on Scotch Creek, a branch of Bush River, adj. said David Pugh, James Dougherty. John Wilkerson Sen'r (Seal), Mary Ann Mary Wilkeson (mark) (Seal), Wit: Robert McClure, John Gottlob Meyer, Jacob Barrett. Proved in Newberry County by the oath of Robert McClure 1 Sept 1788 before Geo Ruff, J.P. Recorded 7 Feb 1789.

A, 596-597: 15 Sept 1786, John Robinson Sen'r of 96 Dist., Newberry County, to John Robinson Jun'r, for £80 sterling, tract in the fork between Enoree & Tyger Rivers in Ninety Six District granted to said John Robinson Senr, 22 March 1769, recorded in Book DDD, page 159. John Robinson (X) (Seal), Wit: Andrew Hunter, Charles Littleton, Hosea Clemmons. Proved 14 Oct 1788 in Ninety Six District by the oath of Andrew Hunter before W. Wadlington, J.P. Recorded 7 Feb 1789.

A, 597-598: 9 July 1788, John Robinson Sen'r of 96 Dist., Newberry County, planter, to John Robinson Jun'r, of same, for £40 sterling, one negro boy named Tony. John Robinson (Seal), Wit: Andrew Hunter, Charles Littleton, Hosea Clemmons. Proved 14 Oct 1788 in Ninety Six District by the oath of Andrew Hunter before W. Wadlington, J.P. Recorded 7 Feb 1789.

A, 599-601: Jonathan Gilbert of Newberry County by bond dated 17 Dec 1785 bound unto Benjamin Heaton & Mercer Babb in the sum of £313 s17 sterling for the payment of £115 s18 d6 by 29 Nov 1786 last past, mortgage of four feather beds, two wagons & Gears, one brass or copper kettle, two iron potts, one Dutch Oven, one black walnut chest, one large trunk, two tables, a dough trough, one woman's saddle, 12 pewter plates, two basons, three dishes, two little one large wheels, six delph plates, turter chairs, two small trunks, one looking glass, one bay horse called Bob, one ditto called George, one sorrel mair, etc., dated 2 Sept 1788. Jonathan Gilbert (Seal), Wit: James Wadlington, Euclidus Longshear (mark), Caleb Gilbert. Proved 3 Sept 1788 by the oath of James Wadlington before Willm Wadlington, J.P. Recorded 9 Feb 1789.

A, 602-604: Lease and release. 3 & 4 March 1778, John Gibbs of Bute County, North Carolina, to Joshua Dinkins of Parish of St. Marks, Craven county, SC, for £400 SC money, tract granted 7 April 1770 to Howell Gibbs, planter, 150 acres in Berkley County in the fork of Broad & Saludy Rivers, on a very small branch of Little River called Mill Creek. John Gibbs (Seal), Wit: John Blanton, Samuel Wiggins. Proved in Fairfield County by the oath of John Blanton 2 Nov 1788 before Isaac Love, J.P. Recorded 20 Feb 1789.

[Page 605 is blank.]

A, 606: Newberry County, Ninety six District. Before Philemon Waters, J. P. for s'd county, appeared Araminta Wilson, admx. of John Musgrove deceased, saith that a certain bond given to said John Musgrove by Michael Dickert for the performance of titles to a tract of land on Saludy River containing 100 acres is burnt, lost, or mislaid, and that she hath no demand against the said Michael Dickert from said Bond, 15 June 178. Recorded 10 Feb 1789.

A, 606-609: Lease and release. 5 & 6 Sept 1778, Matthew Tully of Camden District, SC, to Henry Anderson of Ninety Six District, planter, for £500 SC money, 182 acres in Craven County on Second Creek adj. Jeremiah Williams, Abraham Anderson, James Warden, Henry Anderson, Daniel Horsey, William Richardson. Matthew Tully (Seal), Wit: Jacob Gilder, Gilbert Gilder, Samuel Isaacks. Proved 10 June 1784 by the oath of Samuel Isaacks before John Lindsey, J.P. Recorded 11 Feb 1789.

A, 610-612: Lease and release. 10 & 11 Jan 1788. Adam Manning of the State of Georgia to Ruth Anderson of Ninety Six District, SC, for £100 SC money, 100 acres originally granted to Adam Manning 26 July 1774 on a small draft of Second Creek adj. Saml Lonam, a bounty warrant, Jeremiah Williams. Adam Manning (mark) (Seal), Wit: John Richardson, Lucrease Gilder (X). Proved by the oath of Lucresa Gilder 7 May 1788 before Robt Rutherford, J.P. Recorded 11 Feb 1789.

A, 613-615: Lease and release. 22 & 23 March 1776, John Lindsey Junior of Berkly County, Ninety Six District, SC, and Elizabeth to Joseph Hampton of Kings Creek, same district and county, for £60 SC money, 41 acres, part of 200 acres on the SE side Enoree River on a branch called Kings Creek, adj. Joseph Davis' old trace now the property of Ann Ross widow, Joseph Hampton. John Lindsey Jun'r (Seal), Elizabeth Lindsey (Seal), Wit: Joseph Brown, Thos Lindsey, Samuel Lindsey, Lewis Hogg. Proved in Newberry County 29 Dec 1788 by the oath of Lewis Hogg before W. Wadlington, J.P. Recorded 12 Feb 1789.

A, 616-618: Lease and release. 18 & 19 Jan 1788. Charles King of settlement of Kings Creek, Newberry County, to Joseph Hampton, Blacksmith, for £21 s7 sterling, 150 acres granted to Charles King 6 Aug 1766 on a small branch of Enoree called Kings Creek, adj. land then claimed by Charles King but now held by Edw'd Finch, grant recorded in Book AAA, page 80. Charles King (Seal), Wit: Bartlett Estes, Sebbeloe Lindsey, Jas Lindsey, Edw'd Wadlington. Proved in Newberry County 24 Dec by the oath of Edw'd Wadlington before John Lindsey, J. P. Recorded 12 Feb 1789.

A, 619-620: 3 Sept 1788, Philemon Waters Esq'r of Newberry County to Isaac Elmore of same, for £40 sterling, part of tract granted to John Musgrove and conveyed to Philemon Waters 2 July 1785, recorded in Book S No. 5, 15 May 1786, on north side Saludy River, 100 acres. Philemon Waters (Seal), Wit: Peter Julin, Thos W. Waters. Proved in Newberry County 3 Sept [1788] by the oath of John Lindsey, J.P. Recorded 13 Feb 1789.

A, 621-623: 13 Aug 178, William Turner of Ninety Six District, planter, and Mary his wife, to Philemon Waters of same, esquire, for £500 old currency, being equal to £71 s3 sterling, whereas William Turner the elder, late of

Saludy in the District aforesaid, father to the above mentioned William, did on 1 Feb 1774 make his will and bequeath all the rest of my lands and negroes to my beloved wife Elizabeth Turner during her life and afterwards the said William departed this life leaving the said will in full force, and included in the said clause and whereas the said Philemon Waters did agree with said Elizabeth Turner for the purchase of the said land and she did actually put him in possession thereof, and whereas since the said agreement the said Philemon Waters has been advised that the said Elizabeth has only a life estate in the said lands, and the reversion is in William Turner, eldest son and heir at law of said William Turner deceased., tract on north side of Big Saludy at the mouth of Bush River adj. land of Edward Brown, land lately of Joseph King but now the property of the heirs of John Lark deceased, and also 60 acres on north side of Big Saludy River adj. John Lark. William Turner (Seal), Mary Turner (mark (Seal), Wit: Thos W. Waters, D. Clary. Proved in open court 1 Sept 1788 by the oath of Thos W. Waters.

A, 624-625: 4 Feb 1789, Thomas Hamilton of Abbeville County, Ninety Six District, planter, to Henry Anderson of Newberry County, district aforesaid, for £25 sterling, 100 acres granted to said Thomas Hamilton, recorded in Auditors office in Book H No. 8, page 179, in Newberry County on waters of Second Creek. Thos Hamilton (Seal), Wit: John Hamilton, John Parker. Proved 9 Feb 1789 by the oath of Jno Hamilton before Robt Rutherford, J. P. Recorded 22 Feb 1789.

A, 625-626: 12 Nov 1788, Thomas hill of Newberry County to John Hill of same, for £5 sterling, 50 acres on waters of Peters Creek between Enoree & Tyger Rivers adj. John Robison, Hancock's land, Thos Hill's spring branch. Thomas Hill (+) (Seal), Wit: Richard Hancock, Barber Hancock, James Waters. Proved in Newberry County 19 Jan 1789 by the oath of Richard Hancock before W. Wadlington. Recorded 23 Feb 1789.

A, 626-628: 20 Jan 1788, William Dawkins of Newberry County to James Baird of same, for £10 sterling, 50 acres in the fork of Broad and Saluda Rivers, part of tract granted to George Dawkins Senior decd for 210 acres 29 May 1773, entered in the Auditor's office in Book M. No. 13, page 67, 27 Oct 1774, recorded in the Secretary's office in Book QQQ, page 286, adj. William Dawkins, Isaiah Shirer, Bartholomew Gaurtman, Michael Lietner, said George Dawkins Senior decd and his wife Chloe Dawkins did by lease & release 24 & 25 Jan 1778 convey said tract of 210 acres to Thomas Dawkins, party to these presents being his Eldest son and heir at law to the said tract. William Dawkins (Seal), Wit: David George, John Dawkins, Sarah George (X). Proved by the oath of David George 11 April 1789 before George Ruff, J. P. Recorded 15 April 1789.

A, 628-629: William Woodall do give and bequeath to my two sons John Woodall and Joseph Woodall, tract on which they now live, 100 acres on a branch on the south side of Guilders Creek called Starks branch, to be equally divided between them when they are both of age, only they are not to make sale of s'd land during their mother's life, dated 28 Oct 1788. Wm Wooddall (Seal), Wit: Jean Dennis (mark), Margret Noland (X). Proved in Winton County by the oath of Jean Dennis before William Sisson 7 April 1789. Recorded 17 April 1789.

A, 630-631: Benedick Koone of Ninety Six District, SC, planter, to give to Christiana Booth, tract of 50 acres in the fork between Broad and Saludy Rivers on a branch of Crims Creek, part of tract granted to Andreas Meyer, 500 acres, which the said Benedick Koone bought of said Andreas Meyer, dated 18 Aug 1788. Benedick Koone (mark) (Seal), Wit: Abraham Chapman (AC), George Risor, Henry Sumers. Proved by the oath of Abraham Chapman 17 Feb 1789 before Robert Rutherford, J.P. Recorded 18 Apr 1789.

A, 631-633: 4 March 1786, James Cato of Newberry County to Andrew Yeargain of same, for £100 sterling, 200 acres in the fork between Broad & Saludy River in the fork of Kings Creek, it being a branch of Enoree River, granted to James Cato Sen'r 23 June 1774, entered in the Auditor Generals office in Book M. No. 13, page 101, 14 Nov 1784 [sic], entered in the Secretary's office in Book QQQ, page 518. James Cato (C) (Seal), Wit: Edward Finch, Abner Casey, James Vardaman. Proved 2 April 1789 by the oath of Edward Finch before Levi Casey, J.P. Recorded 20 April 1789.

A, 633-636: Lease and release. 1 & 2 Dec 1788, Charles Neill, of Newberry County, planter, to William Speakman Jun'r of same, for £75 sterling, 150 acres on south side of Bush River commonly known by the name of Charles Neills old place. Charles Neill (Seal), Mary Neill (X) (Seal), Wit: James Lindsey, Thomas Speakman, William Speakman Sen'r (mark). Proved 3 March 1789 by the oath of James Lindsey before W. Wadlington, J.P. Recorded 20 April 1789.

A, 636-637: 16 Feb 1789, James Vardaman, planter, of Newberry County, 96 District, to William Smith, farmer, for £60 sterling, tract on south side Enoree River granted to James Vardaman 5 June 1786, entered in Book LLLL, page 437, 200 acres. James Vardaman (Seal), Jean Vardaman (X) (Seal), Wit: Wit: W. Malone Sen'r, George Johnson, Simon Park (P). Proved by the oath of Simon Park 21 Feb 1789 before Robert Rutherford, J.P. Recorded 24 April 1789.

A, 638: State of South Carolina, Newberry County. William Johnston of Newberry County for £55 sterling to John Johnston, planter, of same, one bay stallion about 15 hands high, 190 years old, a lump in his breast, a blaize in his forehead, a full blooded horse, 17 Jan 1788 the original bill of sale given by James Sharp to me, dated 29 Jan 1788. William Johnston (Seal), Wit: Benjamin Butler (+), Elizabeth Butler (+). Proved in Newberry County by the oath of William Johnston 9 May 1789 before John Lindsey, J.P.

A, 639-641: Lease and release. 7 & 8 Jan 1787, Abraham Gray, of Laurens County, Ninety Six District, sadler, to Charles King of Newberry County, same district, for £100 sterling, 103 acres on Indian Creek adj. land laid out to Abraham Pennington, John Garret, unknown owners, granted to said Gray 2 May 1785, recorded in Book DDDD. Abraham Gray (Seal), Wit: John Odell, William Finch, Wm Gray. Proved 27 Jan 1787 before Levi Casey, J.P., by the oath of Wm Finch. Recorded 18 May 1789.

A, 642-645: Lease and release. 7 & 8 Jan 1788, William Wadlington of Newberry County, Ninety Six District, to William Gilreath of same, planter, for £100 sterling, 200 acres in Berkly County in the fork between Broad & Saludy Rivers on a small branch of Kings Creek adj. James Murphy, recorded in Book OOO, page 473, granted 2 April 1773 to William Wadlington. W. Wadlington (Seal), Wit: Robert Rutherford, Thomas Mathis, Henry Slappy. Proved in Newberry County by the oath of Henry Slappy 16 May 1789 before Robert Rutherford, J.P. Recorded 19 May 1789.

A, 645-648: Lease and release. 18 Oct 1786, Robert Gillam of Newberry County to Daniel Clark of Edgefield County, for £50 sterling, 200 acres granted to Joseph Freeman 26 Sept 1772 adj. Robert Gillam, Samuel Proctor, Sarah Proctor, conveyed by Joseph Freeman to Robert Gillam. Robert Gillam (Seal), Wit: John Jones (+), Delph Day (mark), Susannah Jones (+). Proved in Newberry County by the oath of John Jones 28 Feb 1789 before James Mayson, J.P. Recorded 19 May 1789.

A, 649-650: 15 Oct 1788, Abel Anderson and Rosanna his wife of Newberry County to William Ragland of Wilks County, North Carolina, for £115 Virginia money, 150 acres in Newberry County on both sides Kings Creek, a branch of Enoree River, being a tract granted to Abel Anderson 18 Jan 1765, entered in the Auditors office in Book G, No. 7, page 219, 26 Feb 1765. Abel Anderson (Seal), Rosanah Anderson (Seal), Wit: Charles Crenshaw, Rosanah Anderson (mark), Rachael Anderson (+). Proved in Newberry County 14 Jan 1789 by the oath of Charles Crenshaw before John Lindsey, J.P.

A, 651-652: 28 Feb 1789, Thomas Gordon, Esqr., to Awbrey Noland, Gentleman, both of Newberry County, for £9 s15 sterling, 13 acres on south side of Tyger River between that river & Enoree on Peters Creek, adj. Noland, Crawls[?], granted by Arthur Dobbs, Gov of NC, to George Robinson 13 Oct 1756 and since purchased by John Mitchel and afterwards purchased by said Thomas Gordon 8 Dec 1785, also granted to John Mitchell by SC 1 March 1775. Thos Gordon (Seal), Wit: N. Kelly, Jesse Gordon, Mary Gordon (+). Acknowledged in open court 4 March 1789. Recorded 19 May 1789.

A, 652-653: Joshua Law of Ninety Six District, Newberry County, Doctor, appoints friend Mercer Babb his attorney, to recover or receive of and from all my customers for ____ and medicine, 11 Feb 1789. Joshua Law (Seal), Wit: James Wadlington, Margaret Wadlington (mark). Proved in Newberry County by the oath of Margaret Wadlington 4 March 1789 before W. Wadlington, J.P.

A, 653-657: Lease and release. 9 & 10 Dec 1785, John Bearden & Mary Simpson his mother of Camden District, SC, to Elizabeth Tinsley of Ninety Six District, for £500 former currency of SC, 200 acres on Little River in Ninety Six District, granted to William Bearden 1 Feb 1768, to which the said John Bearden and Mary Simpson his Mother became seized by virtue of being sole heir at law to William Bearden deceased. John Bearden (Seal), Mary Simpson (X) (Seal), Wit: John Golding, Richard Golding, James Tinsley. Proved by the oath of James Tindsley 2 March 1789 before William Caldwell, J.P. Recorded 20 May 1789.

A, 657-661: Lease and release. 28 & 29 Dec 1784, William Sutcliff of St. Johns Parish, SC, to John Wallace of Ninety Six District, for £20 sterling, 100 acres on Goosepond Creek, waters of Saluda in Ninety Six District, adj. Robert Diton, Thomas Clark, estate of James Dyson decd, granted to William Sutcliff 11 Jan 1773, recorded in Book FFF, page 133. William Sutcliffe (Seal), wit: Richard Morris, Thomas Threadcraft, Silvester Sutcliff. Proved 5 Jan 1785 by the oath of Richard Morris before George Ruff, J.P. Recorded 21 May 1789.

A, 661: Darcus Largent of Newberry County, Ninety Six District, for £45 14 3 paid at or before 8 Nov 1785 by John Wallace of same district and county, negro girl named Peggy about 14 years of age, dated 8 Nov 1785. Darcus Largent (+) (Seal), Wit: Wm Anderson, Samuel Savage. Recorded 28 May 1789.

A, 662: Amry Day of Laurance County, Ninety Six District for £40 sterling to John Wallace of Newberry County, negro girl named Venus about 15 years of age, dated 31 May 1788. Amry Day (X) (Seal), Wit: John Saterwhite, Robert Gillam. Recorded 28 May 1789.

A, 663: South Carolina, Newberry County. Before Robert Gillam, J. P., appeared Comfort Stephens and saith that William Winchester Jun'r was born out of wedlock and before she the said Comfort and William Winchester Sen'r was married and that William Winchester Jun'r was no heir to the estate of William Winchester Sen'r but that Daniel Winchester is the Real Heir, 11 March 1787. Comfort Stephens (C). Robert Gillam, J.P.

Richland County. Before me A. B. Ross, J. P. for said county, appeared a woman named Sarah Majors and make oath that William Winchester Jun'r son of Comfort Polson now Stephens was born before wedlock to her knowledge, 7 Aug 1788. Sarah Majors (+), A. B. Ross, J.P.

Before A. B. Ross appeared Sarah Majors and saith that Comfort Winchester now Comfort Stephens was married to William Winchester Sr nearly a year after William Winchester Jun'r was born & that Daniel Winchester is her son and born in wedlock, 7 Aug 1788. Sarah Majors (+), A. B. Ross, J.P. Recorded 29 May 1789.

A, 664: South Carolina, Newberry County. Thomas Burton had sold all my property both in my house & out of doors to Charles Lowry for £100 sterling, 15 Aug 1788. Thomas Burton (Seal), Wit: John Lowry, Charles Lowry. Recorded 29 May 1789.

A, 664-667: 8 Nov 1774, Jacob Farington of Craven County, SC, Ninety Six District, Blacksmith, to Sarah Speak of same, widow, for £150 SC money, 100 acres on waters of Indian Creek granted to said Jacob Farington on Pattersons Creek adj. William Cannon, John Patterson, Mr. Cashaw, Thos Wadlington, Charles King, Jas Catter in Berkly County. Jacob Farington (Seal), Wit: John Hudgins, Samuel Davis, James Lindsey. Proved 3 Sept 1788 by the oath of James Lindsey before John Lindsey, J.P. Recorded 22 June 1789.

A, 667-668: 2 March 1789, Mary, wife of William Turner of Ninety Six, SC, relinquished dower for indenture 13 Aug 1788 to Philemon Waters for 750 acres on north side Saludy River adj. Edward Brown, Joseph King not property of heirs of John Lark, also tract of 60 acres on north side Big Saludy River adj. John Lark. Mary Turner (mark) (Seal) before James Mayson and Jacob Rt's Brown, J.P. Acknowledged by private examination 2 March 1789.

A, 669-672: Lease and release. 3 March 1789, Thomas Brooks of Newberry County, Ninety Six District, farmer, & Susannah his wife, to Margaret Pearson and Enoch Pearson, extx & exr. of the will of Benjamin Pearson, decd., for £100 SC money, 200 acres on a branch of Saludy call'd Beaver Dam adj. land of Caleb Gilbert, James Johnson, certified 5 Sept 1769 by John Caldwell, D.S. Thomas Brooks (Seal), Susanna Brooks (Seal), Wit: James Goodman, Abel Pearson, Robert Pearson. Proved in Newberry County by the oath of James Goodman 3 March 1789 before Thos. W. Waters, J.P. Recorded 24 June 1789.

A, 673-675: Lease and release. 12 & 13 March 1788, Joseph Summers of Ninety Six District to Giles Chapman of same, for £50 sterling, 125 acres on the waters of Bush River adj. Timothy Thomas, Joseph Mooney, John Mills, Enoch Pearson, Joseph Summers, at the wagon road leading to Charleston. Joseph Summers (Seal), Wit: Thos. W. Waters, William Summers, Richard Clagg. Proved by the oath of Thos W. Waters 5 March 1789 before J. Robt's Brown. Recorded 26 June 1789.

A, 676-679: Lease and release. 17 & 18 Oct 1786, John Wallace of Newberry County to Allen Cox of same, for £50 sterling, 100 acres on the bounty adj. land surveyed for Robert Dillon, Thomas Clark, granted to William Sutcliff 6 Feb 1773 and conveyed to said John Wallace 29 Dec 1784. John Wallace (Seal), Wit: Wm Anderson, Timothy Cooper, Thomas Farquhar. Proved 2 March 1789 by the oath of Wm Anderson before James Mayson, J.P. Recorded 29 June 1789.

A, 679-680: John Edwards of Newberry County, Ninety Six District, for £40 sterling to Elizabeth Turner of same, two horses, one yearling mare colt, three negroes Frank, Lydda, and Moses, three cows & calves, two sows & pigs, two feather beds & furniture, one iron pot, one Dutch oven, one plow & plow Irons, one Loom, two pewter basons, six plates, 6 March 1789. John Edwards (Seal), Wit: Samuel Thomas, Elizabeth Cotton (mark). Proved by the oath of Samuel Thomas 28 April 1789 before Mercer Babb, J.P. Recorded 30 June 1789.

A, 680-681: South Carolina, Newberry County. Whereas an action of debt was some time ago commenced by Thomas Dugan in the County Court of Newberry for the sum of £10 against Francis Strother and James Strother and a recovery of £10 and costs obtained by said Thomas Dugan, now Robert Gillam, Sheriff, for £34 sterling sells to Joseph Goodman a negro man named Harry about 25 years old pited with the small pox, dated 22 April 1787. Robert Gillam (Seal), Wit: Paul Caldwell. Acknowledged in court 4 June 1789. Recorded 30 June 1789.

A, 681-685: Lease and release. 31 Oct & 1 Nov 1788, Samuel Waller of Newberry County, planter, and Elenor his wife, to Thomas Davis of Laurance County, both Ninety Six District, and settlement of Indian Creek, for £60 sterling, 250 acres on waters of Indian Creek adj. land of Deadly Bond, Moses Kirkland, granted 23 Jan 1773, recorded in Book NNN, page 52, memorial entered in Book M. No. 12, page 223, 8 __ 1773. Samuel Waller (X) (Seal), Elenor Waller (mark) (Seal), Wit: William Tinney, John Lindsey, Thomas Loftin. Proved 3 March 1789 by the oath of John Lindsey before W. Wadlington, J.P. Recorded 3 July 1789.

A, 686-687: Sarah Horsey of Newberry County for natural affection to Gabriel Anderson & Mary Anderson his wife, one negro man and one negro woman named Primis & Betty, with four children Samson, Nancy, Davy & Debby, 6 May 1789. Sarah Horsey (S) (Seal), Wit: Rob't Powell, John Pope. Proved 1 June 1789 by the oath of Robert Powell before John Lindsey, J.P. Recorded 7 July 1789.

A, 687-688: Sarah Horsey of Newberry County for natural affection to Joseph Rutherford a black cow and calf; to Sarah Hogg a bed and bed cloaths; all the rest of my goods & chattles to Gabriel Anderson, with four children Samson, Nancy, Davy & Debby, 7 May 1789. Sarah Horsey (S) (Seal), Wit: Rob't Powell, John Pope. Proved 1 June 1789 by the oath of Robert Powell before John Lindsey, J.P. Recorded 7 July 1789.

A, 688-691: Lease and release. 21 & 22 Sept 1787, Col. John Lindsey of Newberry County to Mark Love of the settlement of Indian Creek, same county, for £150 SC money, tract granted 5 Oct 1784 to John Lindsey, 271 acres on the old fort branch of Indian Creek adj. Thodorous Feltman now held by James Sproul, Abraham Gray, John Pennington now held by George Akins, recorded in Book AAAA, page 67. John Lindsey (Seal), Elizabeth Lindsey (Seal), Wit: Richard Speake, Samuel Spray, James Lindsey. Proved 1 March 1789 by the oath of Richard Speake and Samuel Spray before W. Wadlington, J.P. Recorded 8 July 1789.

A, 692-695: Lease and release. South Carolina, Ninety Six District. 30 & 31 May 1788, Benjamin Willson of Laurance County, settlement of Duncans Creek, to Providence Williams of Newberry County, settlement of Indian Creek, for £200 sterling, 200 acres granted 12 Apr 1771 to John Cobb, recorded in Book HHH, page 119, on Bush River or Bush Creek adj. William Gary, a Dunrymple [sic for Dalrymple], Henry Middleton, John Gary son of Charles Gary., conveyed by William Johnston to Benjamin Willson. Benjamin Willson (Seal), Elizabeth Willson (+) (Seal), Wit: James Lindsey, John Gary, William Brooks (X). Proved by the oath of James Lindsey 3 March 1789 before W. Wadlington, J.P. Recorded 8 July 1789.

A, 695-699: Lease and release. 13 & 14 Sept 1787, Alexander Gambill of Newberry County, to Dudly Bonds of the settlement of Indian Creek, same county, planter, for £100 sterling, 150 acres, part of tract of 250 acres granted to Charles McBride 20 Oct 1772, recorded in Book MMM, page 376, entered in the Auditors Office in Book M. No. 12, page 48, 18 Oct 1772, on a small branch of Enoree called Indian Creek adj. Adam Shille, John Lofton, Moses Kirkland, Samuel Waller. Alexander Gambill (Seal), Wit: James Willson, Wm. Blackburn, Stephen Sparks (+). Proved 19 July 1788 by the oath of James Willson before John Lindsey, J.P. Recorded 8 July 1789.

A, 699-700: John Robinson Sen'r of Newberry County, planter, for £30 sterling to Ridley Vessels of same, one negro girl named Annaky, one featherbed, dated 8 Aug 1788. John Robinson (+) (Seal), Wit: Charles Littleton, William Wadlington Jr. Proved by the oath of Charles Littleton 26 Nov 1788 before W. Wadlington, J.P. Recorded 9 July 1789.

A, 700-704: Lease and release. 21 & 22 Feb 1788, John Abernathy of Newberry County, and Rhoda his wife, to Dudly Bonds of the settlement of Indian Creek of same, for £20 sterling, tract granted 5 June 1786, recorded in Book KKKK, page 655, 100 acres on waters of Indian Creek adj. Richard Brooks, Robert Brooks, Dudly Bonds, Samuel Waller. John Abernathy (Seal), Rhoda Abernathy (X) (Seal), Wit: James Wilson, James Lindsey, James Johnston. Proved 19 July 1788 by the oath of James Wilson before John Lindsey, J.P. Recorded 9 July 1789.

A, 704-706: 30 Apr 1789, Henry Liles and Ann his wife of Newberry County to George Ashford of same, for £85 sterling, 150 acres in the fork between Broad and Saludy Rivers on south side of Broad River adj. Robert Buzzard, tract originally granted to Jacob Felker and transferred by him to Joseph Brown 20 & 21 Apr 1783, and from Joseph Brown & Keziah his wife to Aaron Cates, 23 March 1785, and by Cates to Henry Liles 24 & 25 April 1786, recorded in secretaries office in Book QQQ, page 54. Henry Liles (Seal), Ann Liles (--) (Seal), Wit: Michael Ashford, Andrew Russell, Redding Ashford. Proved by the oath of Michael Ashford before W. Wadlington, J. P., 30 April 1789. Recorded 20 July 1789.

A, 707-710: Lease and release. 26 & 27 Jan 1789, William Anderson of Newberry County and wife Elizabeth to John Floyd of same, for £300 sterling, 60 acres, part of 100 acres granted to John Lucas 16 Sept 1774, on a branch of Little River called Sandy Run adj. Andrew Erwin, Robert Johnston, John Sims, James Goggans, William Anderson, also 150 acres a part of a tract of 250 acres granted to William Anderson 10 Jan 1770 on south side of south fork of Sandy Run adj. William Pitts, making out 210 acres. William Anderson, Elizabeth Anderson (X), Wit: John Anderson, William Anderson (X), George Goggans. Proved in Newberry County by the oath of George Goggans 2 March 1789 before Robert Rutherford, J.P. Recorded 10 July 1789.

A, 711-715: Lease and release. 18 & 19 May 1773, Joseph Freeman of Berkley County, SC, planter, to Robert Gillam of same, for £50, 250 acres on a small branch of Saludy River adj. Robert Gillam, Samuel Proctor. Joseph Freeman (Seal)m, Wit: John Caldwell, Joseph Crews, Joseph White. Proved 28 Feb 1773 by the oath of Joseph White of Ninety Six District before James Mayson, J.P. Recorded 30 July 1789.

A, 716-719: Lease and release. 23 & 24 Feb 1778, Abraham Gray of Ninety Six District, planter, and Mary his wife, late Mary Pennington and James Bright of same (executors of the will of Jacob Pennington, late of Berkley County, SC, decd), to Reuben Flannagan of same district, for £800 SC money, 200 acres on Indian Creek a branch of Collins's River,and 50 acres on Indian Creek adj. said Pennington, James Ronals. Abraham Gray (Seal), Mary Gray (Seal), James Bright (Seal), Wit: Levi Casey, John Pennington, Ruth Pennington. Proved 31 July 1784 by the oath of John Pennington before Levi Casey, J.P. for Ninety Six District.

A, 720-721: 7 May 1789, Sarah Horsey of Newberry County, to Josiah Rutherford of same, for £12 sterling, 100 acres made over unto the late Daniel Horsey by J. Pearson Jun'r, on a small branch of Broad River called Second Creek but now called Williams's Creek in the fork of Broad & Saludy. Sarah Horsey (S) (Seal), Wit: Gabriel Anderson, John Pope, Robt Powell. Proved 1 June 1789 by the oath of Robert Powell before John Lindsey, J.P. Recorded 8 Aug 1789.

A, 722: Sarah Horsey of Newberry County, for natural affection to Josiah Rutherford of same, one negro named James, dated 6 May 1789. Sarah Horsey (S) (Seal), Wit: Robt Powell, John Pope. Proved 1 June 1789 by the oath of Robert Powell before John Lindsey, J.P. Recorded 10 Aug 1789.

A, 723-724: 7 May 1789, Sarah Horsey of Newberry County, to John Hogg of same, for £10 sterling, part of 147 acres platted to the late Daniel Horsey in the fork of Broad & Saludy on a small branch of Broad River called Second Creek not five feet broad and one deep adj. Flora Brown, Jacob Gilder, land laid out by Bounty warrants, Samuel Lonam, Daniel Horsey, Paul Williams, John Armstrong, 100 acres. Sarah Horsey (S) (Seal), Wit: Gabriel Anderson,

John Pope, Robt Powell. Proved 1 June 1789 by the oath of Robert Powell before John Lindsey, J.P. Recorded 12 Aug 1789.

A, 725: Sarah Horsey of Newberry County, for natural affection to Sarah Hogg of same, one negro girl named Sally, dated 6 May 1789. Sarah Horsey (S) (Seal), Wit: Robt Powell, John Pope. Proved 1 June 1789 by the oath of Robert Powell before John Lindsey, J.P. Recorded 12 Aug 1789.

A, 726-731: Lease and release. 4 & 5 June 1785, John Towles Jun'r, Real Heir and Admr. of Oliver Towles decd's estate in Ninety Six District, to Isaac Crouther in Ninety Six, Storekeeper, for £200 s5 sterling, tract granted 28 Aug 1772 to Robert Brown, 100 acres in Berkley County and said Robert Brown 17 & 18 June 1773 did convey to Oliver Towles, and by another grant dated 9 Sept 1775 to Joseph Grayham, 100 acres in Berkley County on the waters of Mill Creek adj. Oliver Towles, Solomon West, and by another tract dated 8 July 1774 to Nathaniel Harris, 400 acres in Berkley County on Little River on the waters of Mill Creek, and said Nathaniel Harris did on 9 & 10 Sept 1776 convey to Oliver Towles, 123 acres part of said 400 acres. John Towles (Seal), Wit: Julius Nichols Jr., Wm. Swift, James Wilson. Proved in Ninety Six District by the oath of Julius Nichols Jr. before William Moore, J.P., 9 June 1785. Recorded 13 Aug 1789.

A, 731-735: Lease and release. 13 & 14 Feb 1789, Isaac Crowther and Margaret Crowther of District of Ninety Six, Edgefield County, to John McGehee of same, for £200 sterling, tract granted 28 Aug 1772 to Robert Brown 100 acres in Berkley County, 100 acres granted to Joseph Graham 9 Sept 1774 on waters of Mill Creek adj. Oliver Towles, Solomon West, and 123 acres, part of another tract granted 8 July 1774 to Natt Harris for 400 acres [see preceding deed]. Isaac Crowther (Seal), Margaret Crowther (Seal), Wit: Richard Pollard, Francis Wilson, Zach'y Meriwether. Proved in Newberry County by the oath of Francis Wilson before Philemon Waters, J.P., 6 May 1789. Recorded 14 Aug 1789.

A, 736-739: Lease and release. 8 & 9 Dec 1783, Abraham Lindsey of the settlement of Enoree, Ninety Six District, to James Blair of same place, for £250 SC money, 200 acres in the fork between Broad & Saludy Rivers on a small branch called Foster's Creek adj. Isaac Lindsey, Daniel Johnson deceased. Abraham Lindsey (Seal), Wit: Mary Stewart, Thomas Lindsey, James Lindsey. Proved 9 Dec 1783 by the oath of James Lindsey before W. Wadlington, J.P. Recorded 18 Aug 1789.

A, 739-744: Lease and release. 26 & 27 Aug 1778, Thomas Wadlington of Ninety Six District to Solomon Nichols of same, for £2000 SC money, 250 acres between Broad & Saludy Rivers on Guilders Creek adj. "Pattent land." Thos Wadlington (Seal), Elizabeth Wadlington (Seal), Wit: James Lindsey, Levi Walter, Joseph Thomas. Proved 28 Aug 1778 by the oath of James Lindsey before John Lindsey, J.P. Recorded 19 Aug 1789.

A, 744-748: Lease and release. 27 & 28 Aug 1778, Thomas Wadlington of Ninety Six District to Solomon Nichols of same, for £400 SC money, 50 acres between Broad & Saludy Rivers on Guilders Creek adj. Danl Gullick, Margaret Harbison, Robert Dugan, granted to Eve Catharine [sic]. Thos Wadlington (Seal), Elizabeth Wadlington (Seal), Wit: James Lindsey, Levi Walter, Joseph Thomas. Proved 28 Aug 1778 by the oath of James Lindsey before John Lindsey, J.P. Recorded 20 Aug 1789.

A, 748-752: Lease and release. 26 & 27 Aug 1778, Thomas Wadlington of Ninety Six District to Solomon Nichols of same, for £2000 SC money, 187 acres on a small branch of Indian Creek between Broad & Saludy Rivers on Guilders Creek adj. Thos Wadlington, Robert Dugan, Jacob Ducket, Eva Cathrine Kessissen, granted 19 Sept 1770 to Margaret Harbison. Thos Wadlington (Seal), Elizabeth Wadlington (Seal), Wit: James Lindsey, Levi Walter, Joseph Thomas. Proved 28 Aug 1778 by the oath of James Lindsey before John Lindsey, J.P. Recorded 24 Aug 1789.

A, 752-753: South Carolina, Ninety Six District, Newberry County. Elizabeth Vaughan for love, good will and affection to my son Olney Mann Dodgen, 200 acres on west side of Sandy Run adj. Hamilton Murdock, granted to William Dodgen 12 April 1771, dated 5 March 1789. Elizabeth Vaughan (O) (Seal), Wit: John Waldrop, Joseph Brown (J), Mary Brown (+). Proved in Newberry County by the oath of Mary Brown 23 May 1789. Recorded 25 Aug 1789.

A, 754-757: 6 June 1765, Roger Pinckney, Provost Marshall of SC, to James Waldrope of same, whereas Charles Carson was lawfully seized of a tract of 250 acres on a branch of Little River, and said Charles Carson together with Aaron Ryley by their Joint Bond or obligation dated 17 Dec 1763 to John Wagner of Charlestown, merchant, in the sum of £5452 SC money for the payment of £2726 like money with lawful interest, and whereas the said John Wagner in the court of common pleas did implead the said Aaron Ryley & Charles Carson in an action of debt for the recovery of the same, and at November term 1763 did recover judgment, and by write of fieri facias, tract was sold to James Waldrope for £300 SC money. Roger Pinkney Pro Mar'l. (Seal), Wit: James Donovan, Joseph Miligan. Proved 27 April 1789 by the oath of Joseph Milligan before Pat Calhoun, J. C. Recorded 25 Aug 1789.

A, 758-761: Lease and release. 21 & 22 1788, William Lee, merchant, of Charleston, and Sarah his wife, to James Mayson of Newberry County, for £46 s13 d4 SC money, 100 acres on north side Saluda River on a small branch thereof, adj. Robert Cunningham, granted on the bounty 12 Sept 1768 to William Simmons and by him conveyed 23 Aug 1773 to said William Lee. William Lee (Seal), Sarah Lee (Seal), Wit: John Hunter, Levi Casey, Richard Maskill. Proved 3 June 1789 in Newberry County by the oath of Levi Casey Esq'r before William Caldwell, J.P. Recorded 26 Aug 1789.

A, 762-765: Lease and release. 23 & 24 Nov 1788, Thomas Gill and Hannah his wife of the State of Georgia to John Moore of Newberry County, for £100 sterling, 150 acres in Newberry County on waters of Mudlick Creek granted to said Thomas Gill 19 Feb 1767. Thomas Gill (Seal), Hanah Gill (+) (Seal), Wit: James Caldwell, Joseph Hushington [Hutchison]. Proved in Newberry County by the oath of James Caldwell 30 May 1789 before William Caldwell, J.P. Recorded 27 Aug 1789.

A, 765-769: Lease and release. 29 & 30 May 1789, William Braswell of Newberry County, planter, to Samuel Waites of same, for £10 SC money, 200 acres in Newberry County on north side Saludy River adj. Andrew Lee, David McLaran, tract granted to John Willson and conveyed to David Braswell 13 & 14 Oct 1765, and from him to his son William Braswell, being his Heir in Law. William Braswell (Seal), Wit: Jacob Harrell, John Waits, Jonathan Wates. Proved in Newberry County by the oath of John Waites 1 June 1789 before Philemon Waters, J.P. Recorded 28 Aug 1789.

A, 770: For the sum of £80 sterling by Braselmann & Co., for one negro fellow Derry, 10 Sept 1789. Rob't Johnston (Seal), Wit: G. Barnes, Danl Henning. Proved by the oath of George Barnes 14 Sept 1789 before John Lindsey, J.P. Recorded 17 Sept 1789.

A, 771-772: 27 Dec 1787, John Chandler & Rachel his wife of Newberry County to Abraham Eddins of same, for £40 sterling, 207 acres in the fork between Broad & Saluda River on Enoree River, a fork of Broad River, granted to said John Chandler 5 Dec 1785 adj. William Calmes. John Chandler (Seal), Rachel Chandler (X) (Seal), Wit: W. Malone, William Sparks, Lewis Hogg. Proved 21 Aug 1789 by the oath of William Malone Senr before Robt Rutherford, J.P. Recorded 29 Sept 1789.

A, 773-775: Lease and release. 18 Sept 1788, James Ham, the lawful heir of Jeremiah Ham deceased, of Spartingburg County, SC, to William Ham of Newberry County, for £10 sterling, 200 acres in Newberry County on waters of Bush River granted to said Jeremiah Ham deceased 28 Aug 1772. James Ham (Seal), Avarilla Ham (mark) (Seal), Wit: James Young, William Mills (X), James Rutherford. Proved 5 Sept 1789 by the oath of James Rutherford before Mercer Babb, J.P. Recorded 30 Sept 1789.

A, 776-779: Lease and release. South Carolina, 96 District. ____ 1789, Benjamin Berry of Newberry County, and Sarah his wife, to Thomas Spray of same, for £40 SC money, 293 acres on waters of Bush River granted to James lindsey 6 Nov 1786 and conveyed to said Benjamin Berry 4 & 5 Dec 1788, part of tract of 100 acres adj. Clement Davis. Benj'a Berry (Seal), Sarah Berry (mark), Wit: Harmon Davis, Reason Davis (X). Proved by the oath of Reason Davis 1 June 1789 before John Lindsey, J.P. Recorded 6 Oct 1789.

A, 780-781: 2 April 1770 [sic], William Young of Ninety Six District, planter, to John Riley of same, for £200 SC money, 200 acres in the fork between Broad and Saludy Rivers on a branch of Gilders Creek, waters of Enoree adj. James Bonds, granted 3 Aug 1774 to said William Young. William Young

(Seal), Wit: James Ballinger, Edw'd Lane. Proved by the oath of James Ballinger 6 April 1776 before Wm Houseal, J.P. Recorded 23 Oct 1789.

A, 782-785: Lease and release. 10 & 11 Jan 1776, Samuel Duncan, yeoman, in Ninety Six District, and Rebeca his wife, to John Ryley, hatter, for £300 SC money, 144 acres on waters of Palmetto branch and Bush Creek adj. Martha Coppock, John Ryley, James Ballinger, Israel Gaunt, granted to Samuel Dunkin 31 Aug 1774. Samuel Duncan (Seal), Rebeca Duncan (Seal), Wit: John Duncan, Nealson Duncan, William Aspenell (O). A Memorial hereof recorded in the Secretaries office in Book SSS, page 352. Proved by the oath of William Aspernell 12 June 1778 before Samuel Fickling, J.P. Recorded 28 Oct 1789.

A, 786-790: Lease and release. 25 & 26 Nov 1774, John Pearson Jun'r of Craven County, SC, to Capt'n Daniel Horsey of same, for £100 SC money, tract granted 9 Jan 1752 to Paul Williams on a small branch of Broad River called Second Creek now called Williams Creek in the fork between Broad and Saluda River, and at the decease of the said Paul Williams the said tract descended to Jeremiah Williams, his eldest son and heir at law, and the said Jeremiah Williams and Jean his wife conveyed for £50 6 & 7 Apr 1755 to Daniel Williams and said Daniel Williams at his last will and testament devised unto his nephew John Pearson, now conveys 100 acres part of 200 acres now laid off between said Daniel Horsey and David Martin. J. Pearson (Seal), Elizabeth Pearson (mark) (Seal), Wit: George Smith, Ann Martin, James Lindsey. Proved 12 Sept 1784 by the oath of James lindsey before John Lindsey, J. P. Recorded 29 Oct 1789.

A, 791: James Moorhead of Ninety Six District, planter, bound to William Baites of same, planter, in the sum of £500 proclamation money, 18 Dec 1778, to make title to 100 acres at the north westermost corner of a tract of 250 acres. James Moorhead (Seal), Wit: James Williams, Philemon Waters. Proved in Ninety Six District by the oath of Philemon Waters 7 Sept 1789. Recorded 29 Oct 1789.

A, 792-793: 18 Nov 1788, William Nicholes of Lexington County, SC, planter, to Levi Manning of Newberry County, planter, whereas said William Nichols stands indebted to said Levi Manning in the sum of £208 s5 sterling, for the payment of £104 s2 28 Feb 1789, mortgage of negro woman named Hanah & her two children Primas, Sharlotte & a negro boy named Carolina & a negro boy named Abraham. William Nichols (Seal), Wit: John Ihly, Rosanah Manning. Proved in Newberry County by the oath of John Ealy of s'd county 18 July 1789 before Philemon Waters, J.P. Recorded 29 Oct 1789.

A, 794-796: 5 Sept 1789, Samuel Pearson of Bush River, District of 96, farmer, to Willm Pearson, son of said Samuel Pearson, for natural love and affection, 350 acres of land on a branch of Bush River called Palmeter Branch adj. William Williams, Thomas Shaw, Valentine Cloud, granted to Michael Dormer and conveyed by him to Philemon Waters by deed and by said

Philemon Waters to James Donnavan and by another deed to said Samuel Pearson. Samuel Pearson (Seal), Wit: Joseph Furnis, Esther Furnis, Sarah Pearson. Proved in Newberry County 5 Sept 1789 by the oath of Joseph Furnis before Mercer Babb, J.P. Recorded 30 Oct 1789.

A, 796-800: Lease and release. South Carolina, Ninety Six District. 21 & 22 Oct 1789, Joseph Griffin of district aforesaid, sole administrator of Col. James Williams deceased, to Caleb Gilbert, planter, of Newberry County, dist. aforesaid, for £70 sterling, 250 acres in Newberry County on a small branch of Saluda River call'd Beaver Dam adj. John Pendals, John Caldwell Esq'r decd, granted to Thomas Hampton 5 May 1773, and conveyed by said Thomas Hampton to Robt Johnston decd, 25 June 1776, which land fell by heirship to his brother William Johnston, and said William Johnston conveyed to Col. James Williams decd 18 Feb 1778. Joseph Griffin (Seal), Mary Griffin (Seal), Wit: Timothy Goodman, John Griffin, William Benton. Proved in Newberry County by the oath of William Burton 29 Oct 1789 before William Caldwell. Recorded 2 Nov 1789.

A, 801-803: Lease and release. 23 & 24 Aug 1789, Samuel Pearson and Mary of Ninety Six District, Newberry County, to William Pearson, for ten shillings, 100 acres of land on waters of Bush River, a branch of Saluda, being a tract formerly granted to Mary Steeddom now Pearson 17 May 1767. Samuel Pearson (Seal), Mary Pearson (mark) (Seal), Wit: Thomas Brooks, Martha Steeddom, Benjamin Pearson. Proved in Newberry County 24 Aug 1789 by the oath of Thomas Brooks before Mercer Babb, J.P. Recorded 3 Nov 1789.

A, 804-807: Lease and release. 5 April 1788, Joseph & Rachel Hampton of Ninety Six District, to Peter Braselmann of same, for one shilling, 100 acres on Kings Creek in Newberry County adj. land of William Wilson, Charles King, Samuel Chandler. Joseph Hampton (Seal), Rachel Hampton (Seal), Wit: Edward Finch, A. J. DeJonge, M. P., George Barnes. Proved in Newberry County by the oath of George Barns 7 Sept 1789 before Robert Brown, J.P. Recorded 4 Nov 1789.

A, 807: State of South Carolina, Newberry County. William Preast of SC appoints friend George Sinkler of Bedford County, Virginia, my attorney to act in my name concerning two tracts of land in Bedford County for which William Callaway has given his obligation for performance of title to William Patterson, dated 29 Oct 1789. Wm Preast (Seal), Wit: Thos Preast. Proved by the certification of W. Malone, Clk Ct., 29 Oct 1789. Recorded 29 Oct 1789.

A, 808-811: Lease and release. 29 July 1788, Jonothan Gilbert of Ninety Six District, and Hanamell his wife, to Cary Gilbert of same, for £100, 200 acres on Beaverdam Creek granted 28 March 1754 to John Clark by North Carolina but since the late resurvey of the boundary line granted by SC to Jonathan Gilbert 22 June 1774. Jonothan Gilbert (Seal), Hanamell Gilbert (Seal), Wit: Daniel Richardson, Samuel Brown. Proved in Newberry County by the oath of Daniel Richardson 19 July 1789 before Philemon Waters, J.P. Recorded 6 Nov 1789.

A, 811-813: 7 Sept 1789, Robert Gillam, Sheriff of Newberry County & Ninety Six District, SC, to Thomas Gordon of same county and state, planter, whereas John Volentine and Thomas McCrackin in the court of Quarterly Sessions and Common Pleas did implied William Winchester in an action of debt in June Term 1788 and obtained judgment, now by writ of fieri facias to levy £79 s15 d1½ sterling, now sheriff sells 250 acres granted to William Winchester 20 Aug 1767, recorded in Book BBB, page 128 in Newberry County between Broad & Saludy Rivers on the Beaverdam, a branch of Bush River, now sold for £90 sterling to Thomas Gordon. Robert Gillam sheriff (Seal), Wit: G. Barnes. J. Coate. Proved 9 Sept 1789 by the oath of John Coate (Little) before Levi Casey, J.P. Recorded 10 Nov 1789.

A, 814: Newberry County. Diana Morgan of the County of Newberry, whereas William Shaw of Cambridge, attorney at Law at the Court held for Ninety Six in April last obtained a judgment at Law against me and my son Joshua Morgan, for the purpose of satisfying the same judgment & Costs amounting to £10 sterling, by my attorney William McGlammery, deliver the following goods: all my crop of Tobacco, corn, buckwheat & cotton, fifteen head of hoggs, has as swallowfork in the right ear and a smooth crop in the left & seven head of sheep of the same mark, two feather beds & furniture, a dish, three basons and five plates, two potts, three bedsteads, four chairs, a chest, two tables, three wheels & a Loom, dated 10 Sept 1789. Diana Morgan (+) (Seal), Wit: Richard Speake. Proved at a court held for Newberry County 10 Sept 1789 by the oath of Richard Speake. Recorded 11 Nov 1789.

A, 815-820: Lease and release. 19 & 20 Dec 1769, Alexander Johnston of Craven County, SC, to William Largent of the county aforesaid, settlement of Indian Creek, for £100 SC money, 100 acres on waters of Indian Creek and on the north fork of Hedleys Creek granted to s'd Alexander Johnston ___ 1769. Alexander Johnston (Seal), Wit: Robert Camron, Daniel Mouro. Proved 20 June 1771 by the oath of Robert Camron before John Johnston, J.P. Recorded 12 Nov 1789.

A, 820-821: Joseph Dawkins of Camden District bound to Alexander Bookter of Ninety Six District in the sum of £240 sterling in gold or silver, 11 Nov 1789, mortgage of four negro slaves one yellow negro woman named Nell and three of her children a boy named Champ, one named Venus & one named Lewis, to work for the use of the £120 sterling until 1 April next. Joseph Dawkins (Seal), Wit: Benjamin Hampton, John Crooks. Proved in Newberry County, 96 District, by the oath of Benjamin Hampton Jun'r and John Crooks 11 Nov 1789 before W. Wadlington, J. P. Recorded 15 Nov 1789.

A, 822-825: Lease and release. 28 & 29 Oct 1788, William Largent of Edgefield County, Ninety Six District, to William Gray of Newberry County, settlement of Indian Creek, for £30 sterling, 100 acres granted to Alexander

Johnston 12 Sept 1768 and recorded in Book DDD, page 603, and a memorial entered in Book I No. 9, page 232, in the fork between Broad and Saludy Rivers on a small branch of Indian Creek called the south fork of Hedley's Creek, not adj. land of John Garrett, land surveyed for Willm. Hancock, land surveyed for James Kenady. William Largent (W) (Seal), Wit: James Lindsey, Robt Brooks, Ansel Bearden. Proved 31 Aug 1789 by the oath of James Lindsey before John Lindsey, J.P. Recorded 16 Nov 1789.

A, 826-827: Joseph Lewis, late of the state of Georgia, Liberty County, for £150 sterling of SC to Robert Tate of Newberry County, two negro men slaves Primus & Jack. Joseph Lewis (Seal), Wit: Ben'a Cobb, James Cobb, Sarah D. Vall. Proved in Newberry County by the oath of Benjamin Cobb 17 Nov 1789 before John Lindsey, J.P. Recorded 21 Nov 1789.

A, 827: Robert Tate for £75 sterling to Richard Speake, both of Newberry County, one sorrel gelding seven years old, one back mare six years old, one sorrel gelding five years old fourteen hands high branded WI on the nigh, and also one black gelding six years old, 15 Sept 1789. Robert Tate (Seal), Wit: Jno Coate, James Tate. Proved in Newberry County by the oath of John Coate 17 Oct 1789 before Mercer Babb, J.P. Recorded 21 Nov 1789.

A, 828-831: Lease and release. 9 & 10 Feb 1789, William Gray of the waters of Indian Creek, Ninety Six District, planter, to Edward Spence of waters of Saludy, Orangeburgh District, by grant dated 12 Sept 1768 to Alexander Johnston on a small branch called the south fork of Headley's Creek, now adj. John Garrett, William Hencock, 100 acres, now conveyed for £45 SC money. William Gray (Seal), Wit: Pt Lowry, Robt Glassgow, James Spence. Proved 31 Aug 1789 by the oath of James Spence before John Lindsey, J.P. Recorded 21 Nov 1789.

A, 831-837: Lease and release. 16 & 17 July 1789, Saml Harris of Newberry County, Bricklayer, to William Swift of the Town of Cambridge, in the County of Abbeville, SC, merchant, for £100 sterling, 150 acres in the County of Laurence on the waters of Mudlick Creek adj. Mary Stedham, William Caldwell, Nathaniel Foshee, granted to Oliver Towles 12 April 1771 and conveyed to George Neely 6 & 7 Sept 1771 by Neely to Gabriel Smithers on 9 & 10 Sept 1779; by Smithers to Samuel Harris 9 & 10 July 1786; also tract of 200 acres in County of Laurance adj. the above mentioned tract adj. Wm Caldwell, lands surveyed by bounty warrants, granted to John Robison to George Neely 16 & 17 Jan 1772; also tract of 150 acres, being one half of a tract of 300 acres granted to Wm. Caldwell 12 Aug 1768 and conveyed by Caldwell to William Dudgeon 18 & 19 May 1772 and conveyed by s'd Wm Dudgeon to Samuel Harris 22 & 23 March 1786. Samuel Harris (Seal), Wit: William Caldwell, James Goodman, J. R. Mayson. Proved by the oath of James Robert Mayson 1 Dec 1789 before Jas Mayson, J.P. Recorded 23 Nov 1789.

A, 837-841: Lease and release. 8 & 9 Sept 1789, Thomas Brooks of Newberry County, District 96, farmer, and Susannah his wife, to George Powel, sadler, of same, for £15 SC money, 124 acres on the drafts of Scotch Creek, a branch of Bush River adj. Benjamin Pearson, Hugh Creighton, John Brooks, one Wyly, granted to John Brooks 21 Apr 1774. Thomas Brooks (Seal), Susanna Brooks (Seal), Wit: Benjamin Worthington, Samuel Pearson. Proved 10 Sept 1789 by the oath of Samuel Pearson before John Lindsey, J.P. Recorded 24 Nov 1789.

A, 841-845: Lease and release. 24 & 25 Aug 1777, William Dudgeon of Ninety Six District, and his wife Elizabeth to John Vaughan, taylor, of same, for £400 SC money, tract whereon the said John Vaughan now resides, 200 acres, part of 300 acres granted to said William Dodgen 12 April 1771 on waters of Little River, adj. David Emory, Hamilton Murdock, Robert Goudy, Thomas Green, Wm. Burton, grant recorded in Book 3 H, page 118. William Dodgeon (Seal), Elizabeth Dodgeon (+) (Seal), Wit: Olleyman Dodgen, Mark Pitts (X), John Broadway (X). Recorded 24 Nov 1789.

A, 845-848: Lease and release. 10 & 11 March 1788, John Reed of Newberry County, taylor, of the settlement of Gilders Creek, and Elizabeth his wife, to John Boyd of same, for £46 s10 sterling, 50 acres, part of 250 acres granted to said John Reed 1 Sept 1768 in the fork between Broad & Saludy Rivers recorded in Book DDD, page 512. John Reed (Seal), Wit: John Blalock Sen'r, Josiah Elliott, James Lindsey. Proved 31 Aug 1789 by the oath of Jas Lindsey before John Lindsey, J.P. Recorded 27 Nov 1789.

A, 849-851: Lease and release. 17 & 18 Feb 1787, Matthias Elmore of Newberry county, Settlement of Bush River, and Elizabeth his wife, to John Boyd of the Settlement of Saludy River, said county, for £100 SC money, 250 acres granted to Stephen Elmore 8 July 1775 on NE side Saludy River adj. land claimed by Stephen Lewis, land laid out on the Bounty, John Turner, recorded in Book RRR, page 133. Matthias Elmore (Seal), Wit: John Wilson, Jacob Barrett, Jas Lindsey. Proved 8 Sept 1789 by the oath of Jas Lindsey before John Lindsey, J.P. Recorded 27 Nov 1789.

A, 852-855: Lease and release. 7 & 8 Sept 1789, James Daugharty Jun'r of Edistoe, District of Orangeburgh, to John Cannon of Newberry County, settlement of Bush River, for £40 sterling, 640 acres granted 3 April 1786, recorded in Book IIII, page 200 to James Daugharty, on south side of Saludy on the east fork of Twenty six mile Creek, and £14 s14 paid to the state, adj. Doctor Hall's land. Jas Daugharty (Seal), Wit: James Lindsey, Ephraim Cannon, Moses Lindsey. Proved 8 Sept 1789 by the oath of Jas Lindsey before John Lindsey, J.P. Recorded 28 Nov 1789.

A, 856-860: Lease and release. 26 & 27 Jan 1772, Adam Keller of Craven County, SC, planter, to Jacob Ringer of same place, planter, for £100 SC money, 200 acres, part of 400 acres granted to Johannes Setzler 12 May 1768 on a small branch of Second Creek, adj. Michael Lominick, Michl Suber, recorded in Book DDD, page 73, and conveyed 5 July 1770 to Adam Keller. Adam Killer (mark) (Seal), Mary Killer (mark) (Seal), Wit: Jacob Glyn (X), Christopher Kriser (Criser) (X). Proved 27 Jan 1772 by the oath of Jacob Glyn before Michl Dickert, J.P. Recorded 10 Dec 1789.

A, 860-864: Lease and release. 21 Dec 1789, Jacob Ringer and Mary his wife of Newberry County, planter, to John Dawkins of same place, planter, for £60 SC money, 200 acres, part of 400 acres granted to Johannes Setzler 12 May 1768 on a small branch of Second Creek, adj. Michael Lominick, Michael Suber, recorded in Book DDD, page 73. Jacob Ringer (Seal), Mary Ringer (X) (Seal), Wit: John Blewer, Sarah Ringer, Wm Dawkins. Proved in Newberry County by the oath of William Dawkins 4 Jan 1790 before George Ruff, J.P. Recorded 14 Jan 1790.

A, 864-865: 23 Oct 1788, Charles & Unice Crenshaw of Newberry County to Peter Braselmann & Company of same, for £32 s12 d6 sterling, 6 acres between Indian & Kings Creek adj. Bailey Chandler, Charles Crenshaw. Charles Crenshaw (Seal), Unice Crenshaw (Seal), Wit: John Dawson, Geo Barnes, Rob't Powell. Proved 7 Sept 1789 by the oath of G. Barnes before B. Brown, J.P.

A, 866-867: 29 Jan 1789, William Wilson of Newberry County to Peter Braselmann of same, for £60 sterling, 190 acres on branches of Kings Creek granted 3 April 1786, recorded in Book KKKK, page 202, adj. Jos. Hampton's corner, John Johnson, Gabl Anderson. William Wilson (Seal), Jane Wilson (I) (Seal), Wit: G. Barnes, D. Henning, John Wilson. Proved 7 Sept 1789 by the oath of G. Barnes before B. Brown, J.P.

A, 868-871: Lease and release. 29 & 30 Oct 1785, John Ridgdell of Long Cain in District of 96, Shoemaker, and Anne his wife, to Joseph Coppock of Bush River, planter, for £100 SC money, 400 acres granted 22 March 1769 to John Ridgedel on a small branch of Saludy River called Bush Creek. John Ridgdell (Seal), Wit: David Mills, Jehue Inmann, John Ridgdell. Proved 2 Sept 1789 by the oath of Jehue Inmann before Mercer Babb, J.P. Recorded 18 Jan 1790.

A, 871-875: Lease and release. 7 & 8 June 1775, Feith Reisinger of the fork between Broad & Saludy Rivers in Ninety Six District, planter, to Thomas Risinger of same place, for £200 SC money, two grants 25 May 1774, 57 acres in Craven county, one grant for a tract of 11 acres being an Island of Broad River adj. Joseph Fisher, the other of 46 acres on SW side said Broad River adj. Joseph Fisher, Jacob Litcey, John ONeal, recorded in Book GGG, the 11 acres on page 89 the 46 acres on page 55. Feith Reisinger [German signature] (Seal), Susannah Reisinger (X) [German signature] (Seal), Wit: Georg Adam Youn [German signature], Thomas Hamiter (TH). Proved in Ninety Six District by the oath of George Adam Youn before Mich'l Dickert 5 Aug 1775. Recorded 18 Jan 1790.

NEWBERRY COUNTY SC DEED ABSTRACTS

A, 876-881: Lease and release. 4 & 5 Oct 1784, Thomas Risinger of Ninety Six District, planter, to William Liles of same, planter, for £35 SC money, two grants 25 May 1774, 57 acres in Craven County, one grant for a tract of 11 acres being an Island of Broad River adj. Joseph Fisher, the other of 46 acres on SW side said Broad River adj. Joseph Fisher, Jacob Litcey, John ONeal, recorded in Book GGG, pages 89 and 55, conveyed to Thos Risinger 7 & 8 June 1775. Thomas Risinger (Seal), Wit: Mich'l Dickert Sen'r, Mich'l Dickert. Proved in Newberry County by the oath of Mich'l Dickert 5 Sept 1789 before Geo Ruff, J.P. Recorded 21 Jan 1790.

A, 881-885: Lease and release. 28 & 29 Sept 1786, Thomas Risinger of Newberry County, planter, to William Liles of same, planter, for £25 sterling, 100 acres granted to Jacob Litsey in Craven County on waters of Broad River adj. Rudolph Bushard, John ONeal, recorded in Book GGG, page 47, conveyed by Jacob Litzey to said Thomas Risinger _____ 1775. Thomas Risinger (Seal), Wit: Mich'l Dickert Sen'r, Mich'l Dickert. Proved in Newberry County by the oath of Mich'l Dickert 5 Sept 1789 before Geo Ruff, J.P.

A, 885-886: So Carolina, Camden District. Salathel Coffee of district aforesaid, hatter, to Samuel Morriss of Frederick County, Virginia, one negro wench named Jude of yellow complection, a piece of one four finger is off, between the age of 17 and 20 years old, for £85 sterling money of SC, dated 6 Nov 1783. Salathel Coffee (S) (Seal), Wit: Isaac King, John Dial (O). Proved in Newberry County by the oath of John Dial 2 Oct 1788 before John Lindsey, J.P. Recorded 27 Jan 1790.

A, 886: So Carolina, Newberry County. Samuel Morriss of state and county aforesaid for £100 to Thomas Williby Waters of same, one negro wench named Jude & a boy Isaac about six years old, dated 14 Jan 1790. Saml Morriss (Seal), Wit: A. Roberson, John Summers. Proved in Newberry County by the oath of Allen Roberson 15 Jan 1790 before P. Waters, J.P. Recorded 27 Jan 1790.

A, 887-890: Lease and release. 10 & 11 Nov 1789, William Smith of Newberry County, of Ninety Six District, planter, and Amelia his wife, to William Richards of same, for £80 sterling, tract on south side of Enoree River granted to James Vardaman 5 June 1786, recorded in Book LLLL, page 437, conveyed by said Vardaman and Jane his wife to William Smith. William Smith (S) (Seal), Amelia Smith (X) (Seal), Wit: William Malone Sen'r, W. Malone Junr. Proved 25 Jan 1790 by the oath of William Malone Sen'r Esq'r before Tho. W. Waters, Esquire, J.P. Recorded 27 Jan 1790.

A, 891-894: Lease and release. 27 & 28 Dec 1787, John Means Esq'r of Newberry County, merchant, to Thos Wadsworth & William Turpin, merchants, for £20 sterling, 34 acres on waters of Second Creek, a branch of Broad River adj. Col. Rutherford's land, John Montgomeries land, John Steel, Joseph Caldwell, granted to Thomas Wadsworth, William Turpin & John Means 7 Aug 1786. John Means (Seal), George Reynolds, Mathew Hall, S.

68

Maverick. Proved 20 May 1788 by the oath of George Reynolds before Daniel Stevens, J. Q. U. Recorded 28 Jan 1790.

A, 894-897: 28 July 1785, Samuel Pearson of Bush River in the district of 96, farmer, to Enoch Pearson, son of said Samuel Pearson, for natural love and affection, 250 acres on a branch of Bush River called Palmeto Branch adj. Hoofman, William Hillburn, granted to Jonathan Wood, and conveyed to John Wagner and by him to William Hillburn and by him to Samuel Pearson. Samuel Pearson (Seal), Wit: Enos Elleman, Rachel Worthington, Benjamin Pearson. Proved 18 Sept 1789 by the oath of Rachel Toland was Worthington before Mercer Babb, J.P. Recorded 29 Jan 1790.

A, 897-901: Lease and release. 1 & 2 Oct 1789, John Hunter of Abbeville County, Ninety Six District, taylor, to Abijah ONeal of Newberry County, planter, in trust for Hugh ONeal, William ONeal, John ONeal, Henry ONeal, and Thomas ONeal, sons of William ONeal deceased, for £50 sterling, 200 acres in Newberry County near the branches of Bush River between Broad & Saludy Rivers. John Hunter (Seal), Wit: Thos W. Furnis, Susana Hunter (O). Proved 7 Dec 1789 by the oath of Thos W. Furnis before Mercer Babb, J.P. Recorded 29 Jan 1790.

A, 901-904: Lease and release. 14 Oct 1788, Daniel Dyson of Newberry County to Thomas Chappel, for £100 sterling, 100 acres granted to Jeane Fullerton on the bounty 6 Feb 1773 and conveyed to Thomas Clark and conveyed from said Thomas Clark to James Dyson adj. Andrew Cooter, Robert Dillon, Thomas Clark, and Saludy River. Da Dyson (Seal), Margaret Dyson (Seal), Wit: Isaac Dyson, Charles Clarke (+), Elizabeth Richmon (X). Proved in Newberry County 7 Dec 1789 by the oath of Charles Clark before Mercer Babb, J.P. Recorded 8 Feb 1790.

A, 905-908: Lease and release. 30 Dec 1788, Jesse Spray, farmer, of the settlement of Beaverdam of Bush River, to John Furnas, Blacksmith, of the same settlement, both of Newberry County, for £75 sterling, 100 acres, part of larger tract of 200 acres granted to Providence Williams, 20 Aug 1767, recorded in Book BBB, page 176, memorial entered in Book H. No. 8, page 276, 12 Sept 1767, at the Beaverdam near Bush River in Craven County conveyed to Samuel Pearson 13 & !4 April 1774 by James Williams, eldest son & heir to Providence Williams, and conveyed to Jesse Spray 9 & 10 May 1787. Jesse Spray (mark) (Seal), Wit: Samuel Spray, Joseph Furnas, Enoch Pearson. Proved in Newberry County 7 Dec 1789 by the oath of Joseph Furnas before Mercer Babb, J.P. Recorded 8 Feb 1790.

A, 909-910: 19 Oct 1789, Thos Gordon, Esq'r, and Elizabeth his wife of Newberry County, to Robert Crenshaw of Union County, SC, for £200 sterling, 132 acres granted by North Carolina originally and then by South Carolina 5 May 1775 to said Thos Gordon. Thos Gordon (Seal), Elizabeth Gordon (mark) (Seal), Wit: Wm Kelly, Jessee Gordan, Eli Gordan. Proved 23

Nov 1789 by the oath of William Kelly before W. Wadlington, J.P. Recorded 9 Feb 1790.

A, 911-912: 19 Oct 1789, Thos Gordon, Esq'r, and Elizabeth his wife of Newberry County, to Robert Crenshaw of Union County, SC, for £60 sterling, 68 acres on south side Tyger River on the north side of Peter's Creek originally granted by North Carolina 17 May 1754 to Jno Gordon, but by the resurvey of the boundary line the above tract of 460 acres falls within Craven County now Newberry County, entered in the Auditors Office 16 Dec 1771. Tho's Gordon (Seal), Elizabeth Gordon (mark) (Seal), Wit: Wm Kelly, Jessee Gordan, Eli Gordan. Proved 23 Nov 1789 by the oath of William Kelly before W. Wadlington, J.P. Recorded 9 Feb 1790.

A, 913-914: South Carolina, Ninety Six District, Newberry County. 7 Dec 1789, John Ragan and his wife Elizabeth to Thomas Brooks of district aforesaid, yoman, for £10 sterling, tract on Bush River, waters of Saludy Rivers, adj. Land of William Pearson, Benjamin Pearson, Jacob Brooks, James Hogg, granted to John Raigain 5 June 1786. John Ragan (Seal), Elizabeth Ragan (X) (Seal), Wit: Hugh ONeal, Mary Raigan (X), George Clark (mark). Proved in Newberry County by the oath of Hugh ONeale 7 Dec 1789 before Mercer Babb, J.P. Recorded 11 Feb 1790.

A, 915-918: Lease and release. 9 & 10 May 1786, Rudolph Bushard of Newberry County, planter, to John Griffin of same place, planter, for £30 sterling, 10 acres, part of 100 acres granted 1 June 1765 to John Ulrick Souter, in Craven County on Broad River, adj. Hans Jacob Keuhn[?], recorded in Book XX, page 12, and said John Ulrick Souter did convey to Rudolph Bushard Sen'r and said Bushard died "intested" and the said 100 acres devolved unto his son Rudolph Bushard Jun'r. Rudolph Bushard (RB) (Seal), Wit: Michl Dickert, Mich'l Dickert Jun'r, Christopher Dickert. Proved by the oath of Michal Dickert. Recorded 11 Feb 1790.

A, 919-922: Lease and release. 17 & 18 March 1773, John Gant of Craven County, SC, planter, to Alex'r Johnston of Berkly County, SC, by grant dated 28 Aug 1772 to John Gant, 200 acres in Berkly County in the fork of Broad and Saludy Rivers on a small branch of Second Creek adj. Elizabeth Montgomery, Jenett Johnston, Alex'r Johnston, William Johnston, Joseph Smith, now conveyed for £25 sterling. John Gant (Seal), Wit: John Johnston, William Johnston, John Weer. Proved 19 March 1773 by the oath of John Weer before Mich'l Dickert. Recorded 16 Feb 1790.

A, 923-924: 14 Oct 1789, George Bartram of Newberry County, SC, to Ulrick Hardman of same, for £85 sterling, tract on Indian Creek adj. George Awbry, widow Glynn, Robert Johnston, Geo. Gordon. Geo. Bartram (Seal), Wit: John Lindsey, J.P., Robt Powell, Caleb Lindsey. Proved 15 Feb 1790 by the oath of Robert Powell before W. Wadlington, J.P. Recorded 18 Feb 1790.

A, 925: South Carolina, Newberry County. John Turner and Delphia his wife of county aforesaid for £60 sterling, to Daniel McKee, one negro man named Carolina, dated 5 Sept 1789. John Turner (+) (Seal), Delphia Turner (+) (Seal), Wit: Jessee Johnson, George Richardson, Tabitha Hudson (+). Proved by the oaths of all three witnesses 29 Jan 1790 before Levi Casey.

A, 926: South Carolina, Newberry County. William Meriwether of county aforesaid for £130 sterling, to Bartlett Saterwhite, one negro woman named Dolly, one boy named Thomas, one child named Sally, and a negro boy named Will, dated 1 March 1789. William Meriwether (Seal), Wit: Cornelius Dendy, John Saterwhite. Proved in Newberry County by the oath of Cornelius Dandy 22 Feb 1790 before William Caldwell, J.P. Recorded 25 Feb 1790.

A, 927: South Carolina, Newberry County. William Meriwether of county aforesaid for £50 s10 sterling, to Bartlett Saterwhite, eleven head of black cattle, four head of sheep, three feather beds and furniture, thirty head of hoggs, dated 20 Feb 1789. William Meriwether (Seal), Wit: Cornelius Dendy, John Satterwhite. Proved in Newberry County by the oath of Cornelius Dandy 22 Feb 1790 before William Caldwell, J.P. Recorded 25 Feb 1790.

A, 928: John Hudgens & Delilah Pennington of Craven County to Oliver Towles of same, one negro girl named Amey, 3 Nov 1777. John Hudgens, Delilah Pennington. Wit: Joseph Goodman, Robert Owens. Recorded 12 March 1790.

A, 928: Jane Towles of Ninety Six District, Newberry County, widow, makes her son Daniel Towles, her attorney to receive a certain negro wench named Fanny now in possession of Jno Davison of the State of North Carolina, 6 Jan 1790. Jane Towles (+), Wit: J. Brown. Recorded 12 March 1790.

A, 929-933: Lease and release. 3 & 4 June 1774, Charles McBride of Ninety Six District, SC, planter, to James Doherty Sen'r of same, planter, for £150 , 100 acres, part of 250 acres granted to Charles McBride 20 Oct 1772 in Berkley County on a small branch of Enoree called Indian Creek not ten feet broad nor one deep adj. land of Adam Shakell, Joseph Loston, Moses Carthlin, Samuel Waters, Isaac Brooks, recorded in Book MMM, page 376. Charles McBride (mark) (Seal), Nancy McBride (mark) (Seal), Wit: William Tyker (+), Jacob Frederick (O), James Daugherty. Proved by the oath of William Tyker 9 June 1774 before Mich'l Dickert, J.P. James Daugherty assigned his right to William Speakman 7 Dec 1785[?], Wit: James Daugherty, Agnes Daugherty (X). Recorded 15 March 1790.

A, 933-934: March 18th 1785. Then Rec'd of John Weadingman full satisfaction for a bond of £75 and interest, Mathew Roberson.

So Carolina, Union County. This day Mathew Roberson came before me John Henderson, J.P., and made oath that he never sign'd a note of hand payable from John Weadingman, 5 Dec 1790. Mathew Roberson (P). Recorded 15 March 1790

A, 934-937: Lease and release. 25 & 26 Dec 1789, William Anderson of Edgefield County to Benjamin Long of Newberry County, for £40 SC money, 183 acres in two separate surveys on Little River and the waters thereof, 103 acres granted to William Anderson 5 Feb 1787 and 80 acres granted to Frederick Ward 4 Sept 1786 and conveyed to said William Anderson by said Frederick Ward. Will'm Anderson (Seal), Wit: David Devenport, Daniel Rogers. Proved in Newberry County by the oath of David Devinport 2 March 1790 before Philemon Waters, J.P. Recorded 15 March 1790.

A, 937-941: Lease and release. 24 & 25 June 1789. William Goggans, planter, of Newberry County, and Rachel his wife, to George Goggans, planter, of same, for £100 sterling, 100 acres in Berkley County on a small branch of Little River called Sandy Run adj. Robert Johnson, granted 1 Feb 1768, recorded in Book BBB, page 430, conveyed 17 & 18 July 1777 from Thomas Edgehill Sen'r to William Goggans. William Goggans (Seal), Rachel Goggans (X) (Seal), Wit: James Goggans, Robert Johnson. Proved in Newberry County by the oath of James Goggans 18 July 1789 before Mercer Babb, J.P. Recorded 15 March 1790.

A, 942-945: Lease and release. 6 & 7 Dec 1789, William Hencock of Newberry County and the Settlement of Tyger River, to David Spence, late of Indian Creek, same county, for £50 SC money, 113 acres granted to William Hencock 5 March 1787, recorded in Book RRRR, page 249. William Hencock (Seal), Wit: Robert Brooks, Archibald Spence, James Lindsey. Proved 21 __ 1789 by the oath of James Lindsey before John Lindsey, J.P. Recorded 16 March 1790.

A, 945-949: Lease and release. 9 & 10 July 1770, Rudolph Bushart of Craven County, SC, millar, to Barnard Mantz of same place, planter, for £500 SC money, tract granted 6 April 1753 to Felix Bushard, 250 acres on Cannon Creek in the fork of Broad River, recorded in Book OO, page 193, conveyed to Rudolph Bushard 8 Sept 1757. Rudolph Bushard (Seal), Marian Bushard (B) (Seal), Wit: Leanard Holtz [German signature], William Dawkins. Proved 8 Aug 1770 by the oath of Leonard Holtz before Michael Dickert, J.P. Recorded 17 March 1790.

A, 950: 28 Feb 1790, Philip Phagans of Newberry County to William Gary of same, for £20 sterling, 40 acres, part of tract of 88 acres on a small branch of Bush River granted Joseph Goodman 6 Nov 1786, recorded in Book QQQQ, page 102. Philip Phagans (Seal), Wit: George Goggans, Daniel Johnson. Recorded 17 March 1790.

A, 951-954: Lease and release. 6 & 7 Nov 1769, Peter Buyer of the fork between Broad & Saludy Rivers in Berkly County planter, to John George Shoemaker of same place, shoemaker, for £50 SC money, tract of 50 acres on a branch of Crims Creek called Counz Creek adj. Francis Hiot, granted to

John Mazer, conveyed 12 & 13 July 1763 to Peter Buyer. Peter Buyer (mark) (Seal), Wit: Franz Heyet[?] [German signature], John Purcell. Proved by the oath of John Purcell 7 Nov 1769 before John Fairchild, J.P. Recorded 18 March 1790.

A, 955-958: Lease and release. 8 & 9 Dec 1773, John Hogg of the settlement of the Enoree in forks of Broad & Saludy Rivers, Craven County, planter, and Sarah his wife to Charles Coats of the same settlement & county, for £100 SC money, 100 acres granted 5 May 1773 to John Hogg on Kelly branch, waters of Enoree River adj. John Green. John Hogg (Seal), Sarah Hogg (X) (Seal), Wit: James Lindsey, Joseph Fish, John Sparks. Proved 14 Dec 1773 by the oath of James Lindsey before John Johnston, J.P. Recorded 12 March 1790.

A, 958: State of So Carolina, Chester County. James Dillard of county aforesaid for £45 sterling, one negro girl named Jude between eleven and twelve years of age, 29 July 1788. James Dillard (Seal), Wit: John Crooks, John Foote. Proved in Newberry County by the oath of John Crooks 16 March 1790 before W. Wadlington, J.P. Recorded 23 March 1790.

A, 959-962: Lease and release. 17 & 18 Feb 1778, William Johnston of Ninety Six District, adm'r of Robert Johnson deceased, to James Williams of same, for £215 SC money, tract of 250 acres on a small branch of Saludy River called the Bever Dam adj. John Pendel, John Caldwell, granted to Thomas Hamton and conveyed to above said Rob't Johnson deceased, 25 June 1776. William Johnston (Seal), Wit: James Griffin, Clemmon Hencock, Daniel Williams. Recorded 25 March 1790.

A, 962-963: By the Hon. William Bull, Esq'r, Lt. Gov of SC, be it known that on 13 April 1782 personally appeared James Kelly of Ninety Six District and Charlotte Churn of said place, who say that said James Kelly for himself that upwards of seven years ago he sold to Jacob Huffman of the same district a tract of land on waters of Guilders Creek adj. Harman Davis, and said James Kelly, and said Charlotte Churn for herself that she was possessed of that titles to the said tract in June last when a party of the enemy came to her house on the Road to Ninety Six took possession of the trunk in which they were and they threw that and other papers in the fire where she believes they were consumed. James Kelly, Charlotte Churn (X). William Bull (Seal).

A, 963-964: South Carolina, Ninety Six District, Newberry County. Elizabeth Vaughan of said district & county for love, god will and affection to my son Olley man Dodgen of same, the five following negroes: Jacob, Phillis, Milly, Jack & Daniel, 10 March 1790. Elizabeth Vaughan (X) (Seal), Wit: Jean Brown (O), Mary Brown (O). Proved in Newberry County by the oath of Jane Brown 16 March 1790 before T. W. Waters, J.P. Recorded 25 March 1790.

A, 964-968: Lease and release. 13 & 20 July 1763, John Mazer of Charles Town to Peter Buyer of Berkley County, for £50 SC money, tract granted 2 Jan 1754 to John Mazer, 50 acres on a branch of Crims Creek called Kountz

Creek adj. Francis Huit, recorded in Book OO, folio 367. Henry Mitsher (mark) (Seal), Wit: Peter Bocquet Jun'r, Casper Philip Byerly (X). Proved by the oath of Casper Philip Byerly 1 Jan 1755 before John Pearson, J.P. in Berkley & Craven County. Recorded 27 March 1790.

A, 969-970: Joel Mabry of Fairfield County, SC, bound to John Turner of Newberry County, in the sum of £500 sterling, 10 Nov 1786, to make title to a tract of 200 acres on Kings Creek in Newberry County formerly possessed by Francis Wafer and sold by said Wafer to William Coast and by said Coats to Joel Mabry. Joel Mabry (Seal), Wit: Bartholomew Turner (mark), Sarah Bonds (+). Proved in Newberry County by the oath of Bartholomew Turner 27 Feb 1790 before W. Wadlington, J.P. Recorded 6 April 1790.

A, 970-973: Lease and release. 8 & 9 Nov 1785, Jacob Brooks of Ninety Six District, to Thomas Brooks of same, for £10 sterling, 200 acres on waters of Bush River, part of 500 acres granted to Jacob Brooks Senr deceased, 19 Sept 1785, adj. Benjamin Pearson. Jacob Brooks (Seal), Mary Brooks (Seal), Wit: Moses Walton (X), Abraham Little, Jabesh Hendricks. This is to certify that Nebo & Samuel Gaunt is agreed that the above said Tho's Brooks's 200 acres is laid out in the NW corner of the above said tract, 31 March 1790. Nebo Gaunt, Samuel Gaunt. Wit: Fred Nance, Jno Lindsey Jun'r. Recorded 6 April 1790.

A, 974-978: Lease and release. 7 & 8 Sept 1757, Felix Bousard in Santee fork, Berkly County, SC, planter, to his son Rudolph Bousard of same place, planter, by grant dated 6 April 1753, 250 acres on Cannon Creek in the forks of Broad River, now conveyed for £500 SC money. Felix Bossart (Seal), Anna[?] Bossart [German signature] (Seal), Wit: Jacob Schuff[?], Peter Crim, J.P. Recorded 6 April 1790.

A, 978-983: Lease and release. 24 & 25 Dec 1775, John Pearson of Craven County, SC, Blacksmith and planter, to Terrence Riley of same, planter, for £150 SC money, tract granted 5 July 1769 to Isaac Morgan, 100 acres in Craven County in the forks of Broad and Saludy Rivers on Cannons Creek adj. James Murphy, Terrence Riley, and said Isaac Morgan for £100 did convey to John Pearson 1 & 2 May 1770. John Pearson (Seal), Jean Pearson (mark) (Seal), Wit: George Ruff, William Runils (+), Jno Pearson. Proved in Ninety Six District by the oath of George Ruff 26 Dec 1775 before Michl Dickert, J.P. Recorded 12 April 1790.

A, 984-988: 27 Oct 1789, Hon. Nicholas Eveliegh & Mary his wife to Rev. Robert Smith, Edward Rutlage, and John Bee Holmes, for five shillings, all those several tracts of land: 50 acres in the District of Ninety Six on south side Saludy River granted to James Mayson 1 Aug 1785 and by him conveyed to Nicholas Eveliegh 17 & 18 Nov following; 440 acres in the district aforesaid adj. lands purchased of Capt. William Anderson surveyed in the name of Joseph Campfield 20 April 1785 granted 1 Aug 1785 and conveyed to said Nicholas Eveleigh 17 & 18 Nov 1785; 279 acres on north side of Saludy bought of Joseph White and conveyed to said Nicholas by the said Joseph White 27 & 28 March 1780; 640 acres in Ninety Six District above the ancient Boundary on Savannah River called the Cove surveyed for said Nicholas Eveleigh by John Purvis testified 3 July 1787; 640 acres bought by said Nicholas Eveleigh of John Harleston on west side Cape Fear River in Brunswick County [North Carolina] conveyed to said Nicholas Eveleigh by Jno Harleston 30 Oct 1779; 700 acres in Ninety Six District 350 acres of which were bought of James & John Martin 15 Aug 1785 on Ninety Six Creek' 329 acres on dry branch of Horns Creek in Ninety Six District granted to John Rutlage 21 July 1775 conveyed by John Purves to said Nicholas Eveleigh about the month of December 1779; 200 acres on Crooked Run a branch of Turkey Creek conveyed by John Purves to said Nicholas Eveleigh about December 1779 granted to Donald Simson about 6 Feb 1773; 100 acres on Rocky Creek sold by Richard Anders Raply to said Nicholas Eveleigh; 350 acres called Horse Shoe on the north side of Saludy River bought of Andrew Rogers & conveyed by him to said Nicholas Eveleigh; 450 acres on Reedy River bought of Daniel Williams & his son Nimrod Williams 9 March 1780; 450 acres purchased of William Furlow composed of 200 acres, 150 acres, 100 acres in Berkly County on north side Saludy River; 500 acres purchased of Alexr Frayser Junr on 4 July 1780 granted to Edward Edwards & on west side Edisto River; 350 acres purchased of Alex'r Frayser within three miles of the former tract in Colleton County granted to James Walker; 515 acres purchased of Richard Andrew Raply as attorney for Joseph Salvador on Black Rocky Creek above Ninety Six and is part of tract granted to William Livingston Esqr; 5689 acres purchased of Richard Andrew Raply 18 March 1780 part of lands granted to said William Livingston on Saludy River in the District of Ninety Six; 3900 acres conveyed by said Richard Anders Raply 29 & 30 April 1778, part of lands granted to William Livingston; 1450 acres on Black Rocky Creek in the District aforesaid, part of land granted to William Livingston and conveyed by said Richard Anders Raply to said Nicholas Eveleigh 29 & 30 April 1778; 3022 acres part of land granted to William Livingston & purchased of said Richard Anders Raply 20 Dec 1777; 1048 acres part of the land granted to said William Livingston conveyed by said Richard Anders Raply to said Nicholas Eveleigh 29 & 30 April 1778; plantation in Craven County on or near the high hills of Santee 1107 acres adj. lands of Benjamin Warring & George Ioor, one undivided moiety of a tract of 1000 acres in the North Britton tract on the high hills of Santee; also tract of 213½ acres on south side Santee in St. Johns Parish adj. lands of Ralph Izard, Mr. Saml Ewing; also 2743 acres on south side Santee in St. James Parish adj. land of Anth. Simmons, Charles Pinckney Esqr; also an undivided moiety of 1375 acres in Craven County bounding the Berkly County line adj. lands of Henry Mouzon; 1000 acre on Peedee River adj. lands of John Stone and Elizabeth Raven; 100 acres in Ninety Six District on a branch of Little Stephens Creek; 400 acres between Saludy and Savana Rivers on Turky Creek.; 100 acres on Lower Bridge Creek, a branch of Horns Creek; 640 acres in Ninety Six district on a branch of Twenty Six Mile Creek, which said ten last mentioned tracts were mortgaged to the said Nicholas Eveleigh by Thomas Eveleigh. Nicholas Eveleigh (Seal), Mary Eveleigh (Seal), Wit:

Thos Bee, Thomas Eveleigh. Proved in Charleston District by the oath of Thomas Eveleigh 19 March 1790 before Dl Mazyck, J.P.

A, 988-989: A List of Sundry Persons, Creditors of Nicholas Eveleigh.

State Loan Office ab't £1000
Hannah Heyward
Rebeca Evance 487
Joseph Alston, B. Huger &
 self my half is 890
R. A. Rapley
Jane Simmons
Coln. Dry 124
Anth'y L. Abbe, B. Huger &
 self, My half about 175
Thomas Cochran 125
Alexander Fraer 97
Ambrus Marr 61
Library Society, B. Huger
 & self, may half abt 524
Isaac DaCosta 73
Esta. Thos Shubrick 345
Jacob Vanbibber 128
John Terrie 396
Jas Laurens T. E. &
 self, my half ab't 320
Daniel Huger
Esta. Henry Crouch 483
Rev'd Rob't Cooper 431
Jas Brown, B. Huger
 & self, my half abt 720
Lewis Lesterjette 254
Esta. Mary Stephens 60
Andrew Rogers
Courfauld & Ogier 101
Ja's & Edw'd Penman 43
Rob't Hazlehurst & Co. 403
Ditto for T. Eveleigh
 as Security 2400
Benj'a Guerard 367
Lockey & Bradford 100
Colcock & Graham 6
Keating & Jas Simmons 27
R'd Bohun Baker ab't 1020
Thos Phepoe 288
Mills 288
Aedanus Burk 288

Wm Brailsford 96
Mich'l Watson 30
J. L. Gervais 90
Hooper & Alex'r 14
George Hooper 26
Doctor Fayssoux 450
 2 Bonds as security for T. Eve-
leigh
½ am't for Bonds to Jas Laurens
 as Security for T. E. 320
Roger Smith for ditto 400
F. E. Mey for ditto in the
 hands of Dr. Clitherall 940
Rawlins Lowndes, B. Huger &
 self, my half about 218

Recorded 24 April 1790

76

A, 989-990: Ephraim Liles Jun'r of Newberry County bound to John Valentine of same, in the sum of £200, 15 March 1790, whereas John Valantine was surety for Ephraim Liles to the executors of Captn. Charles King for £96 sterling for which said Ephraim Liles hath mortgaged a negro man named Jack, one woman slave named Cate, three feather beds, with household furniture, one bay horse, etc. Ephraim Liles (Seal), Wit: Thos Gordon, John Liles. Proved in Newberry County by the oath of Maj'r Thos Gordon 15 April 1790 before W. Wadlington, J.P.

A, 990-991: State of South Carolina, Ninety Six District. John Pitts of district aforesaid bound to William Mangum of same in the sum of £160 sterling, 8 April 1789, to make title to tract of 100 acres in Newberry County on the main Charlestown Road adj. land of William Mangrum. John Pitts (Seal), Wit: Charles Griffin, Daniel Pitts. Proved in Newberry County by the oath of Daniel Pitts Ju'r before James Mayson & J. R. Brown, justices, 21 April 1790. Recorded 9 April 1790.

A, 992-993: 25 July 1784, Thomas Johnston to Catrine Butler, daughter of said Tho's Johnston, for natural love and affection, one negro wench about four years old named Nell at my wife Elizabeth's death. Thos Johnston (Seal), Wit: Henry Butler (mark), Mary Butler (+). Proved in Ninety Six District by the oath of Henry Butler 23 April 1785 before Jno Hunter, J.P. Recorded 14 May 1790.

A, 994-999: 8 & 9 Sept 1789, John Coate of Newberry County & Susanna his wife to James Mayson, Philemon Waters, Robert Rutherford, William Caldwell, Jacob Roberts Brown, Esquires, and other justices of the county of Newberry, for £10, two acres for the purpose of erecting a court house, goal and other buildings for the use of the public, on a small hill to the west of the Dwelling House of said John Coats, on waters of Bush River. John Coats (Seal), Susannah Coats (Seal), Wit: Benjamin Long, James Yancey. Recorded 25 May 1790.

A, 1000-1001: 24 April 1790. Clemen Davis Ju'r of Newberry County & Settlement of Beaverdam branch, to Andrew Felts of same settlement, for £10 sterling, 45 acres adj. said Davis, Wm Winchester, Charles Cade[?], granted to said Clemen Davis 5 Feb 1787, recorded in Book SSS, page 66. Clem't Davis (Seal), Wit: James Lindsey, James Walker. Proved 7 May 1790 by the oath of James Lindsey before John Lindsey, J.P. Recorded 11 June 1790.

A, 1002-1006: Lease and release. 25 Aug 1778, John Rankin of Ninety Six District, planter, to Abel Thomas, farmer, of same, for £650 SC money, 300 acres granted 10 Feb 1775 to John Rankin, on a small branch of Cannons Creek, recorded in Book GGG, page 138. John Rankin (I) (Seal), Wit: Edward Thomas, Isaac Thomas, Timothy Thomas. Proved in Newberry County 7 June 1790 by the oath of Isaac Thomas before Mercer Babb, J.P. Recorded 28 June 1790.

A, 1006-1008: 29 Jan 1789, Noah Bond & Fanny his wife of Newberry County, planter, to Nathaniel Henderson & Davis Sims, in copartnership, of same, for £50 sterling, tract on a branch of Enoree River called Beaver Creek including a Mill seat on said creek, 45 acres, granted to Richard Bond 5 June ____. Noah Bonds (Seal), Fanney Bonds (+) (Seal), Wit: Reuben Sims, John Grasty, Thos Grasty. Proved in Newberry by the oath of Reuben Sims 19 Nov 1789 before Geo Ruff, J.P.

A, 1009-1011: 21 Dec 1787, Reuben Jones & Marthy his wife of the Province of Georgia, farmer, for £100, to Nath'l Henderson of Newberry County, SC, carpenter, 100 acres in the fork between Tyger & Enoree River adj. Robert Duncan, Thomas Gordon. Reubin Jones (Seal), Wit: John Stewart, Philip James, David Sims. Proved in Newberry County by the oath of John Stewart 19 Nov ____ before George Ruff, J.P. Recorded 15 July 1790.

A, 1011-1015: Lease and release. 7 & 8 Jan 1778, Simon Ridlehuber of Ninety Six District, planter, to George Michael Ridlehuber of same, planter, by grant dated 3 Sept 1754 of 300 acres in Craven County on a branch of Cannons Creek adj. Hemeter, Christian Leiver, Anthony Staggs, recorded in Book PP, page 225, now conveyed for £200 SC money. Simon Ridlehuber (X) (Seal), Wit: Ulrich Meyer [German signature], George Eigelberger [German signature], Martin Frick [German signature]. Proved by the oath of Ulrick Myer 20 Jan 1778 before Mich'l Dickert, J.P. Recorded 15 July 1790.

A, 1016: South Carolina, 96 Dist., Newberry County. John Chandler Sr., planter, of county aforesaid, for £90 sterling to John Chandler Jun'r, a negro boy named Lewis about 7 years old, one other negro boy named Charles about five years old, one sorrill stallion with one hind foot white & a star in his forehead six years old, dated 12 Jan 1789. John Chandler (Seal), Wit: James Waters, Richard Bonds (X), John Waller. Proved in Newberry County by the oath of John Waller 13 March 1790 before W. Wadlington, J.P. Recorded 16 July 1790.

A, 1017-1020: Lease and release. 22 May 1787, Israel Gaunt and his wife Hannah Gaunt of Ninety Six District, to Enoch Pearson of same, for five shillings sterling, 14 acres in the fork between Broad & Saludy Rivers on waters of Bush River, granted to Israel Gaunt 5 Oct 1786, recorded in Book OOOO, page 622. Israel Gaunt (Seal), Hannah Gaunt (Seal), Wit: Daniel Smith, Isaac Jinkins, Char's Thompson. Proved in Newberry County 7 June 1790 by the oath of Daniel Smith before Mercer Babb, J.P. Recorded 17 July 1790.

A, 1021-1025: Lease and release. 15 Dec 1786, John Riley of Newberry County, Ninety Six District, SC, hatter, & Rachel his wife, to Enoch Pearson of same, farmer, for £13 s10 SC money, 27 acres, part of 350 acres granted to said John Riley 28 Aug 1767 on Bush River in Berkly County adj. land of Cloud, John Hammer; said 27 acres adj. Enoch Pearson, John Riley, heirs of Gilliland, by plat certified by P. Waters, D. S., 24 Aug 1786. John Rily (X)

(Seal), Wit: Daniel Smith, Isaac Jinkins, Hezekiah Riley. Proved in Newberry County 7 June 1790 by the oath of Daniel Smith before Mercer Babb, J.P. Recorded 18 July 1790.

A, 1025-1029: Lease and release. 3 & 4 June 1790, Captain Thomas Stark of Newberry County, to John Thomas, planter, of same, for £70 sterling, 293 acres granted to Stark 3 April 1786, recorded in Book KKKK, page 191, adj. land of William Crow, land claimed by Jonothan Neill, Jonathan Taylor, Robert McAdam, and said William Stark conveyed to Thomas Stark. Thomas Stark (Seal), Wit: James Lindsey, William Crow, George Hughes. Proved 8 June 1790 by the oath of James Lindsey before Robt Rutherford, J.P. Recorded 20 July 1790.

A, 1029: Newberry County. Personally appeared Ruth Lewallen and made oath that she was lawfully married into Daniel MaclDuff by one Col. John Clark, dated 24 Feb 17890. Ruth Lewallen (X), before W. Wadlington, J.P. Recorded 17 Aug 1790.

A, 1030: Mary Graham of Newberry County for natural love and affection to my son Jesse Graham Riley, my third of negroes & land and also my right of administration on the estate of George Graham deceased, 13 Aug 1790. Mary Graham (+) (Seal), Wit: Jeremiah Williams, James Graham. Proved 28 Aug 1790 by the oath of James Graham before Robert Rutherford, J.P. Recorded 30 Aug 1790.

A, 1031-1034: Lease and release. 5 & 6 Sept 1774, James Ray, planter, of Berkley County, SC, to Abraham Right, weaver of Craven County, SC, for £500 SC money, 200 acres in fork between Broad & Saludy Rivers on Indian Creek adj. Henry Hendricks, granted 5 Oct 1756. James Ree (Seal), Agness Ree (X) (Seal), Wit: Robert Dears, Samuel Lucas, William Willson. Proved in Ninety Six District by the oath of Samuel Lucas before Thos Wadlington, J.P., 10 Sept 1774. Recorded 31 Aug 1790.

A, 1035-1038: Lease and release. 24 & 25 May 1790, William Tate, Esqr., of District of Ninety Six, to Willm Irby of Newberry County, for £200 sterling, 200 acres, part of tract granted 2 July 1751, recorded in Book NN, page 108, to William Singfield, conveyed by William Singfield to William Turner Sen'r (decd), part of which was left to Absolem Turner by the will of William Turner, and since conveyed by William Turner Jun'r & John Turner to Robert Tate, and by Robert Tate conveyed to William Tate, adj. Tho's Brown, on Saluda River (formerly called Santee). Wm Tate (Seal), Wit: Robt Tate, Edward Thweatt, Rich'd Speake. Proved in Newberry County 14 May 1790 by the oath of Richard Speake before John Lindsey, J.P. Recorded 3 Sept 1790.

A, 1039-1041: Lease and release. 23 & 24 May 1786, Robert Tate of District of Ninety Six to William Tate of same, Robert Tate of Ninety Six District to William Tate of same, for £200 sterling, 5000 acres and upwards, conveyed to Robert Tate and others by a certain Miles Jennings, on waters of Saludy

River: 460 acres on the north side adj. to Saludy River opposite to Saludy Old Town, 260 acres purchased from the Commissioners of Forfeited Estates being lately the property of David Turner; the second parcel 100 acres purchased by said Robert Tate from John Turner as co-heir of Absolom Turner decd, the third parcel of 100 acres purchased by said Robt Tate form James Cook who purchased the same from William Turner as co-heir with the aforesaid John Turner of Absalom Turner decd. Rob't Tate (Seal), Wit: James Tate Jun'r, James Allen (I). Proved by the oath of James Tate Jun'r 28 June 1786 before Robert Rutherford, J.P.

A, 1042-1044: Lease and release. 1 & 2 Dec 1788, George Litsey, planter of Newberry County, to James Beard of same, planter, for £20 sterling, tract granted 5 Nov 1787 to George Litsey, 46 acres on waters of Cannons Creek adj. Henry Wicker, Charles Bondrake, Peter Stockman, Peterman. George Litsey (Seal), Wit: Michl Dickert Sen'r, Jacob Litecy (IL), Peter Dickert. Proved in Newberry County by the oath of Mich'l Dickert Sen'r 23 July 1790 before Geo Ruff, J.P. Recorded 12 Nov 1790

A, 1045-1047: Lease and release. 1 & 2 Sept 1790, George Watson of Newberry County, shoemaker, to Rosanah Russell of same, widow, for £10 SC money, 23 acres on north side Saludy River below the ancient Boundary on waters of Bush River granted to John Duncan 4 Dec 1786, conveyed by said John Duncan to Geo Watson 4 Aug 1787, recorded in Book A, page 560 in Newberry County. George Watson (Seal), Wit: Robt McClure, Richard Clegg. Proved in Newberry County by the oath of Robert McClure 1 Nov 1790 before Tho W. Waters, J.P. Recorded 15 Nov 1790.

A, 1048-1049: 14 Aug 1790, William Malone & Sarah his wife of Newberry County to William Richards of same, for £40 sterling, tract of 100 acres on waters of Enoree River granted to Daniel Johnston and conveyed to william Malone Senr 31 Dec 1779, and by said Malone granted to his son William Malone by deed 2 Dec 1786, also 36 acres adj. Bartholomew Johnston. W. Malone (Seal), Sarah Malone (+), Wit: W. Malone Sen'r, Jas Russell, W. Malone Minor. Proved 2 Nov 1790 by the oath of W. Malone Sen'r before Robt Rutherford, J.P. Recorded 16 Nov 1790.

A, 1050: William Speakman, planter, of Newberry County, for love, good will and affection to my brother Thomas Speakman of same, 100 acres on Indian Creek adj. Charles McBride, and a roan mare the property of William Speakman deceased, dated 6 Sept 1790. William Speakman (Seal), Wit: James Kenady, Jas Wilson, Mathew Wilson.

A, 1050-1052: 23 April 1790, Benjamin Hampton and Ann his wife of Newberry County to Lewis Hogg of same, for £50 sterling, tract of 250 acres in the fork between Broad & Saludy Rivers on a branch of Broad River call'd Enoree River, granted to said Benj'n Hamton 7 June 1774. Benj'a Hampton (Seal), Ann Hampton (Seal), Wit: W. Malone Sen'r, Bartho'w Johnston, W

Malone. Proved 2 Nov 1790 by the oath of William Malone Sen'r before Robert Rutherford, J.P. Recorded 17 Nov 1790.

A, 1052-1055: Lease and release. 30 & 31 March 1789, Daniel Winchester of Newberry County, settlement of Bush River, hatter, to his brother Willeby Winchester of same settlement, farmer, for £50 SC money, 125 acres, part of tract of 250 acres granted to William Winchester deceased 22 Aug 1763, which land fell unto said Daniel Winchester being the surviving heir of the above William Winchester, being on a small branch of Bush River. Daniel Winchester (Seal), wit: Ezekiel Williams, Ruth Lindsey, James Lindsey. Proved 7 Sept 1790 by the oath of James Lindsey before Philemon Waters, J.P. Recorded 25 Nov 1790.

A, 1055-1059: Lease and release. 13 Feb 1790, Henry Coats to Robert Gilliam, for £100 sterling, 350 acres on a small branch of Saludy River known by the name of Goospond adj. Joseph Freeman, granted to said Coats 19 Nov 1772. Henry Coats (mark) (Seal), Wit: Jno Dooly, Thos Dooly, William Campbell. Proved in Burk County, Georgia 30 July 1790 by the oath of William Campbell before Charles Harvey, J.P. Recorded 26 Nov 1790.

A, 1059-1063: Lease and release. 6 & 7 Aug 1779, Joseph Hays, Blacksmith, of Ninety Six District, to John Mangrum, planter, of same, for £200 SC money, 100 acres in Berkly County, Ninety Six District, on waters of Little River, half of 200 acres granted 19 June 1772 to Elizabeth Johnston and conveyed by Elizabeth Johnston to Joseph Hays 23 & 24 Feb 1773, on the south side of the Main County Road from Rebourns Creek to Charleston, adj. land of John Pitts, David Richardson. Jos. Hays (Seal), Wit: Daniel Williams, Samuel Goodman, James Goodman. Proved in Newberry County by the oath of James Goodman 4 Oct 1790 before William Caldwell, J.P. Recorded 27 Nov 1790.

A, 1063-1065 & 1075-1076: Lease and release. 4 & 5 Dec 1788, James Lindsey of Ninety Six District, Settlement of Indian Creek, to Benjamin Berry of Settlement of Bush River, for £70 Virginia money, 293 acres on waters of Bush River granted to James Lindsey 6 Nov 1787, recorded in Book QQQQ, page 119, adj. Clement Davis, Jacob Huffman, Joshua Reeder. James Lindsey (Seal), Wit: John Cross, Robert Dunnon (mark), John Boyd (O). Proved in Newberry County 6 Nov 1786 [sic] by the oath of John Cross before John Lindsey, J.P. Recorded 13 Dec 1790.

A, 1065-1068: Lease and release. 9 & 10 Aug 1790, Simon Wicker of Newberry County, planter, to Thomas Parrott of same, planter, for £25 sterling, 100 acres on waters of Enoree River granted to Michael Wingart 21 May 1772, recorded in Book LLL, page 291, conveyed by Michael Wingart and Mary his wife to Adam Mack 15 & 16 Jan 1773, and by said Adam Mack to Mathias Wicker deceased 15 & 16 Jan 1772 [sic], and by his will said 100 acres devolved into the possession of his son Simon Wicker. Simon Wicker (W) (Seal), Wit: Ephraim Liles, Jno Parrott, Michl Dickert Sen'r. Proved in

Newberry County by the oath of John Parrott 25 Oct 1790 before Geo Ruff, J.P. Recorded 13 Dec 1790.

A, 1069-1070: 13 Nov 1787, Ferrel Riley of Richman County, Georgia, to Edward Finch of Newberry County, SC, for £135 sterling, 150 acres in Newberry County on a branch of Cannons Creek, a branch of Broad River, granted to James Murphey 13 Oct 1767, recorded in Book BBB, page 312. Ferrel Riley (Seal), Wit: Levi Coursey, Aggatha Brooks, Thomas Riley. Proved 6 Sept 1790 in Newberry County by the oath of Thomas Riley before John Lindsey, J.P. Recorded 23 Dec 1790.

A, 1070-1075: Lease and release. 7 & 8 Feb 1768, Edward Murphy, planter, and Sarah his mother, in Berkly County, SC, to Isaac Morgan of same, planter, for £50 SC money, 150 acres on waters of Cannons Creek in Craven County adj. John Pearson, granted to James Murphy, father to said Edw'd Murphy, 30 Oct 1767. Edw'd Murphy (Seal), Sarah Murphy (mark) (Seal), Wit: Daniel Horsey, Sarah Horsey, Elizabeth Lindsey. Proved 28 March 1769 by the oath of Daniel Horsey before Jonathan Gilbert, J.P. in Craven County. Recorded 24 Dec 1790.

A, 1076-1081: Lease and release. 25 & 26 Dec 1775, John Pearson of the forks of Broad & Saluda Rivers in Craven County, SC, Ninety Six District, Blacksmith, to Terrence Riley of same forks, planter, for £350 SC money, tract granted 30 Oct 1767 to James Murphey, 150 acres in Craven County on a branch of Cannons Creek, recorded in Book BBB, page 313, and conveyed 7 & 8 Feb 1768 from Edward Murphy, eldest son of said James Murphy & Sara his mother, to Isaac Morgan, and Isaac Morgan 1 & 2 May 1769 to John Pearson. John Pearson (Seal), Jean Pearson (mark) (Seal), Wit: George Ruff, John Grayham, Micajah Harrison. Proved in Ninety Six District by the oath of George Ruff 26 Dec 1775 before Michl Dickert, J.P. Recorded 12 Feb 1791.

A, 1081-1085: Lease and release. 27 Aug 1782, Captn. Charles King, late of District of Ninety Six, to Isaac Morgan of Ninety Six District, by grant to Joseph Davis on south east side of Kings Creek now adj. William Hambleton, John Lindsey, Joseph Hampton, 150 acres and sold by execution by Robert Stark, then sheriff of District aforesaid at the suit of John Glyn, conveyed to Charles King, now conveyed for £450 SC money. Charles King (Seal), Wit: James Lindsey, George Speake, John Speake. Proved 27 Nov 1790 by the oath of James Lindsey before Jno Lindsey, J.P. Recorded 12 Feb 1791.

A, 1085-1086: Jacob Oxner of Newberry County, farmer, for good will & affection to his son Martin Oxner, 75 acres in the fork of Broad & Saluda Rivers, also to my sons Jacob Oxner, Mich'l Oxner & Joseph Oxner, each 75 acres also to my loving daughters & Sons Jacob, Michl, Joseph, Nancy, Rachel, Molly & Susanah, all my stock of horses, cattle, hogs, to be equally divided between them; also to my son in law Henry Kelch, 50 acres. to my son Michl Oxner, all my household furniture of potts, pewter, in my present dwelling house, dated 28 Dec 1790. Jacob Oxner (IO) (Seal), Wit: Peter Little, Henry Kelch (+). Proved in Newberry County by the oath of Peter Little 28 Dec 1790 before Geo Ruff, J.P. Recorded 4 Jan 1791.

A, 1087-1090: 5 April 1782, Frederick Sheffer of Ninety Six District, planter, and Elizabeth his wife, to Peter Stockman of same, farmer, for £500 SC money, 200 acres in Ninety Six District on a branch of Crims Creek, waters of Broad River adj. Christopher Remenstin, Jacob Fulk, Henry Habold, Adam Guinger[?], recorded in Book NNN, page 435. Fred. Sheffer, Eliz'a Sheffer. Wit: Jcaob Folmer, John Sweetenburgh, Geo Jacobson. Proved in Orangeburg District by the oath of Jcaob Folmer 6 April 1782 before Michal Leitner, J.P. Recorded 14 Feb 1791.

A, 1090-1093: Lease and release. 15 & 16 Sept 1780, Hans Adam Zigler of Orrangeburgh District, SC, planter, to Peter Stockman of Ninety Six District, tanner, for £250 SC money, 150 acres between Broad & Saluda Rivers granted to Nicholas Zeigler adj. Jacob Lights, recorded in Book PP, page 145, whereas said Nicholas Zeigler died intestate, and his eldest son Hans Adam Zigler became heir at law. Hans Adam Ziglar (mark) (Seal), Wit: John Kinard (IK), Johannes _____ [German signature], Michael Dickert. Proved in Ninety Six District by the oath of John Kinard Jun'r 16 Sept 1780 before Michal Dickert, J.P. Recorded 15 Feb 1791.

A, 1094-1095: 18 Jan 1790, Mathew Mabin of Rutherford County, North Carolina, to Peter Stockman of Newberry County, SC, for £50, 100 acres on south side of Broad River on a branch of Cannons Creek adj. John Buzzard, John Michal. Mathew Mabin (Seal), Wit: Ulrich Kuhn [German signature], Francis Cunningham, John Earle. Proved in Lexington County, SC, by the oath of Ulrick Koon 1 May 1790 before John Hampton, J.P. Recorded 16 Feb 1791.

A, 1095-1098: Lease and release. 9 March 1790, Barnard Mantz of Orangeburg District, SC, to John Adam Summers of same, for £100, tract granted 6 April 1753 to Felix Bousard, 250 acres on Cannons Creek, recorded in Book OO, page 193, and transferred to Rudolph Bousard 7 & 8 Sept 1775, and he conveyed to Barnard Mantz 9 & 10 July 1770. Barnard Mantz (Seal), George Mantz (Seal), Wit: Benedick Moyer, Jno Moyer. Proved in Lexington County by the oath of John Moyer 31 Dec 1790 before John Hampton, J.P. Recorded 16 Feb 1791.

A, 1099-1102: Lease and release. ___ 1790, Jacob Huit & Cristena his wife of SC to John Adam Summer of Orangeburgh District, storekeeper, for £15 sterling, grant dated 2 Jan 1754 to John Mazer or Henry Mitsker, 50 acres in the fork between Broad & Saluday Rivers on a branch of Crims Creek called Kountz Creek adj. Francis Huit, recorded in Book OO, page 367, and said 50 acres transferred to Peter Buyer by said John Mazer 12 & 13 July 1763, and Peter Buyer did transfer to John George Shoemaker 6 & 7 Nov 1769, and said John George Shoemaker died intestate whereby his daughter Cristena, lawful wife of said Jacob Huiet, being the only child became her at law to her said father's estate. Jacob Huit (+), Cristine Huit (Seal), Wit: Benedick Moyer John Moyer. Proved in Lexington County by the oath of John Moyer 31 Dec 1790 before John Hampton, J.P. Recorded 16 Feb 1791.

A, 1102-1106: Lease and release. 16 & 17 Nov 1788, George Gray, Robert Moore, George Mounts, Rosanah Glyn of Newberry County, SC, to Adam Summer of Lexington County, miller & dealer, for £50, 100 acres adj. Robert William Moore, James Shepherd, on waters of Cannons Creek, part of 200 acres granted to first named George Gray. Rosanah Glyn (Seal), Wit: Jas Tinsley, Johannes Meyer [German signature], Benedict Meyer [German signature]. Proved in Lexington County by the oath of John Moyer 31 Dec 1790 before Jno Hampton, J. P. Recorded 17 Feb 1791.

A, 1106-1107: 11 Nov 1790, Elizabeth Vaughn of Newberry County to Oliman Dodgen, her son of same, for natural love and affection, one negro woman Phillis & her three children and a negro man named Jacob; also 200 acres of land, and after his death to go to his son James Dodgen. Elizabeth Vaughn (+) (Seal), Wit: Daniel Pitts Jun'r, Aaron Potts, Edward Pitts. Proved in Newberry County by the oath of Daniel Pitts Jun'r 13 Jan 1791 before J. Roberts Brown. Recorded 18 Feb 1791. [See page 1147 for additional proof.]

A, 1108-1110: Lease and release. 5 & 6 March 1790, Joseph Wright of Newberry County, Millright & Charity his wife to Abijah ONeal of same, planter, in trust for the use of Hugh Oneal, William ONeal, John ONeal, Henry ONeal, & Thomas Oneal, minors, sons of William ONeal deceased, for £50 SC money, 250 acres on a small branch of Saluda River call'd Bush Creek adj. Thomas Shaw, granted to said Joseph Wright 30 July 1767. Joseph Wright (Seal), Charity Wright (C) (Seal), Wit: Thomas Right, Jemima Right, Milly Layton (mark). Proved 19 July 1790 by the oath of Thomas Right before Mercer Babb, J.P. Recorded 30 May 1791.

A, 1111-1112: 26 Nov 1790, David Dickson of Green County, Georgia, to John Lake of Newberry County, SC, for £40 sterling, 100 acres on a small branch of Tyger River call'd Peter's Creek, granted to James Croll 19 March 1773. David Dickson (Seal), wit: Thos Gordon, Jas Waters, Tho's Lake (+). Proved 17 Dec 1790 by the oath of Thomas Lake before W. Wadlington, J.P. Recorded 6 June 1791.

A, 1112-1114: Lease and release. 8 & 9 April 1789, Woodrick Miers of Lexington County to Philaman Waters of Newberry County, for £10 sterling, 530 acres on waters of Big Saluda adj. Reuben Morgin, Jonathan Waters, Genl Huger, granted to said Woodrick Miers 4 Sept 1786. Woodrick Myers (Seal), wit: Mary Scurry, Landon Waters (mark), Jurdon Morrel (mark). Proved in Newberry County by the oath of Mary Scurry 11 Feb 1789 before Thos. W. Waters, J.P. Recorded 6 June 1791.

A, 1114-1115: 12 Dec 1789, Benjamin Berry of Newberry County, planter, to William Caldwell of same, planter, for £18 sterling, 193 acres, part of 293 acres granted to James Lindsey and conveyed to said Benjamin Berry by said Lindsey, recorded in Grant Book QQQ, page 119 adj. Joshua Reader, Clement Davis, Job Oins. Benjamin Berry (Seal), Wit: John Boyd (O), David Boyd, Joseph Caldwell (K). Proved 12 Dec 1789 by the oath of Joseph Caldwell before Robert Rutherford, J.P.

A, 1116-1117: 31 May 1788, James [sic, for Samuel] Lindsey & Elizabeth his wife of Newberry County to Charles Crenshaw of same, for £200 sterling, 193 acres on Kings Creek, part of tract granted to George Wiles 27 Aug 17651 conveyed by said Geo Wiles to Isaac Pennington & willed by Isaac Penington to his daughter Charity, being the wife of Charles King & conveyed by Charles King & Charity to John Lindsey Jun'r, and by John Lindsey Jun'r to John Lindsey Sen'r, then to his son Samuel Lindsey. Samuel Lindsey (Seal), Elizabeth Lindsey (Seal), Wit: Thos Williams, Caleb Lindsey, Geo Wells Proved in Newberry County by the oath of Thos Williams 8 June 1790 before Robert Rutherford, J.P. Recorded 7 June 1791.

A, 1117-1118: 14 Oct 1790, Levi Casey of Newberry County, SC, to Joseph Herndon of Wilkes County, South [sic, for North?] Carolina, for £20 sterling, 40 acres on south side Duncans Creek, part of tract granted to Levi Casey 5 Dec 1785 adj. William Dickson. Levi Casey (Seal), Wit: Charles Crenshaw, Benjamin Summer, Nathaniel Burdine. Proved in Newberry County by the oath of Charles Crenshaw 14 Oct 1790 before Levi Casey, J.P. Recorded 7 June 1791.

A, 1119-1121: Lease and release. 15 & 16 Feb 1790, Joseph Wright of Newberry County, Millright, to Isaac Mills of same, for £10 sterling, 300 acres on waters of Saluda River adj. Timothy Thomas, James Patty, said Joseph Wright, Shaw, granted to said Joseph Wright 6 Aug 1787. Jos. Wright (Seal), Wit: Peter Julien, Phil. Waters, John Wright. Proved 16 May 1790 by the oath of Peter Julien before Mercer Babb, J.P. Recorded 8 June 1791.

A, 1121-1122: Elizabeth Turner, the surviving widow of William Turner decd, of Ninety Six District, Newberry County, for love, good will & tender affection to my granddaughter Rebekah Turner of same, a female black slave named Charlotte aged about 4 years next Christmas, dated 27 Jan 1791. Elizabeth Turner (Seal), Wit: William Irby, Benj. Long. Proved in Newberry County by the oath of Capt. William Irby before Jacob Roberts Brown, J.U.C. Recorded 8 June 1791.

A, 1122: Elizabeth Turner, the surviving widow of William Turner decd, of Ninety Six District, Newberry County, for love, good will & tender affection to my grandson Richard Turner Jun'r, now residing in Edgefield County, SC, a female black slave named Hams aged 20 years more or less, dated 27 Jan 1791. Elizabeth Turner (Seal), Wit: William Irby, Benj. Long. Proved in

Newberry County by the oath of Capt. William Irby before Jacob Roberts Brown, J.U.C. Recorded 8 June 1791.

A, 1123: Elizabeth Turner, the surviving widow of William Turner decd, of Ninety Six District, Newberry County, for love, good will & tender affection to my grandson William Turner Junior, , a female black slave named Hams aged 20 years more or less, dated 27 Jan 1791. Elizabeth Turner (Seal), Wit: William Irby, Benj. Long. Proved in Newberry County by the oath of Capt. William Irby before Jacob Roberts Brown, J.U.C. Recorded 8 June 1791.

A, 1124-1125: South Carolina. John Thornton of Ninety Six District bound to John O'Neal in the sum of £7000 SC money, 10 Aug 1773, to make title to 350 acres on a branch of Mudlick formerly laid out for Zachariah Tinessy. John Thornton (Seal), Wit: Henry ONeal. June 8th 1776, I do assign over the bond to William ONeal. s/John ONeal. Recorded 8 June 1791.

John Thornton of Craven County, SC, carpenter, appoint my friend William O'Neal of said county, my true & lawfull attorney to make title to 300 acres whereon I now live between Ranks's Creek & a branch of Mudlick Creek call'd the dry lick fork, part of 350 acres laid out for Zachariah Tinesey & elapsed by me the said Thornton, 27 April 1772. John Thornton (Seal), Wit: Mary ONeal, Isaachar Willcocks. Recorded 9 June 1791.

A, 1125: State of South Carolina, Newberry County. John Sudder does give up all right and title of William Auther estate deceased to William Wilson, received of William Wilson full satisfaction. Mr. Benjamin Arthur. Sir please to pay William Willson, John Sudder's part of William Arthur's estate, 21 Feb 1791. John Sudder. Wit: Jo Penington, Evans Robert (X), James Johnston (B). Recorded 8 June 1791.

A, 1125-1128: Lease and release. 25 & 26 Oct 1790 William Mazyck & Isaac Mazyck of Charleston, Residuary Legatees of the late William Mazyck deceased, to Philiman Waters of Newberry County, for £125 SC money, 200 acres on north side Saludy River adj. land granted to Michal Tickert [sic, for Dickert], Valentine Coudey, Patrick McDugan, James Morehead, granted to the late William Mazyck 14 Sept 1771. William Mazyck (Seal), Isaac Mazyck (Seal), Wit: John Cordes, Paul De St. Julien Ravenal. Proved 26 Oct 1790 by the oath of Paul De St. Julian Ravenal before Peter Freneau, J.P. Recorded 9 June 1791.

A, 1128-1130: 5 May 1791, Boltus Neece (the lawful heir of Conrad Neese deceased), of Mecklinburgh County, North Carolina, to William Chapman of Newberry County, SC, for £35 sterling, 100 acres in Newberry County in the fork of Broad & Saluda Rivers on south branch of Cannons Creek adj. Samuel Chapman, Abraham Thompson, Charles Burton, Robert Hannah, and was laid off on the bounty unto Doroty Neece 3 Feb 1773. Baltus Nees [German signature] (Seal), Francis Neese (mark), Wit: Daniel Little, John B. Mitchell.

Proved in Newberry County by the oath of John B. Mitchell before Geo Ruff, J. N. C. Recorded 17 June 1791.

A, 1130-1132: Lease and release. 8 & 9 March 1791, William Tate of District of Ninety Six, Esquire, to James Tate Junior of same, for £300 sterling, 266 acres in Newberry County on north side Saludy, opposite to the place called Saludy Old Town. William Tate (Seal), Wit: William Irby, Caleb Lindsey, Rich'd Speake, Susannah Tate. Proved in Newberry County by the oath of William Irby 17 May 1791 before J. R. Brown, J. N. C.

A, 1132-1133: 22 Nov 1787, John Lindsey of Newberry County to Charles Crenshaw of same, for £21 sterling, tract on waters of Kings Creek, 27½ acres, part of tract of 209 acres granted to said Lindsey whereon he now lives on north side Kings Creek adj. Charles Crenshaw, William Hamilton, Chandler. John Lindsey (Seal), Wit: Edward Finch, Jesse Brown. Recorded 1 July 1791.

A, 1133-1136: Lease and release. 6 & 7 May 1791, Thos. W. Waters of Newberry County, and Fanny his wife, to Henry Dunn of same, for £150 sterling, tract on north side Saluda River at John Turner's corner, adj. Wm. Clary, heirs of John Davis dec'd, granted to Stephen Elmore 8 July 1774, recorded in Book RRR, and fell to Mathias Elmore, son & heir to Stephen Elmore, and sold by him to John Boyd and John Boyd conveyed to Thomas Willoughby Waters. Thos W. Waters (Seal), Fanny Waters (Seal), Wit: George Campbell, William Jackson (mark). Proved in Newberry County by the oath of William Jackson 16 May 1791 before Mercer Babb, J.P. Recorded 23 Aug 1791.

A, 1136-1137: 2 May 1790, Bartlett Brooks of Newberry County & Elizabeth his wife to Thomas Wadsworth & William Turpin, merchants, for £20 SC money, 118 acres below the old Indian line on the N side of Saluda River on waters of Little River adj. John Satterwhite, Robert Gilliam, Isaac Mitchel, granted to Bartlett Brooks 6 Dec 1790, recorded in Book C No. 5, page 110. Bartlett Brooks (Seal), Elizabeth Brooks (mark) (Seal), Wit: William Caldwell, John Robison. Proved in Newberry County by the oath of William Caldwell 29 July 1791 before Robert Gilliam, J.P. Recorded 23 Aug 1791.

A, 1137-1138: Anna Mary Boushard of County of Newberry for love, good will and affection, to my son Mathias Heir [Hair, Heer] of same, 100 acres where he now lives, formerly of my husband Peter Heir deceased, 16 Nov 1790. Anna Mary Bushard (+) (Seal), Wit: Wm Houseal, Frederick Davis, John Reichard [German signature]. Proved in Newberry County by the oath of John Richard (mark) 27 July 1790 before Geo Ruff, J. N. C. Recorded 24 Aug 1791.

A, 1138-1141: Lease and release. 7 & 8 March 1791, John James of Newberry County, blacksmith, to Robert Brooks of same, planter, for £55 sterling, 217 acres, part of 260 acres granted 5 Feb 1785, recorded in Book OOOO, on waters of Indian Creek adj. John James, Nathan Brown (decd), Roberts & Killpatrick, William Gray, James Bonds. John James (Seal), Elizabeth James

(Seal), Wit: James Lindsey, T. Wilson, Thomas Larger. Recorded 26 Aug 1791.

A, 1141-1142: 9 Nov 1791, Robert Brown of Newberry County, wheelright, to John James of same, blacksmith, for £100 sterling, 56 acres, part of 100 acres granted to Robert Grown 9 Nov 1774 on Guilders Creek. Robert Brown (Seal), Wit: William Wilson, Ptk. Lowry, W. Webster. Proved in Newberry County by the oath of William Wilson 6 Aug 1791 before Edw'd Finch, J. P. Recorded 26 Aug 1791.

A, 1143: Edwin Conway of Newberry County for love & Affection to my daughter Agatha Conway, three negroes Catoe[?], Fanny & Betty, one bed and furniture, and one gilded looking glass, dated 22 July 1791. Edwin Conway (Seal), wit: Jas. Creswell, R. Watts. Proved by the oath of Creswell and Richard Watts 28 July 1791 before Robert Gilliam, J.P. Recorded 29 Aug 1791.

A, 1143-1146: Lease and release. 13 & 14 Jan 1791, Jacob King of Newberry County to Thomas Stark of Gilders Creek, same county, for £20 sterling, 145 acres on a branch of Indian Creek adj. Patrick Lowry, William Tinney, Davis, William Woodall, Thomas Stark, recorded in Book LLLL, page 186. Jacob King (Seal), Elizabeth King (Seal), Wit: Penington King, Thomas Lindsey. Proved 28 July 1791 by the oath of Thomas Lindsey before Providence Williams, J.P. Recorded 29 Aug 1791.

A, 1147: Daniel Pitts Jun'r, Aaron Pitts, and Edward Pitts prove deed from Elizabeth Vaughan deceased to Olleman Dodgen her son & James Dodgen son of said Olleman, dated 11 Nov 1790... 30 Aug 1791, before Robert Gilliam, J.P. Recorded 30 Aug 1791.

A, 1148-1150: Lease and release. 11 & 12 March 1790, Jacob Houber of Orangeburgh District, Sc, planter, to George Reyzor Jun'r of Ninety Six District, planter, for £22 sterling, tract granted 27 Aug 1751 to Mary Ann Seaman, 50 acres in the fork between Broad and Saluda Rivers on waters of Crims Creek, recorded in Book NN, page 138, said Mary Ann Seaman was the lawful wife of Martin Hidle, and said Martin hidle transferred 50 acres to Jacob Houbert 19 & 20 Dec 1786. Jacob Hauberd (Seal), Wit: John Kounts, Martin Reyzor, George Reyzor Sen'r. Proved by the oath of John Kounts 22 March 1790 before John Hampton, J.P.

A, 1151-1154: Lease and release. 9 & 10 Jan 1780, Nathaniel Harris of Ninety Six District to Robert Gilliam of same, for £1000 SC money, 100 acres on waters of Mudlick Creek, waters of Little River, only part of that tract granted to said Nathaniel Harris 8 July 1774, adj. William Anderson, said Gilliam, Grayham. Nathaniel Harris (Seal), Wit: James Caldwell, Harris Gilliam. Proved by the oath of James Caldwell 11 Dec 1783 before Bartlett Satterwhite, J.P. Recorded 1 Sept 1791.

NEWBERRY COUNTY SC DEED ABSTRACTS

A, 1154-1157: Lease and release. 24 & 25 Nov 1790, Thomas Lehre of Charleston to John Johnston of Newberry County, for £59 d8 sterling, 566 acres granted 4 Dec 1786 on Indian Creek in Ninety Six District, adj. William Layent, Francis Burrows, William Kilpatrick, John Reid, John Garrett, Henry Roberts, widow Evans, Hancock, William Sampson. Thomas Lehre (Seal), Wit: John Griggs, Hugh Marshell. Proved 14 July 1791 by the oath of Hugh Marshel before P. Williams, J.P. Recorded 3 Sept 1791.

A, 1157-1161: Lease and release. 4 & 5 March 1791, Mark Love of Newberry County, to Hugh Marshell of same, for £62 s12 sterling, tract granted 5 Dec 1785 to John Lindsey, 135½ acres, half of tract of 271 acres on the old fort branch of Indian Creek adj. Theodorus Feltmet now held by James Sproul deceased, Abraham Penington but now Thomas Duckett, George Akins, recorded in Book AA, page 67, and said John Lindsey & Elizabeth his wife conveyed to Mark Love on 1 & 2 Sept 1787. Mark Love (Seal), Wit: Jno. B. Bennet, Micajah Bennet. Proved 14 July 1791 by the oath of Micajah Bennett before P. Williams, J.P. Recorded 6 Sept 1791.

A, 1161-1164: Lease and release. 23 & 24 June 1788, Abraham Gray of Laurence County, SC, and settlement of Enoree to Hugh Marshell of Newberry County, settlement of Indian Creek, for £20 sterling, 108 acres granted to Abraham Gray 5 June 1786 on waters of Indian Creek adj. Mark Love, Isaac Evans, Jacob Penington, Henry Roberts, recorded in Book LLLL, page 92. Abraham Gray (Seal), Wit: George Eakins, James Sproull, Mark Love. Proved 14 July 1791 by the oath of Mark Love before P. Williams, J.P. Recorded 6 Sept 1791.

A, 1164-1165: Samuel Beaks of Newberry County, settlement of Indian Creek, planter, to Ann Gray & Providence Williams, executors of John Gary deceased, one chesnut brown horse, one dark brown gelding, two feather beds & furniture, one cow & Calf, one weaving cloth loom, dated 9 April 1791. Samuel Beaks (Seal), Wit: James Lindsey, Benjamin Neill (mark). Proved 29 July 1791 by the oath of James Lindsay before Mercer Babb J.P. Recorded 7 Sept 1791.

A, 1165-1166: 21 Sept 1790, Simon Reeder Jun'r and his wife Leesly[?] Reeder of Newberry County, planter, to Benjamin Berry of same, planter, for £40 sterling, 100 acres, part of 250 acres granted to Simon Reeder & conveyed to Simon Reeder Jun'r. Simon Reeder (Seal), Lucinty Reeder (X) (Seal), Wit: Robert Brown, Elizabeth Brown (X). Proved in Newberry County by the oath of Robert Brown 10 Aug 1791 before Elisha Ford, J.P. Recorded 7 Sept 1791.

A, 1167-1170: Lease and release. 13 & 14 July 1785, Simon Reeder Sen'r to Simon Reeder Jun'r of settlement of Kings Creek, for £200 SC money, 100 acres, part of 250 acres in Craven County on Kings Creek adj. Clement Davis, Charles King, Thomas Lindsey, John Woodall. Simon Reeder Sen'r (+) (Seal), Wit: Richard Tear, David Reeder (R), James Lindsey. Proved by the oath of David Reeder 5 Aug 1791 before Edw'd Finch, J.P. Recorded 7 Sept 1791.

A, 1170-1171: Joseph Dawkins for £140 sterling paid 11 Nov 1789 to Alexander Bookter, five negro slaves one yellow woman about 35 years of age named Nelly, and four of her children one boy named Champ about 18 years of age, one ditto named Lewis about 54 years of age, one girl named Venus about three years of age, one ditto named Jackey which now sucks eight months old, dated 1 June 1791. Joseph Dawkins (Seal), Wit: John Turner, John Crooks. Proved in Newberry County by the oath of John Crooks 26 July 1791 before Edw'd Finch, J.P. Recorded 8 Sept 1791.

A, 1171-1172: 16 April 1791, William Coats of SC to John Turner Sen'r, for £70 sterling, tract in Newberry County on south side Enoree River on Kings Creek, granted to Francis Wafer 14 Aug 1772, grant entered in Book MMM, page 478, 200 acres, conveyed to William Coats 5 & 6 Jan and recorded in Book Co. No. 4, page 216. Barton Coats (X) (Seal), Netty Coats (Seal), Wit: James Waters, Bartholomew Turner, Richard Hughins. Proved in Newberry County by the oath of James Waters 6 July 1791 before Edw'd Finch, J.P. Recorded 9 Sept 1791.

A, 1173-1174: 13 Dec 1790, Andrew Russell & Jean Russell his wife of Newberry County to Aaron Cates of same, for £25 sterling, 20 acres on south side of Second Creek, part of tract granted to Edward Connerly 30 Sept 1774, conveyed to John Malone 8 Aug 1784, and from said Malone to Andrew Russell 29 June 1790. Andrew Russell (Seal), Jeannet Russell (+) (Seal), Wit: W. Malone Sen'r, Andrew Swan. Proved 19 Aug 1791 by the oath of W. Malone Sen'r before Edward Finch, J.P. Recorded 10 Sept 1791.

A, 1174-1176: 26 March 1771, John Embree of Berkley County, planter, to David Jenkin, William Right, Moses Embree & Enos Elleman of same county, planters, by grant dated 28 Jan 1771 to Conrad Imunick [sic, for Emick?] for 300 acres in Berkley County on Bush River, conveyed by Conrad Imunick to John Embree 16 Nov 1771. John Embree (Seal), Wit: Samuel Pearson, Samuel Chapman, David Mote. Proved in Craven County by the oath of Samuel Chapman 10 July 1772 before Samuel Cannon, J.P. Recorded 22 Sept 1791.

A, 1177-1178: 9 Aug 1791, John Price Sen'r of Newberry County, Ninety Six District, to John Price Jun'r of same, for natural love & Affection to my son John Price Jun'r, all my right, title, claim to my real and personal estate (only he is to maintain me & my wife & Children as long as I shall live). John Price (I) (Seal), Wit: Fred'k Nance, William Finch, Hezekiah Riley. Proved in Newberry County by the oath of Fred'k Nance 13 Aug 1791 before Geo Ruff, J. N. C. Recorded 23 Sept 1791.

A, 1178-1180: Before George Ruff, Esquire, 9 Sept 1789, Susannah Coats, wife of John Coats, relinquished dower to James Mayson, Phileman Waters, Robert Rutherford, William Caldwell, Jacob Robert Brown, Esquires, and the other justices of Newberry County, to the tract for the purpose of erecting the court house & other public buildings. Geo Ruff (Seal). Recorded 23 Sept 1791. Plat included by P. Waters, D. S., and William Caldwell, D. S.

A, 1180-1181: Jacob Brooks of Saluda in the District of Ninety Six, bound to Zebulon Gaunt of Bush River, gentleman, in the sum of £1000 sterling, 20 Sept 1783, to make title to 550 acres (excepting 200 acres sold by Jacob Brooks to Thomas Brooks), granted to Jacob Brooks Sen'r decd, on both sides Bush River adj. now by lands in possession of Joseph Thompson, Benjamin Pearson, William Pearson, Samuel Kelly, Mercer Babb, William Gilliam. Jacob Brooks (Seal), Wit: Joseph Thompson, Abel Insco. Proved by the affirmation of Joseph Thompson 26 June 1790 before Mercer Babb, J.P.

A, 1182-1186: Lease and release. 16 & 17 Dec 1791, William Brooks, son & heir of Jacob Brooks, & Ann his wife, Vachael Clary & Mary his wife, executors to said Jacob Brooks, for £500 SC money, to Samuel Gaunt of Newberry County, 350 acres, part of 550 acres on Bush Creek at the time of surveying in Berkley County adj. land of Thomas Cooper, Stephen Ellmore, George Campbell, granted to Jacob Brooks Senr 19 Sept 1758 and Jacob Brooks Sen'r did on 8 & 9 Nov 1762 convey said 550 acres to Jacob Brooks Jun'r. William Brooks (Seal), Ann Brooks (X) (Seal), V. Clary (Seal), Mary Clary (Seal), Wit: Saml Kelly Sen'r, Nebo Gaunt. Proved in Newberry County by the affirmation of Nebo Gaunt 19 Dec 1791 before Elisha Ford, J.P. Recorded 28 Dec 1791.

A, 1187: Joseph Brown and Keziah his wife of District of 96, for £32 s12 d6 sterling to Alexander Bookter, negro boy named Kent, dated 23 March 1785. Joseph Brown (Seal), Kezia Brown (X) (Seal), Wit: Wm. Malone Sen'r, Joseph Dawkins. Recorded 2 Jan 1792.

A, 1188: Vachael Clary of Edgefield County, Ninety Six District, bound to Samuel Gaunt of Newberry County, in the sum of £200 SC money, 12 June 1790, if Mary Clary, wife of said Vachael Clary, & widow of Jacob Brooks deceased, & admrx, shall make renunciation of dower. Vachel Clary (Seal), Wit: Saml Kelly Sen'r, Zimri Gaunt. Proved in Newberry County by the affirmation of Zimri Gaunt before Mercer Babb, J.P. Recorded 5 Jan 1792.

A, 1189: Received 2 Sept 1787 of Samuel Gaunt at Sundry Times to the amount of £50 s10 d7 sterling, it being her third of the estate of Zebulon Gaunt deceased. Mary Gaunt (X). Proved in Lancaster County, SC, by the oath of Michael Ganter 7 May 1790 before John Kershaw, J.P. Recorded 5 Jan 1792.

A, 1189-1190: Ephraim Liles Jun'r of Ninety Six District, Newberry County, bound to John Gorree of same, planter, in the sum of £122 sterling, 20 May 1791, mortgage of negro boy slave named Ned about 15 years of age, one stud horse, and other cattle until 1 Jan 1793. Ephraim Liles (Seal), Wit: Edwd

Kelly, Williamson Liles. Proved in Newberry County 13 Nov 1791 by the oath of Edward Kelly before Reubin Sims, J.P. Recorded 7 Jan 1792.

A, 1191-1192: 17 Oct 1791, Richard Speak, Sheriff of Newberry County, & District of 96, to Thomas Gordon of same, planter, whereas James Rogers brought suit against Arthur McCrackin & became dismiss'd at Plaintiff's Costs for want of a Legal demand, recorded in Order Book A, Sept Term 1786, and said Arthur McCrackin defendant did obtain judgment against the said James Rogers to be levied of the goods, etc., of James Rogers, now on 1 October 1791 a tract of 200 acres granted to John Biddy 1 Jan 1785 and by him conveyed to Danl McKelduff & from him to James Rogers on Tyger River, now conveyed for £8 210 sterling to Thomas Gordon. Richard Speak Shff (Seal), Wit: James Campbell, William Finch. Proved in Newberry County by the oath of William Finch 18 Oct 1791 before Robert Gilliam, J.P. Recorded 7 Jan 1792.

A, 1193-1194: 22 Aug 1791, John Speak of Newberry County, to Jean Sproul, widow of James Sproul decd, and late admx., of same county, for £5 sterling, 100 acres laid unto Theodurus Feltmat decd on waters of Indian Creek adj. John Pearson, now property of Mark Love, Jacob Pennington now property of Thos Duckett, George Akins, Thomas Wadlington, John Lindsey, granted 6 May 1773, recorded in Book FFF, memorial entered in Book M No. 13, page 29, 29 Sept 1774, said Jacob Buzard did convey to John Speak 12 Aug 1791, and by letters of admn. dated 28 July 1791 said John Speak conveys to Jean Sproul. John Speake (Seal), Wit: Robt McClintock, John Odell, James Lindsey. Proved 29 Aug 1791 by the oath of James Lindsey before P. Williams, J.P. Recorded 20 Jan 1792.

A, 1195: 5 Sept 1791, John Speak of Newberry County, to Levi Casey of same, for £100, 576 acres on Fowlers Branch, a branch of Duncans Creek below the Indian Boundary, recorded in Book ZZZ, page 315. John Speak (Seal), Wit: Jos Herndon, William Ragland, Ed'wd Finch, J.P. Recorded 21 Jan 1792.

A, 1196: 5 Sept 1791, Levi Casey of Newberry County to Benjamin Herndon of Wilkes County, North Carolina, for £400 Virginia money, 576 acres granted to John Speak on Fowlers Branch, a branch of Duncans Creek below the Indian Boundary, recorded in Book ZZZ, page 315. Levi Casey (Seal), Wit: Jos Herndon, William Ragland, Ed'wd Finch, J.P. Recorded 21 Jan 1792.

A, 1197-1200: Lease and release. 6 & 7 Sept 1790, Joseph Kennerly of Lexington County, SC, to Geo Ruff, Esqr., merchant, for £150 sterling, tract granted 29 Nov 1750 to Henry Coleman, 450 acres in Berkley County in the fork between Broad & Saludy Rivers, recorded in Book MM, page 13, and after the s'd Henry Coleman deceasing devolved unto his sons Herman & Conrad Coleman, and they conveyed to Jos Frederick Dubber 9 & 10 Dec 1773, and as s'd Frederick Dubber deceased indebted to Richard Stark, said tract was sold by Edmd Martin, sheriff, unto Joseph Kennerly, 30 Nov 1785.

Joseph Kennerly (Seal), Wit: Joseph Caldwell, David Ruff, Henry Ruff. Proved in Newberry County by the oath of David Ruff.

A, 1201-1202: Abel Jones Horsey of District of Orangeburgh District, to Mary Hogg widow, his sister, all lands there were given to me by my honored father Daniel Horsey deceased, by his last will and testament, and that will fall to me at he death of my mother Sarah Horsey, living in the District of 96 on William s Creek, also six slaves: Primas, Bett, Sampson, Sam, Nance & Jim. Abel Jones Horsey (Seal), Wit: John Miller, Absolom Lake. Proved by the oath of John Miller before Henry Young, J. P., 7 Dec 1781. Recorded 3 Feb 1792.

A, 1202-1203: South Carolina, Newberry County. 24 Oct 1791. Jacob King to Thomas Lindsey for £50 sterling, one bright bay mare, one black colt, two feather beds & furniture, one dutch oven & pot, stock of Hoggs in number about 24, corn about 50 barrels. Jacob King (Seal), Wit: Clement Gore, Pennington King. Proved 5 Nov 1791 by the oath of Pennington King before P. Williams, J.P. Recorded 24 Feb 1792.

END OF DEED BOOK A

The first 32 pages of Deed Book B are missing and were missing at the time of the LDS microfilming and at the time that the WPA transcripts were made. Fortunately, however, there are "memorialized records" of these deeds, Newberry County being one of four counties for which such records exist. The memorialized records, from the originals at the South Carolina Archives, for the missing deeds are included below.

"State of South Carolina, County of Newberry. Agreeable to an Act of Assembly of this State Passd the 17th day of March 1785, I heareby Return the following Memorials of deeds & other Conveyances Proved in open Court & otherways Proved as the law directs & Recorded in the Clerks Office &C from the Sixth of January 1792. by W. Malone & his Deputy C. C."

Michael Livingston to William Houseal, Lease & Release, dated 15th & 16th days of Septem'r 1774 for 250 acres of land on Cannons Creek in Newb'y County, Consid'n £200 old So. Currency, Proved the 28th Jan'y 1775 & Recorded the 12th March 1792.

William Stephens to George Latham, Mortgage dated 27th of Feb'y 1792 for 200 acres of Land on Little River, Newb'y County, £100 Sterling, Proved the 25th day of Feb'y 1792 & Recorded the 29th of March 1792.

John Johnston to James Sproull, Deed dated 25th of Feb'y 1792 for 157 Acres of Land on Indian Creek, Newberry County, Consid'n £30 sterling. Proved the third day of March 1792 & Recorded the 29th of March 1792.

Thomas Brandon to William Hendrix & Henry Hill Deed dated the 1st of Jan'y 1789 for 100 acres of Land in Newb'y County, Consid'n £50 sterling, Proved the 30th day of Nov'r 1791 & Recorded the 29th of March 1792.

Abel Pearson to Henry Hill Deed dated 14th day of Feb'y 1792 for 124 Acres of Land on Enoree River, Newb'y County, Consid'n £30 sterling. Proved the 15th day of Feb'y 1792 & Recorded the 2d of April 1792.

Jean Sproul to James & Charles Sproul Deed dated 22 day of Dec'r 1792 for 232 Acres of Land on Ind'n Creek, New'by County, Consid'n (Affection &C). Proved the 16th day of March 1792 & Recorded 2d April 1792.

Daniel Horsey to William Darby, Lease & Release dated the 21st & 22 days of March 1785 for 100 acres of Land in Newb'y County, Considn'n £200 Curr't Money. Proved the 23rd of Dec'r 1791 & Recorded the 3d April 1792.

Alexander Robison to Amory Day. Bill of Sale dated the 12th day of June 1785 for one Negro Girl Named Venus aged 12 years, £70 sterling. Proved the 28th day of Feb'y 1792 & Recorded 6th of April 1792.

Thomas Lewis to Ann Lewis lease & Release Dated the 19th & 20th days of May 1771 for 100 Acres of Land on Sesteh Creek, Newberry County. £100 So Currency. Proved the 18th day of Oct'r 1791 & Recorded the 6th of April 1792.

John Riley to Isaac Jinkins lease & Release 31st of Oct'r & 1st day Nov'r 1791 for 74 Acres of Land on Sesteh Creek, Newb'y County £30 sterling. Proved the 18th day of February 1792 & Recorded the 7th of April 1792.

John Clark to Ephraim Ledbetter, Deed dated 9th of April 1768 for 200 acres of Land on the Beaverdam, Newb'y County, £20 Procklamation Money. Proved the 16th of July 1769 & Recorded the 9th day of April 1792.

Ephraim Ledbetter to Abraham Odom Sen'r lease & Release 13th & 14th day of March 1770 for 200 acres of land on beaverdam Creek, Newb'y County £250 Curr't Money. Proved the 13th day of March 1770 & Recorded the 9th day of April 1792.

Reuben Flannigan to Thomas Duckett Deed dated 2d day Jan;'y 1790 for 200 acres of land on Ind'n Creek, Newberry Creek, Consid'n £150 sterling. Proved the 2d day of August 1790 & Recorded 10th of April 1792.

Executors of Charles King (Dec'd) to Thomas Duckett, Deed dated the 2d day Janr'y 1790 for 103 acres of land on Ind'n Creek, Newberry County, £60 sterling. Proved the 2d day of August 1790 & Recorded the 10th day of April 1792.

John Adam Summer to Adam Shealy, Lease & Release Dated the 23rd & 24th day of September 1791 for 520 acres of land on Waters of Crims Creek, Newberry County, £75 Curr't Money. Proved the 3d day of Jan'ry 1792 & Recorded the 11th of April 1792.

B, 33-34: 18 Dec 1792. Dempsey Odom to Jonathan Gilbert of SC, for £250 SC money, 200 acres on south side of Broad River on Beaver dam branch, granted to John Clark 8 March 1754 by North Carolina. Dempsey Odom (Seal), Wit: Michael Watson, William Ward. Proved by the oath of W. Ward before Moses Kirkland Dec'r 1773. Recorded 11 April 1792.

B, 34: Dorus Feltmet bound to John Lindsey Jun'r in the sum of £500 SC money, 5 March 1773, to make title to 100 acres. Dorus Feltmet (T) (Seal), Wit: James Lindsey, Samuel Lindsey, John Williams (mark).

B, 35-37: Lease and release. [date torn off from deed book, dated 23 & 24 Feb 1792 in memorialized records], Henry Wilson of Newberry County, to John Sterling of same, for £50 sterling, 10 acres in Ninety Six District on a branch of Sandy Run adj. Henry Butler, granted 7 __ 1789, recorded in Book BBB, page 543. Henry Wilson (Seal), Wilmoth Wilson (X) (Seal), Wit: Moses Butler

(+), John Wilson (X). Proved in Newberry County by the oath of Moses Butler 28 Feb 1791 before Geo. Ruff, J. N. C. Recorded 12 April 1792.

B, 38: 13 Dec 1791, Francis Howell of Newberry County to James Goggans of same, one negro man Daniel about 13 years of age. Francis Howell (Seal), Wit: George Goggans, Harrel Felton. Recorded 12 April 1792.

B, 39: John Voluntine Latener of Newberry County for love, good will and affection to John Richardson of same county, 50 acres adj. Jacob Kapperman, dated 7 April 1791. John Volentine (IEL) (Seal), Wit: Jacob ____ [German signature], John Reason, David Ruff. Acknowledged in open court 18 Oct 1791. Recorded 16 April 1792.

B, 40: Francis Krouse to Christiana Barbara Priester (natus Kroomer), tract of 150 acres, dated 14 April 1784. Francis Krouse (+) (Seal), Wit: Joachim Bulow, Jacob Halman [German signature], Jesse Wilson. Proved in Newberry County by the oath of Jacob Halman 12 Nov 1791 before Geo ruff, J. N. C. Recorded 16 April 1792.

B, 41: Ephraim Liles of Newberry County for £35 sterling to Alexander Bookter, sorrel stud by the name of Limbrick, about 14 hands & three inches high, 25 Feb 1792. Ephraim Liles (Seal), Wit: Peter Staley, Benjamin Hampton. Recorded 24 April 1792.

B, 41-42: James Edrington of Camden District bound to Alexander Bookter of Ninety Six District in the sum of £22 sterling, at the rate of one pound one shilling & nine pence to a Guinea, and Eight pence to a dollar, 29 Dec 1791, to repay £11 sterling old & silver coin at the above rates, mortgage of negro Tom about 16 years old. James Edrington (Seal), Wit: Noah Bonds, Samuel Dawson, Christopher Edrington. Recorded 24 April 1792.

B, 42-44: Lease and release. 24 & 25 Aug 1791, James Morehead of Burk County, North Carolina, to Philemon Waters Sen'r of Newberry County, for £60 sterling, 100 acres granted to said James Morehead 12 Aug 1768 and recorded in Book DDD, page 392 in the County of Newberry, also tract granted to James Morehead Senr dec'd father to said James Morehead in 1768, 250 acres on north side Saluda River on a branch called Hawlick Creek. Jas Morehead (Seal), Wit: W. W. Waters, Henry Baits (+). Proved by the oath of Westwood Waters 8 Sept 1791 before Peter Julin, J.P.

B, 44: Amory Day of Edgefield County, SC, blacksmith, for £__ sterling, to William Day, Tavern Keeper of Newberry County, one set of Blacksmith tools, one bellows, one anvill, one vice, one beek Iron, one pair of Tongs two Sledge hammers, two Hand Hammers, one box of Punches, Chizles, Files & C., 15 Oct 1791. Amory Day (+) (Seal), Wit: James Taylor (X), ___ Brown. Recorded 21 April 1792.

B, 45: 22 Sept 1791, Thomas Gordon Sen'r to John Volentine & Thos McCrackin, for £90 sterling, 250 acres granted to William Winchester 20 Aug 1767, recorded in Book BBB, page 128, on Beaverdam branch of Bush River. Thos Gordon (Seal), Wit: Charles Prewit, H. Kelly. Recorded 26 April 1792.

B, 46-47 and 52: 31 Aug 1768, Fight Reisinger of Second Creek in Berkly County, planter, & Susannah his wife, to William Davis of Second Creek, planter, by grant dated 28 Aug 1767 to Fight Reisinger, 150 acres on Second Creek in Berkly County, now conveyed for £150 SC money. Feith Reisinger (Seal), Susanah Risinger (mark) (Seal), Wit: John Godfrey, George Grayham. Proved in Berkley County by the oath of George Grayham before John Ford, J. P., 15 Dec 1768. Recorded 27 April 1792.

B, 48-50: Lease and release. 11 & 12 Aug 1791, William Irby of Ninety Six District, Newberry County, to Thomas Brown of same, for £23 16 sterling, 119 acres, part of tract of 435 acres granted to said William Irby 7 Nov 1785, recorded in Book 4F, page 269. William Irby (Seal), Wit: Jos Goodman, Elizabeth Brown (mark). Proved in Newberry County by the oath of Joseph Goodman 12 Aug 1791 before Robert Gilliam, J.P. Recorded 27 April 1792.

B, 50-51: 28 Nov 1791, John Turner and Fathy his wife of Newberry County to William Calmes of same, for £100, 200 acres on Kings Creek, part of tract granted to Francis Wafer. John Turner (Seal), Wit: Benjamin Hampton, Robert Rutherford Jun'r, Alexander Turner. Proved by the oath of Benjamin Hampton 20 March 1792 before Edward Finch, J.P. Recorded 28 April 1792.

B, 53-55: Lease and release. 9 & 10 Sept 1789, Patrick Carmichal, weaver, and Elizabeth his wife, of Newberry County, to Joseph Gaunt of same, for £30 SC money, 150 acres granted to said Patrick Carmichal 17 March 1772 on waters of Bush River adj. said Carmichal, Israel Gaunt, William Aspernell. Patrick Carmichal (Seal), Elizabeth Carmichal (mark) (Seal), Wit: Giles Chapman, Thomas Reagan, William Thompson. Proved in Newberry County by the oath of William Thompson before Robert Gilliam. Recorded 28 April 1792.

B, 56-58: Lease and release. 14 & 15 April 1783, John Burney, weaver, of Ninety Six District, to George Montgomery of same, distiller & planter, for £90 SC money, 250 acres on a small branch of Second Creek a branch of Broad River adj. William Dawkins, Geo Montgomery, David Dunn. John Burney (mark) (Seal), Wit: Adam Glazier, Ainsworth Middleton (mark), David Ruff. Proved 15 April 1783 by the oath of Adam Glazier before Geo. Ruff, J. P. Recorded 28 April 1792.

B, 59-61: Lease and release. 27 & 28 Oct 1778, John Colvin of Ninety Six District, and Mary his wife, to Thomas Clark, weaver, for £100 SC money, tract granted to George Goggans 20 Feb 1771, recorded in Book GGG, page 227, 250 acres, conveyed 10 Nov 1773 to said John Colvin. John Colvin (Seal), Mary Colvin (Seal), Wit: James Abernethy, Job Colvin, John Abernathy.

Proved by the oath of Jobe Colvin 2 March 1789 before William Caldwell, J.P. Recorded 2 May 1792.

B, 62-64: Lease and release. 9 & 10 Nov 1773, George Goggans of Ninety Six District, to John Colvin of same, for £276 SC money, 250 acres granted to George Goggans 20 Feb 1771. George Goggins (Seal), Wit: John Satterwhite, Jean Caldwell, Isham East. Proved by the oath of Isham East 27 Jan 1777 before Thomas Wadlington, J.P. Recorded 3 May 1792.

B, 65-66: 24 Sept 1791, George Long & Catherine his wife of Newberry County to Adam Shealy of same, for £50 sterling, 21½ acres on a branch of Crims Creek, granted to George Long 22 Jan 1759, recorded in Book TT, page 102. George Long (GL), (Seal), Catherina Longen[?] (mark) [German signature], Wit: Johannes Schele [German signature], Johann Kuhn [German signature]. Proved 5 Jan 1791 by the oath of John Shealy before John Hampton, J.P. Recorded 4 May 1792.

B, 66: South Carolina, Newberry County. Jacob King for £120 to Pennington King, one negro woman named Jean about 18 or 19 years of age & a negro boy Peter about 14 or 15 years of age, dated 22 Oct 1791. Jacob King (Seal), Wit: John Smith, Nathan Anderson. Proved 5 Nov 1791 by the oath of John Smith before P. Williams, J.P.

B, 67: South Carolina, Newberry County. Edward Kelly of county aforesaid for £60 sterling, to Andrew Hunter of same, tract being one half of tract granted to Francis Awberry in Newberry County in the fork between Enoree & Broad River on Peter's Creek, adj. Awbry Noland, Mr. Foster, Nathan Davis, dated 25 May 1791. Edward Kelly (Seal), Wit: John Maxedon, N. Kelly, James Waters. Proved 27 Feb 1792 by the oath of John Maxedon before Reuben Sims, J.P. Recorded 4 May 1792.

B, 68-69: 28 Dec 1791, James Lester of Newberry County, planter, to Dianna Morgan of same, for £10, 35 acres, part of a grant to said James Lester 5 Feb 1787, 365 acres, on waters of Saluda on a branch called Big Creek adj. J. Summers, Martin Caymet, James Lester. James Lester (I), Wit: Rich'd Clegg, James Johnston. Proved in Newberry County by the oath of James Johnston 5 May 1792 before Peter Julien, J.P. Recorded 11 May 1792.

B, 69-70: 1 Feb 1792, James Shearer & Theadotia his wife of Newberry County to John & Andrew Johnston of same, for £45 s14 d3 sterling, tract of 200 acres granted to said James Shearer, recorded in Book IIII, page 350 on Heddley's Creek of Indian Creek. James Shearer (Seal), Theadotia Shearer (X) (Seal), Wit: Robert Anderson, John Johnston. Proved in Newberry County by the oath of John Johnston 3 May 1792. Recorded 11 May 1792.

B, 71-73: Lease and release. 29 & 30 Sept 1791. Philemon Waters Sen'r of Newberry County, to George Baldre, planter, of same, for £10 SC money, pat of tract of 250 acres on Hawlick Creek purchased by James Morehead and conveyed by him unto said Philemon Waters 24 Aug 1791. P. Waters (Seal), Wit: Henry Baits (+), Henry Tate. Proved in Newberry County by the oath of Henry Baits before Peter Julin, J.P., 10 Dec 1791. Recorded 11 May 1792.

B, 73-74: 1 Oct 1791, Bartholomew Johnson and wife Jean of Burk County, Georgia, to William Collingsworth of Newberry County, for £100 sterling, 200 acres on a branch of Enoree River called Gossetts Creek, part of two tracts, one granted to Daniel Johnston deceased 20 Jan 1772 and was willed by him to Bartholomew Johnson, the other granted to Bartholomew Johnston 6 June 1785. Barthol'w Johnson (Seal), Jeane Johnson (X) (Seal), Wit: W. Malone Sen'r, Robert Stell, Stephen McCraw. Proved 31 Dec 1791 by the oath of W. Malone before Edw'd Finch, J.P. Recorded 11 May 1792.

B, 75: Elizabeth Turner, wife of William Turner dec'd of Ninety Six District, for tender affection, regard, love & good will to my granddaughter Elizabeth the daughter of Benjamin & Precilla Long, one negro girl named Beckah about 2 years of age, dated 6 Dec 1791. Elizabeth Turner (Seal), Wit: William Irby, Willis Pruit (W). Proved in Newberry County 29 Feb 1792 by the oath of William Irby before Mercer Babb, J.P. Recorded 11 May 1792.

B, 76: Elizabeth Turner, wife of William Turner dec'd of Ninety Six District, for tender affection, regard, love & good will to my grandson William Henry Long, son of Benjamin & Precilla Long, one negro boy named Frank about nine years old, dated 6 Dec 1791. Elizabeth Turner (Seal), Wit: William Irby, Willis Pruit (W). Proved in Newberry County 29 Feb 1792 by the oath of William Irby before Mercer Babb, J.P. Recorded 11 May 1792.

B, 77-79: Lease and release. 27 & 28 Dec 1791. James Goggans of Newberry County to John Sterling of same, for £90 sterling, 135 acres on a branch of Little River called Sandy Run, part of tract of 150 acres granted to Robert Johnson dec'd 13 Aug 1766 and conveyed by William Johnson son to said Robert Johnson Sen'r decd to Robert Johnson Jun'r then to Joseph Smith 12 & 13 Sept 1777, and from Joseph Smith to James Goggans 22 & 23 July 1778. James Goggans (Seal), Mary Goggans (+) (Seal), Wit: B. Brown, George Goggins, Charles Gary (C). Recorded 12 May 1792.

B, 80-82: Lease and release. 1 Aug 1777, Samuel Nelson of Ninety Six District to Thomas Brooks of same, for £27 s10 SC money, 50 acres on waters of Little River, waters of Saluda River, part of tract of 150 acres formerly granted to said Samuel Nelson 2 June 1769. Samuel Nelson (Seal), Cathrine Nelson (mark) (Seal), Wit: James Brooks, James Wright, John Wright. Proved by the oath of John Right 31 Aug 1791 before Elisha Ford, J.P. Recorded 12 May 1792.

B, 83-86: Lease and release. 4 & 5 July 1788. Michael Hamiter of Charleston District, to George Michael Ridlehuber of Newberry County for £50 sterling, 120 acres in two separate tracts, 100 acres on Cannons Creek adj. Uldrick Slight, Christian Lever, Henry Callman, Charles Sigler, part of 300 acres granted to Thomas Hamiter 3 September 1754 of which Thomas Hamiter transferred 100 acres to his son George Simon Hamiter 3 & 4 February 1775, and said George Simon Hamiter transferred to Michael Hamitor 3 & 4 November 1786, granted recorded in Book PP, page 192; and 20 acres, part of 250 acres granted to Charles Siglar 2 Jan 1754 on Cattail branch of Cannons Creek adj. land of Uldrick Sligh, recorded in Book OO, page 397, and devolved by Charles Siglar to his son John Sigler & transferred by him unto George Simon Hamitor 5 Aug 1784 and by said George Simon unto Michael Hamitor 3 & 4 Nov 1786. Michael Hamiter (MH), Ann Mary Hamiter (Seal), Wit: Geo Long (GL), Geo Riser. Receipt witnessed by John Cannon and Michael _____ [German signature]. Proved in Lexington County by the oath of George Riser [signed in German, Georg Reiser], 31 Dec 1790 before Jno Adam Summer, J.P. Recorded 12 May 1792.

B, 87-89: Lease and release. 18 & 19 Feb 1791, Christiana Rooth alias Koone of Ninety Six District, to George Koone of same, planter, for £40 sterling, 50 acres, part of 200 acres on waters of Crims Creek, granted to Andreas Myers 12 Feb 1755, recorded in Book PP, page 366, conveyed from said Myers unto Benedick Koone and said Koone conveyed the same unto Christiana Rooth now Koone, 18 Aug 1788, recorded in Book A, page 630. Christiana Koone (X) (Seal), Wit: John Folk, Peter Stockman, Henry Koon (mark). Proved in Newberry County by the oath of John Folk before Geo Ruff, J. N. C., 15 July 1791. Recorded 12 May 1792.

B, 90-93: Lease and release. 6 & 7 Dec 1790, John Duglass of Edgefield County, Ninety Six District, SC, planter, to Shadrack Carter of Newberry County, for £80 SC money, 200 acres, part of 400 acres granted to Jacob Kelly 2 Feb 1754. John Duglass (I) (Seal), Wit: William Langford, Jacob Langford, George McCollester (+). Proved in Newberry County by the oath of William Langford 28 Nov 1790 before Peter Julin, J. P. Recorded 12 May 1792.

B, 94-96: Lease and release. 18 & 19 Jan 1792, Horatio Griffin & Patsey his wife of Newberry County, to Mark Smith of same, for 100 guineas, 78 acres, part of 200 acres granted to Edward Brown 12 June 1751 and conveyed by him to Horatio Griffin and his wife on Big Saluda on the east side of Big Creek adj. John Musgrove, Wallice Jones. Horatio Griffin (Seal), Patsey Griffin (X) (Seal), Wit: Jacob Smith, W. W. Waters, John Ryle. Proved in Newberry County by the oath of John Ryle 8 March 1792 before Peter Julin, J.P. Recorded 19 May 1792.

B, 97-99: Lease and release. 18 & 19 Jan 1792, Philemon Waters Sen'r of Newberry County to Mark Smith of same, for £60 sterling, 76 acres on north side Big Saluda River, granted to John Musgrove (decd) 19 June 1772.
P. Waters (Seal), Wit: Horatio Griffin, John Ryle, John Lewis (X). Proved in Newberry County by the oath of John Ryle 8 March 1792 before Peter Julin, J.P. Recorded 19 May 1792. Plat included showing land adj. William Jones, Horatio Griffin, Wallice Jones.

B, 100-101: 3 April 1792, Philliman Waters of Newberry County to John Cunningham of Charlestown, for £5 SC money, tract of 750 acres on north side big Saluda River at the mouth of Bush River, adj. Joseph King, granted to William Turner and conveyed by him to said Philliman Waters. P. Waters (Seal), Wit: Robert G. Harper, Johnson Haygood. Proved in Charleston District by the oath of Johnson Haygood 14 April 1792 before Stephen Ravenell, J.P. Recorded 31 May 1792. Mortgaged to Philliman Waters to John Cunningham for £100.

B, 102-104: Lease and release. _____ 1791, Col. Philliman Waters of Newberry County to Philliman Waters of same, for £100 sterling, tract of 200 acres on north side Saluda River above Buffalow Creek, formerly conveyed to said. Col. P. Waters from Lewis Peterman& Susannah his wife, 19 Jan 1772;. also 50 acres on north side Saludy River adj. Presnell, granted to sd. Col. Philliman Waters, 21 Jan 1785. P. Waters (Seal), Wit: David Richardson, Daniel Perkins. Proved in Newberry County by the oath of David Richardson 21 May 1792 before Peter Julin, J.P. Recorded 14 June 1792.

B, 105-106: Michael Abney of Newberry County, Ninety six District, planter, for £100 SC money to George Latham, merchant, of same, all the goods, household stuff & implements, horses, cattle hoggs, and items mentioned on the schedule hereunto annexed, 7 May 1792. Michael Abney (Seal), Wit: Sam. Kelly Sen'r, Francis Atkins. Proved by the affirmation of Samuel Kelly Sen'r 11 May 1792 before Elisha Ford, J.P. Recorded 4 July 1792.

B, 106: Charles Collins of Ninety Six District, bound 7 Oct 1779 in the sum of £5000 SC money, to Thomas Jones of same, to make title to a tract in Berkly in the Forks between Broad & Saluda on Second Creek whereon Thomas Jones now lives. Charles Collins. Wit: John Lindsey, Isaac Morgan, John Balinger. Proved 1 May 1792 by the oath of Isaac Morgan before Geo. Ruff, J. N. C.

B, 107-109: Lease and release. 23 & 24 June 1775, Joachim Bulow of District of Ninety Six, Minister, to Barnard Mantz, George Eigleberger & George Hertel, Elders of the Congregation tot he Decending [sic, for Dissenting] Church of St Paul of same, for £20 SC money, 50 acres, part of 200 acres granted to Joachim Bulow on waters of Crims Creek adj. Tobias Legron, Andrew Thomas, Michael Kibler, Jacob Durr, Willia Houseal. Joachim Bulow (Seal), Wit: William Houseal, Charles Binnicker, Martin Single. Proved by the oath of Martin Singley before Wm Houseal, J.P., 14 Aug 1776. Recorded 5 July 1792.

B, 110-111: 17 Aug 1791, Thomas Johnston of Newberry County to Jehue Johnston for natural love and affection, 83 acres, part of 250 acres granted to James Johnston 14 Dec 1754. Thos Johnston (Seal), Wit: William Goggans, John Johnston, Daniel Johnston. Proved by the oath of William Goggans before Mercer Babb, J.P., 22 May 1792. Recorded 10 July 1792.

B, 111-112: 17 Aug 1791. Thomas Johnston of Newberry County to John Johnston for natural love and affection, 83 acres, part of 250 acres granted to s'd Thomas Johnston 14 Dec 1754, adj. John Johnston. Thos Johnston (Seal), Wit: William Goggans, John Johnston, Daniel Johnston. Proved by the oath of William Goggans before Mercer Babb, J.P., 22 May 1792. Recorded 10 July 1792.

[N. B. The grant referred to in the two previous deeds is in the name of Thomas Johnston (not James Johnston) and is found on Royal Grants, Volume 6, page 171, at the South Carolina Archives.)

B, 113: 8 Feb 1792. Seth Hatcher of Newberry County to Daniel Raymond & Ann his wife (my beloved sister, 20 acres adj. land of William Gold's land, Benjamin Conwill & said Seth Hatcher, part of 200 acres when granted but now less by reason of an old grant taken a part thereof & now remains about 60 acres & a small tract I bought of William Gould of ten acres. Seth Hatcher (Seal), Linney Hatcher (mark) (Seal), Wit: Chesley Davis, James Black. Proved by Chesley Davis 26 March 1792 before Peter Julin, J.P. Recorded 10 July 1792.

B, 114-116: Lease and release. 26 & 27 Jan 1792, John Lindsey Esqr. of Newberry County, Ninety Six District, to Samuel Lindsey of same, for £150 sterling, 150 acres, part of 209 acres granted to said John Lindsey 2 Oct 1786 near Long Lane adj. Samuel Lindsey, William Wilson, Gabriel Anderson & William Hamilton, granted recorded in Book MMM, page 625. John Lindsey (Seal), Wit: William Irby, James Lindsey, Ab'm Lindsey. Proved by the oath of James Lindsey 23 __ 1792 before Edw'd Finch, J.P. Recorded 17 July 1792.

B, 117-119: Lease and release. 26 & 27 Jan 1788, Abel Anderson Sen'r of the settlement of Kings Creek, Newberry County, to Samuel Lindsey of same, for £100 sterling, 250 acres in the fork between Broad & Saludy Rivers on a branch called Kings Creek, waters of Enoree, adj. said Anderson, Samuel Clowny & granted to Abel Anderson 29 April 1786, recorded in Book CCC, page 99. Abel Anderson (Seal), Wit: Rosanah Anderson (Seal), Wit: Caleb Lindsey, John Lindsey Jun'r, James Lindsey. Proved by the oath of James Lindsey 31 Aug 1789 before John Lindsey, J.P. Recorded 17 July 1792.

B, 120-122: Lease and release. 16 & 17 March 1774, John Wright of Ninety Six District & Jemima his wife to James Douglas of same, for £211 s10 SC money, 200 acres on waters of Little River, one of the north branches of Saluda River adj. Jenet Stewart, granted to John Wright 5 May 1773. John Wright (Seal), Jemima Wright (Seal), Wit: Thomas Brooks, Elizabeth Brabant, John Carson (X). Proved by the oath of John Carson 19 March 1774 before Robt Dillon, J.P. Recorded 19 July 1792.

B, 123-125: Lease and release. 20 & 21 Sept 1790, Daniel Winchester of Newberry County to Abraham Beach alias Winchester, of same, for £50 sterling, 125 acres, part of 250 acres granted to William Winchester 20 Aug

1763 and from him unto Joseph Winchester his eldest son & by the death of Joseph Winchester unto Daniel Winchester, being the heir at law, on a small branch of Bush River. Daniel Winchester (Seal), Wit: John Abernathy, Isaac Toland, James Lindsey. Proved by the oath of James Lindsey before John Lindsey, J.P., 11 Oct 1790. Recorded 20 July 1792.

B, 126-127: 18 July 1792, John Edwards of Newberry County to George Latham & Saml Kelly Sen'r, both of Newberry County, for £200 SC money, moiety of tract of 500 acres granted to Enoch Anderson adj. Benjamin Long, Joseph Toles, Thomas Speakman, for the term of 500 years. John Edwards (Seal), Wit: John Kelly Sen'r, Abijah Gaunt. Proved by the affirmation of John Kelly before Elisha Ford, J.P., 21 July 1792. Recorded 23 July 1792.

B, 128-130: Lease and release. 28 & 29 Jan 1792, John Lindsey, Esquire, of Newberry County, to Caleb Lindsey of same, for £100 sterling, 500 acres on waters of Indian Creek on Georges branch adj. said John Lindsey, Daniel Blackburn, Evan & Clement Davis. John Lindsey (Seal), Wit: Joseph Towles, Edward Williams, Thos Williams. Proved by the oath of Thomas Williams 26 July 1792 before Elisha Ford, J.P. Recorded 23 Aug 1792.

B, 131: South Carolina, Newberry County. Jacob Cromer Sen'r of county aforesaid for good will and affection to my son George Cromer of same, goods and chattles [list included], 27 Aug 1792. Jacob Cromer Sen'r (mark), Wit: David Ruff, Peter Wagner. Proved in Newberry County by the oath of Peter Wagner 27 Aug 1792 before David Ruff, J.P. Recorded 27 Aug 1792.

B, 132-135: Lease and release. 22 & 23 March 1791, Philiman Waters, Esq., of Newberry County to Henry Creek of same, for £25 SC money, 128 acres, part of 500 acres granted to William Mazyck 14 Sept 1771 and conveyed by William Mazyck & Isaac Mazyck to said Philiman Waters 25 Oct 1790 on north side Saluda River adj. John Waites, William Taylor, Patrick McDugan. P. Waters (Seal), Wit: A. Robison, William Pope. Proved by the oath of Allen Robison 23 March 1792 before Peter Julien, J.P. Recorded 29 Aug 1792.

B, 136-137: 10 Feb 1792, Nathaniel Abney to Joseph Goodman, both of Newberry County, for £60 sterling, 141 acres, part of 500 acres granted to Enoch Anderson 13 dec 1751 and conveyed to William Turner, and he deceased did will to his daughter Ann, one half of tract adj. land of William Turner & Nathl Abney, being now the eldest son of her body, conveys to Joseph Goodman. Nathaniel Abney (X) (Seal), Wit: William Caldwell, Joseph Towles, George Brown, John Thweatt. Proved by the oath of William Caldwell & George Brown 31 July 1792 before Robert Gilliam, J.P. Recorded 30 Aug 1792.

B, 138-139: 27 March 1790, Gilbert Gilder of Newberry County, planter, to Jeremiah Williams of same, for £30 sterling, 100 acres granted to Mathew Tully, 118 acres in the fork between Broad & Saluda Rivers on waters of Kings Creek adj. Thomas Cross, Henry Thompson, Thomas Cross Sen'r. John

Wilson, recorded in Book SSS, page 474. Gilbert Gilder (Seal), Wit: Enoch Anderson, Nicholas Lattiner (Z), John Volentine Lattener (IE). Proved in Newberry County by the oath of Enoch Anderson 22 July 1791 before Edward Finch, J.P. Recorded 30 Aug 1792.

B, 140-142: Lease and release. 9 & 10 March 1796, Mathew Tully of Orangeburgh District to Gilbert Gilder of Ninety Six District, Newberry County, for £150 SC money, 118 acres in the fork between Broad & Saluda Rivers on waters of Kings Creek adj. Thomas Cross, Henry Thompson, Thomas Cross Sen'r. John Wilson, granted 31 Aug 1774, recorded in Aud'rs Office Book M No. 13, page ___, 24 Feb 1775, grant recorded in Book SSS, page 474. Mathew Tully (Seal), Wit: Alexander Miller, Isaac Gilder (I). Proved 19 Sept 1789 by the oath of Alexander Miller before John Lindsey, J.P. for Newberry County. Recorded 30 Aug 1792.

B, 143-144: 3 May 1792, Elisha Rhodes of Newberry County to Thomas Gibson, farmer, for £30 s2 sterling, 103 acres on a small drought of Indian Creek, waters of Enoree River, part of 227 acres granted to said Elisha Rhodes 5 June 1786, surveyed 22 Oct 1785, adj. William Nimmons, Elisha Rhodes, recorded in Book NNNN, page 185. Elisha Rhodes (+) (Seal), WiT: John Beard, William Hendrix (X), William Kelly. Acknowledged by Elisha Rhodes 30 May 1792 before Edward Finch, J.P. Recorded 31 Aug 1792.

B, 145-147: Lease and release. 26 & 27 July 1791. James Daugherty Jun'r, Deputy Surveyor, of Orangeburg District, to John Robertson of Newberry County, for £100 sterling, 100 acres granted to James Daugherty 13 Oct 1772 on a branch of Second Creek adj. George Grayham, George Dawkins, Joseph Smith. James Daugherty (Seal), Wit: David Ruff, George Daugharty, Nathan Boyd. Proved by the oath of David Ruff 27 July 1791 before George Ruff, J.P. Recorded 31 Aug 1792.

B, 148-150: Lease and release. 30 Sept & 1 Oct 1790, William Gary Jun'r of Newberry County, but late of Laurence County, to William Gary, minor son of John Gary deceased, for £55 SC money, 100 acres, part of 200 acres granted to William Gary deceased & left by him the deceased to his two sons Charles & William Gary Jun'r by his will dated 1 Feb 1768, on a small branch called Bush Creek, now Bush River, adj. land of Providence Williams, Thomas Gary, Robert McAdam, recorded in Book AAA, page 420, and in Book H. No 8, page 177 2 April 1786 [sic]. William Gary Jun'r, Hannah Gary (Seal), Wit: Providence Williams, Luezea Lindsey, James Lindsey, William Gary, Thos Gary. Proved 23 June 1792 by the oath of James Lindsey before Providence Williams, J.P. Recorded 31 Aug 1792.

B, 151-152: 26 March 1792, Benjamin Anderson in Green County, Georgia, to Charles Crenshaw of Newberry County, SC, for £100 sterling, 200 acres on both sides Indian Creek granted to Abraham Anderson 22 Nov 1764 recorded in Book G, No. 7, page 263, 22 nov 1761, recorded in Book YY, page 128, and heir by Joshua Anderson, he being the only son to Abraham Anderson & said land now coming under his will & heired by Benjamin Anderson. Benjamin Anderson (Seal), Wit: Sally Veazey (A), Jesse Veazey, Reuben Chiles. Proved in Newberry County by the oath of Reuben Chiles 28 May 1792 before Edw'd Finch, J.P. Recorded 5 Sept 1792.

B, 152: I certify that I have run a tract of land in Newberry County on Indian creek granted to and in possession of Peter Braselman & C. R. Edson and delivered to Mr. Peter Brazelman, __ June 1792. Geo. Barnes. Wit: Robt Powell. I do hereby certify that I have no Claim to the above mentioned land but are willing to give a quit claim. Long lane, 16 April 1791, C. R. Edson. Recorded 6 Sept 1792.

B, 153-154: 19 May 1791, Gabriel Anderson, planter, of Newberry County to Peter Brasilman of same, merchant, for £10 sterling, 10½ acres near long lane between Indian & Kings Creek, adj. land of Jacob Frost, said Gabriel Anderson. Gabriel Anderson (Seal), Wit: John Cary Royston, Robert Powell. Proved by the oath of Robert Powell before Edw'd Finch, J.P., 26 June 1792. Recorded 5 Sept 1792.

B, 155-156: 18 Dec 1789, Joseph Hampton & Rachel his wife, of Newberry County, to Peter Brasilman of same, for £200 sterling, 250 acres on Kings Creek adj. land of Edward Finch, Peter Brasilman, John Turner, Simon Park; purchased by Joseph Hampton in two separate tracts from the late Charles King & the present John Lindsey Esquire. Joseph Hampton (Seal), Rachel Hampton (Seal), Wit: Rob't Powell, Geo Barnes. Proved in Newberry County 26 June 1792 by the oath of Robert Powell before Edw'd Finch, J.P. Recorded 6 Sept 1792.

B, 157-158: 6 Oct 1791, William Wilson of Newberry County, to Peter Braselman of same, merchant, for £43 sterling, 43 acres near the long lane between Indian and Kings Creek. William Wilson (Seal), Wit: Daniel Henning, Bailey Chandler, Robert Powell, Edward Finch, J.P. Recorded 6 Sept 1792.

B, 159-161: Lease and release. 18 & 19 July 1791, Samuel Ruble of the Western Territories, South of the Ohio River, Hockins County, to William McDowell of Newberry County, SC, for £37 s10 sterling, 75 acres on a small branch of Bush River adj. William Murdock, Samuel Duncan, William McDowell, part of 250 acres granted to Peter Ruble 22 March 1769 and left by his will to Samuel Ruble his son. Samuel Ruble (Seal), Wit: William Murdock, Isaac Right, Susanah Hollingsworth (X). Proved 22 July 1791 by the affirmation of William Murdock before Mercer Babb, J.P. Recorded 7 Sept 1792.

18 & 19 July 1791, Samuel Ruble of the Western Territories, South of the Ohio River, Hockins County, to William Murdock of Newberry County, SC, for £37 s10 sterling, 75 acres on a small branch of Bush River adj. William Murdock, Samuel Duncan, William McDowell, part of 250 acres granted to

Peter Ruble 22 March 1769 and left by his will to Samuel Ruble his son. Samuel Ruble (Seal), Wit: William Murdock, Isaac Right, Susanah Hollingsworth (X). Proved 22 July 1791 by the affirmation of William McDowell before Mercer Babb, J.P. Recorded 7 Sept 1792.

B, 164-165: 15 Feb 1786, William Hewston Sen'r of Ninety Six District, Newberry County, to the Trustees or Elders of the Presbyterian Congregation, Rev'd Robert McClintic, pastor, one acre of land which said John Hewston purchased of Francis Shearer, near the old fields where the Burial place of the said Frances Shearer's family is, to building a house of worship thereon & a burial place and free use of the Spring. John Hewston (Seal), Wit: John Thomas, Adam Chambers, Patrick Lowry. Proved 31 July 1792 by the oath of Patrick Lowry before Providence Williams, J.P. Recorded 10 Sept 1792.

B, 165: William Maffit, planter, of Ninety Six District, bound to James Maffit in the sum of £5000 sterling, 18 April 1785, to make title for 200 acres of land adj. tract laid out for William Moore upon condition the said James Maffit pays to said William Maffit £7 s12 sterling by 22 March 1787. William Maffit (Seal), Wit: John Abernathy, John Cannon. William Maffit assigned this bond to Samuel Cannon deceased by the oath of _____ 30 July 1792 before Providence Williams, J.P. Recorded 10 Sept 1792.

B, 166-167: 23 May 1789, William Goggans & Rachel his wife of Newberry County to William Burton for £50 sterling, 100 acres on waters of Beaverdam, surveyed originally for Benjamin Burton and granted 18 Aug 1776, recorded in Book 4 O, page 22, granted to John Robinson and conveyed to William Goggans & Rachel his wife. William Goggans (Seal), Rachel Goggans (X) (Seal), Wit: Gibson Burton, James Burton, Feby Gibson (mark). Proved in Newberry County 23 June 1792 by the oath of Gibson Burton before Mercer Babb, J.P. Recorded 10 Sept 1792.

B, 168-170: Lease and release. 12 & 13 Apr 1778, Thomas Wadlington of Berkley County, SC, to Joseph Thomas of same, for £600 SC money, 200 acres on a small branch of Enoree called Kings Creek adj. land of Jacob Guilder, Jacob Duckett, Margaret Huston, granted to Thomas Wadlington 19 Sept 1770, recorded in Book FFF, page 232, memorial entered in Book K No. 10, page 262. Thomas Wadlington (Seal), Elizabeth Wadlington (Seal), Wit: James Lindsey, Daniel Brown, Notley Thomas. Proved 25 Aug 1781 by the oath of James Lindsey before John Lindsey, J.P. Recorded 10 Sept 1772.

B, 171-173: Lease and release. 15 & 16 Aug 1781, Joseph Thomas of Berkley County, SC, to William Gray of same, for £600 SC money, 200 acres on a small branch of Enoree called Kings Creek adj. land of Jacob Guilder, Jacob Duckett, Margaret Huston, granted to Thomas Wadlington 19 Sept 1770, recorded in Book FFF, page 232, memorial entered in Book K No. 10, page 262. Joseph Thomas (Seal), Elizabeth Thomas (+) (Seal), Wit: James Lindsey, Notley Thomas, Jean Carr. Proved 27 Aug 1781 by the oath of James Lindsey before John Lindsey, J.P. Recorded 11 Sept 1772.

B, 174-175: 31 July 1792, William Gray of Laurence County to Samuel Burdine of Newberry County, for £600 SC money, 200 acres on a small branch of Enoree called Kings Creek adj. land of Jacob Guilder, Jacob Duckett, Margaret Huston, granted to Thomas Wadlington 19 Sept 1770, recorded in Book FFF, page 232, memorial entered in Book K No. 10, page 262, conveyed to Joseph Thomas, then to William Gray. William Gray (Seal), Wit: Robert Johnston, Nathan Anderson, James Lindsey. Proved 31 Aug 1781 by the oath of James Lindsey before John Lindsey, J.P. Recorded 11 Sept 1772.

B, 175: James Roach of Newberry County for £6 sterling to John Windel which is coming to John Coats of same, the crop (except the value of nine shillings), now growing on the plantation of John Windle, planter, 9 June 1792. James Roach (+), Wit: John Windel, Mary Wilson (mark). Recorded 11 Sept 1792.

B, 176-178: Lease and release. 11 & 13 Nov 1790, William Nelson, of Orange County, North Carolina, planter, to William Taylor of Ninety Six District, farmer, for £100 SC money, 100 acres granted to said William Nelson 5 May 1773 adj. John Caldwell. William Nelson (Seal), Wit: James Brooks, Charity Cook, Susanah Hollingsworth (X). Proved in Newberry County 17 July 1795 by the affirmation of James Brooks before Mercer Babb, J.P. Recorded 12 Sept 1792.

B, 179-181: Lease and release. 19 & 20 Aug 1771, Tacitus Gaillard of Berkley County, SC, planter, to Benjamin Moore of Craven County, SC, planter, for £200 SC money, 200 acres on a branch of Mudlick called Pages Creek adj. Benjamin Farrar, granted to Isaac Porcher 2 May 1770. Tacit's Gaillard (Seal), Wit: Ann Savage, Moses Price. Proved 3 Feb 1772 by the oath of Moses Price before John Savage, J.P. Recorded 12 Sept 1792.

B, 182-184: Lease and release. 3 & 4 Feb 1780, Nathaniel Harris of Ninety Six District, to Thomas Burden of same, for £500 SC money, 25 acres on Mudlick Creek, waters of Little River adj. Thomas Turner, granted to said Nathaniel Harris 8 July 1774. Nathl Harris (Seal), Wit: Robert Lang, Isaac Davinport, John Caldwell. Proved 3 Feb 1780 by the oath of Robert Lang before John Satterwhite, J.P. Recorded 13 Sept 1792.

B, 182-184: 21 Nov 1791, John Cannon of Newberry County to Patrick Lowry of same, for £50 sterling, 200 acres on Indian Creek, granted to John Cannon 2 Aug 1768. John Cannon (I) (Seal), Wit: Hugh Boyd (IB), Josiah Elliott. Proved by the oath of Josiah Elliott before Providence Williams, J.P. Recorded 29 Sept 1792.

B, 184: William Malone, Esqr. This is to inform you that I have rec'd full satisfaction for the Bond & Mortgage of Philleman Waters by the hands of Mr. Joseph Bieller. John Cunningham. Charleston, Feb. 4th 1793. Recorded 20 Feb 1793.

B, 187-189: Lease and release. 7 & 8 Feb 1774, Benjamin Moore of Ninety Six District, planter, to Thomas Burdin, planter, of same, for £200 SC money, 200 acres on a branch of Mudlick called Pages Creek adj. Benjamin Farrar, granted to Isaac Porcher 2 May 1770. Benjamin Moore (Seal), Wit: John Satterwhite, Oliver Towles, John Norris. Proved by the oath of John Satterwhite 19 Aug 1774 before John Caldwell, J.P. Recorded 24 Sept 1792.

B, 190-192: Lease and release. 27 Dec 1791, Thomas Green, planter, of Laurence County, SC, to William Green, Gunsmith of Newberry County, for £150 sterling, 150 acres, part of 200 acres granted to Thomas Green 2 Aug 1771, recorded in Book 3 I, page 30. Thomas Green (Seal), Wit: William Dodgen, John Golding, Henry Weaver (H). Proved 3 July 1792 by the oath of William Dodgen before Mercer Babb, J.P. Recorded 24 Sept 1792.

B, 193-194: 23 Nov 1791, Van Davis of Newberry County to Patrick Lowry of same, for £100 sterling, 100 acres, part of 200 acres in the fork between Broad & Saludy Rivers on a branch of Indian Creek called Guilders Creek, granted to said Van Davis 7 Aug 1767 on NW side Davis's Creek, recorded in Aud'rs office, in Book H. No 8, page 272. Van Davis (Seal), Wit: James Tinsley, John Johnston. Proved 25 Nov 1791 by the oath of James Tinsley before Providence Williams, J.P. Recorded 24 Sept 1792.

B, 194-195: South Carolina, Newberry County. Michael Abney bound to Joseph Goodman in the sum of £500 sterling, 11 Feb 1792, against any claim of Michael Abney to a tract 141 acres that Joseph Goodman purchased of Nathaniel Abney, being wiled to Ann Abney by William Turner and sold by Nathaniel Abney by heirship to Joseph Goodman son of said Nathaniel Abney. Michael Abney (Seal), Wit: Joseph Towles, John Abney (X). Recorded 20 Sept 1792. Proved by the oath of Joseph Towles 3 Sept 1792 before Robert Gilliam, J.P.

B, 195: William Musgrove, Westward and Philimon Waters Jun'r of Newberry County, bound to Allen Robison of same, in the sum of £200 sterling, 22 March 1792, to abide by the award of arbitration and determination of Mercer Babb, Elisha Ford, Wallice Jones, Mark Smith & Peter Julin or any three of them, by 1 May next. William Musgrove, W. W. Waters, Phil. Waters. Wit: Thos W. Waters. Recorded 24 Sept 1792.

B, 196: Mercer Babb, Elisha Ford, Wallice Jones, Mark Smith & Peter Julin, whereas there is a dispute depending between William Musgrove and Allen Roberson concerning a quarrel or trespass & they by their bonds 22 March 1792 are bound to keep the award and final determination, now we published our award: said Robison is to pay unto William Musgrove by 1 Jan next £5 and costs, such as Doctors Bills, that have occurred by the said wound at the house of Henry Creek on 14 October last past, 22 March 1792. Costs are to Henry Tate Senr $10, to Arraminta Wilson $10. Recorded 24 Sept 1792.

B, 197-198: 2 June 1795, Richard Watts, Sheriff of Newberry County, to William Johnston Sen'r of same, planter, whereas said William Johnston did on 15 May 1786 bring suit against the admx. of Daniel Glyn deceased in the sum of £96 sterling, four shillings and six pence, and obtained judgment 2 June 1789, and by write of fieri facias, sheriff sells 150 acres, and as there being several judgments against the lands of said David Glen, 15-0 acres being run by survey containing 220 acres, land granted to John Johnston 19 June 1772, and conveyed to David Glyn 11 Oct 1779, now sold for £46 sterling. R. Watts (Seal), Wit: William Satterwhite, Ephraim Cannon. Proved in Newberry County by the oath of Ephraim Cannon 27 July 1792 before David Ruff, J.PO. Recorded 25 Sept 1792.

B, 199-200: 7 April 1792, George Awberry of Newberry County to Col. Thomas Brandon of Union County, for £50 sterling, 100 acres on south side Enoree River adj. John Gordon, Nicholas Butler, granted 1 Jan 1761 to Tobias Hicks and conveyed by him to Henry Awberry. George Awberry (Seal), Wit: Samuel Otterson, Thos Gordon Jun'r. Proved in Union County by the oath of Samuel Otterson 4 Sept 1792 before H. Means, J.P. Recorded 2 Oct 1792.

B, 201-202: 9 April 1792, Thomas Gordon of Newberry County to Col. Thomas Brandon of Union County, for £50 sterling, 100 acres on south side Enoree River adj. Joshua Anderson, granted 17 Oct 1762 to Cateren Brustill but now Cateren Edwards & conveyed by her son Benjamin Fulehener heir at law, herself, to Mr. Thomas Gordon 30 May 1786. Thos Gordon (Seal), Wit: Samuel Otterson, Benjamin Gordon. Proved in Union County by the oath of Samuel Otterson 4 Sept 1792 before H. Means, J.P. Recorded 2 Oct 1792.

B, 203-205: Lease and release. 11 & 12 Dec 1778, Francis Davis of Ninety Six District, to Mary Furnace of same, for £300 SC money, 100 acres granted to Francis Davis on Bush Creek, recorded in Book HHH, page 313, adj. Hugh Creighton. Francis Davis (Seal), Wit: Saml Kelly, Daniel Perkins. Proved in Newberry County by the affirmation of Samuel Kelly 9 Oct 1792 before J. Brown, J. N. C. Recorded 2 Oct 1792.

B, 206-207: 3 Oct 1792, Edward Kelley, planter, of Newberry County, planter, to Robert Kennedy, Taylor of same, for £50 sterling, 75 acres in the fork between Enoree & Broad Rivers, part of tract granted to Francis Awberry for 150 acres 9 Sept 1774, recorded in Book SSS, page 595, adj. Andrew Hunter, Robert Kennedy. Edward Kelley (Seal), Mary Kelley (+) (Seal), Wit: David Shelton, Samuel Dawson, John Noland. Proved 3 Oct 1792 by the oath of John Noland before Reuben Sims, J. P. Recorded 31 Oct 1792.

B, 208-210: 15 Aug 1770, Ralph McDugal, exr. of the will of Henry Glass and heir at law to said Henry Glass deceased, to James Golden of Berkly County, farmer, by virtue of the will of said Henry Glass, said Ralph became seized of a tract of 200 acres in Craven County adj. John Mills, granted 28 July

1779[sic]. Ralph McDugal (X) (Seal), Wit: Wm. Anderson, John Gow, John Caldwell. Proved by the oath of John Caldwell 27 Aug 1770 before Robert Cunningham, J.P. Recorded 14 Nov 1792.

B, 211: 15 Nov 1792. George Montgomery of Newberry County, to my daughter Elizabeth and son in law David Glynn of same, two negroes named Joe and Lettuce, also three horses, one wagon, five head of cattle, nine hoggs, three sheep, with my crop of corn, dated 15 Nov 1792. George Montgomery (M) (Seal), Wit: William Malone Sen'r, Joseph Caldwell. Proved in Newberry County by the oath of Joseph Caldwell before Edw'd Finch, J.P., 15 Nov 1792. Recorded 17 Nov 1792.

B, 212: 12 Nov 1792, Barber Hencock of Newberry County to Thomas Hardy of same, for £50, 96 acres adj. Thomas Hill, John Hill, John Lake, Thomas Hardy. Barber Hencock (Seal), Wit: Freeman Hardy, James Hardy, John Grasty. Proved in Newberry County 16 Nov 1792 by the oath of James Hardy before Reuben Sims, J.P. Recorded 17 Nov 1792.

B, 213-214: 25 July 1792, John Cureton bound to Thomas Wadsworth & William Turpin, merchants, 18 May 1791, said Cureton by two bonds amounting to £69 3½ sterling, payable to Peter Skrine, for better securing said bonds, mortgage of negro man Arther about 32 years of age, a girl Mima about ten years of age, and a negro man Georgia about 19 years of age. John Cureton (Seal), Wit: Danl Symmes, Silvester Bill. Proved by the oath of Daniel Symmes __ Nov 1792 before Robert Gilliam, J.P. Recorded 3 Dec 1792.

B, 215-216: Katy Thweatt and Edward Thweatt, of Newberry County, bound to Thomas Wadsworth & William Turpin, merchants, 7 Aug 1792, mortgage of negro Jimmy born over sea about 45 years of age, a wench Sarah born about 25 years ago, a wench Suckely country born about 22 years of age, for securing sum of £92 12 s5 by four bonds. Kt. Thweatt (Seal), Edward Thweatt (Seal), Wit: Danl Symmes. Proved by the oath of Daniel Symmes 1 Nov 1792 before Robert Gilliam, J.P. Recorded 3 Dec 1792.

B, 217: 11 Nov 1792, Charles Coats, planter, and Ann his wife, of Newberry County, to Walter Goodman, merchant, for £50 sterling, 100 acres on south side Enoree in the fork between Broad & Saludy River, on a draft of Kelly's branch, waters of Enoree, adj. John Green, granted to John Hogg, and from him conveyed to said Coats. Charles Coats (Seal), Ann Coats (Seal), Wit: W. Wadlington, Wm. Calmes, Edw'd Finch, J.P. Recorded 3 Dec 1792.

B, 218-219: 20 Nov 1792, Edmund Martin of Edgefield County, to Sims Brown of Newberry County, for £100 sterling, 200 acres on Kings Creek, waters of Enoree. Edmond Martin (Seal), Wit: John Martin, Robert Gilliam Sen'r. Proved 20 Nov 1792 in Edgefield County by the oath of John Martin before W. Anderson, J. E. C. Recorded 3 Dec 1792.

B, 220-222: Lease and release. 20 & 21 Oct 1791, Ann Waring of St. Georges Parish, SC, to Edmund Martin of Edgefield County, SC, for £56 s 5, four tracts of land: one tract of 65 acres in Granville county on Savannah River on the long Reaches, adj. Glebe Setro, Thomas Filpot, William Webster; 300 acres in Berkly County on Little River adj. Thomas Edghill, John Simmons, William Turner; 100 acres on Peters Creek adj. heirs of Daniel Crawford; 200 acres in Berkley County on a small branch of Enoree River called Kings Creek; the said four tracts granted to Richard Waring, late husband of said Ann Waring in 1771. Ann Waring (Seal), Wit: P. A. Smith, Jno Martin. Proved 12 Nov 1792 in Edgefield County by the oath of John Martin before W. Anderson, J. E. C. Recorded 4 Dec 1792.

B, 223: James Grayham of Ninety Six District, Newberry County, sold to Alexander Bookter, planter, of same, for £55 sterling, one negro wench named Salley. James Grayham (Seal), Wit: Peter Statley, Wm. Finch. Proved in Newberry County 5 Oct 1792 by the oath of Peter Statley before Reuben Sims, J.P. Recorded 11 Dec 1792.

B, 224: We the legatees of the estate of Abraham Anderson deceased in consequence of Levi Anderson having paid each of us four shillings & eight pence sterling, all our right to 200 acres on both sides main Waggon Road adj. land of Gabriel Anderson, Levi Anderson & Robert Mars on Indian Creek, 27 July 1792. Thos Gordon (Seal), Elizabeth Gordon (Seal), Abel Anderson (Seal), Gabriel Anderson (Seal), Jesse Anderson (Seal), Nathan Anderson (Seal), Abra'm Anderson (Seal), George Gordon (Seal), Wit: Adam Glazier, John Volentine. Proved 12 Nov 1792 in Newberry County by the oath of John Voluntine before Edw'd Finch, J.P. Recorded 11 Dec 1792.

B, 225: 4 March 1790, Samuel Cannon to Ephraim Cannon, both of Newberry County, for £5 sterling, 29 acres on waters of Cannons Creek, part of grant to James Thompson adj. John Maypoles, Ephraim Cannon, memorial entered in Book L No. 11, page 84 on 23 Oct 1771. Samuel Cannon (Seal), Wit: William Cannon, Lidda Cannon (X), Eliz'a Cannon. Proved in Newberry County by the oath of William Cannon 5 Aug 1791 before P. Williams, J.P. Recorded 11 Dec 1792.

B, 226: John Rodmire and Francis Chiles & John Domney of Berkley County bound to John Cannon of same, in the sum of £40, 30 July 1753, to make title to 100 acres upon bounty by warrant on waters of Santee, by way of lease & release before 30 July next. John Rodmire (X) (LS), Francis Chiles (LS), John Domney (LS), Wit: Samuel Cannon, Ephraim Cannon. October 28, 1716. I do assign my whole right & title to my son Ephraim Cannon. John Cannon (I). Wit: Abraham Carradine. Proved by the oath of Abraham Carradine 27 Feb 1764 before Jno Pearson, J.P. Recorded 11 Dec 1792.

B, 227: South Carolina, Berkley County. Before William Hopton, J. P. in county aforesaid, appeared Michal Colyon of Charlestown in the same county, tavern keeper, who stated that Conrad Moyer late of Forks of Broad River now deceased came to Charles Town about two months ago to take out a plat and grant for 100 acres of land that while the said Conrad Moyer was in Charleston he fell sick at the house of this deponent and in about a week died there that while he was so sick he desired this deponant to go to the Secretaries office for said plat & grant for him as he was disabled to go himself by such sickness which this deponent did accordingly & paid to the Secretary Two pounds two shillings for his fees for the same, that the said Conrade Moyer on his death bed sold told this deponent that he had sold the said land to John Cannon of the Forks of Broad River, planter, for some cattle, which cattle he had received from the said Cannon, that he the said Conrade Moyer desired this deponent in case he died of that his sickness to take the cattle that he had so sold his Land for as his own for the Expence that he was at with him in his sickness and that he would deliver the plot and grant of the said 100 acres of land to the said John Cannon & make a title for the same to him but that the said Conrade Moyer died without making any will in writing that he knows of nor has any other Effects that he knows of but those Cattle which he is informed are not worth administring for, that this deponant hath delivred the said Plat & Grant to the said John Cannon, which Land is now produced to me the plat is certified 27 Sept 1753 by George Hunter Surveyor General & the Grant bears date 12 Feb 1755... dated 12 June 1755. Michal Colyon, William Hopton. Henry Stos[?] of Charleston, Baker, also made oath that he heard the said Conrod Moyer within an hour before he died that he had sold his land for cattle... 12 June 1755. Recorded 11 Dec 1792.

B, 228: Plat headed South Carolina, Ninety Six District, Newberry County. At the Joint request of John Robison and ___ Robison, I have admeasured unto __ Robison 57 acres, being her third of a tract now in possession of said John Robison in the fork of Enoree & Broad Rivers on a small branch of the Enoree River, 6 Nov 1790 by Geo. Harbert, D.S. (Robert Wilson shown as adjacent land owner.) Recorded 11 Dec 1792.

B, 229: John Chandler of Newberry County, planter,for £20 SC money, to John Clark of same, planter, one negro boy named James, dated 8 Feb 1790. John Chandler (Seal), Wit: John Chandler (mark, William Chandler. Proved by the oath of John Chandler 6 March 1790 before W. Wadlington, J.P. Recorded 11 Dec 1792.

B, 230-231: 23 March 1790, James Vardaman of Newberry County, planter, & Jane Vardaman his wife, to John Clark, farmer, for £5 sterling, tract on south side Enoree River below the line, 440 acres granted to said James Vardaman 5 Sept 1786, certified 8 Nov 1785, recorded in Book FFF, page 42. James Vardaman (Seal), Wit: Barth'w Johnston, William Wilson, George Johnson. Proved 3 Sept 1789 by the oath of George Johnston before W. Wadlington, J.P. Recorded 12 Dec 1792.

B, 232: 3 Oct 1789, James Daugharty of Orange County, <u>South</u> Carolina, to David Cannon of Newberry County, for £40 sterling, 150 acres on waters of

Cannons Creek, part of 500 acres granted to James Dougharty 7 May 1787, adj. James Grayham, Alston, John Caldwell, Joseph Caldwell. James Dougharty (Seal), Wit: Ephraim Cannon, Daniel Caldwell. Proved in Newberry County by the oath of Dan: Caldwell 12 Sept 1792 before David Ruff, J.P. Recorded 12 Dec 1792.

B, 233-234: 25 Aug 1792, Joseph Furnas of Newberry County, to Abel Insco of same, for £50 sterling, 100 acres on Scotch Creek, a branch of Bush River, adj. Hugh Creighton, formerly granted to Francis Davis 18 May 1881, recorded in Book K No. 10, page 477. Joseph Furnas (Seal), Sally Furnas (Seal), Wit: James Insco, Thomas W. Furman. Proved 25 Aug 1792 by the oath of James Insco before Elisha Ford, J.P. Recorded 12 Dec 1792.

B, 235-236: 2 June 1792, Richard Watts, Sheriff of Newberry County, to Ephraim Cannon of same place, planter, whereas William Johnston did on 15 May 1786 did bring suit against the admrs. of David Glyn, decd, in the sum of £96 s4 d6 sterling, and obtained judgment against the said admrs., 2 June 1789, and by writ of fieri facias said Richard Watts did sell 254 acres, granted to Mary Frost and conveyed 5 Feb 1773 to John Johnston and on 4 Sept 1778 conveyed to David Glyn deceased, now sold for £50 sterling. R. Watts (Seal), Wit: Fred Nance, William Satterwhite, William Johnston. Proved 27 July 1792 in Newberry County by the oath of William Johnston before David Ruff, J.P. Recorded 13 Dec 1792.

B, 237-238: Whereas Benjamin Few of the State of Georgia by bond to William Thomas Linton of South Carolina in the peal sum of 2000 pounds of inspected tobacco at Augusta condition to make titles for 2070 acres, and said bond has not been comply'd with unto William T. Linton, now said William T. Linton for £1000 sterling paid by Robert Tate of SC in Newberry County, assigns his rights and appoints said Robert Tate his lawful attorney to receive of said Benjamin Few the lands which titles are to be made of, 10 Nov 1792. Wm. T. Linton (Seal), Wit: Wm. Jones, John Eaton, W. Hall. Proved in Newberry County by the oath of John Eaton 31 Dec 1792 before Edw'd Finch, J.P. Recorded 31 Dec 1792.

B, 239-240: 2 June 1792, Richard Watts, Sheriff of Newberry County, to Ephraim Cannon of same place, planter, whereas Ephraim Cannon and Elenor his wife, joints administrators of the estate of John Caldwell (deceased), did on 20 Dec 1789 bring suit against the admrs. of David Glyn, decd, in the sum of £21 s17 d7 sterling, and obtained judgment against the said admrs., and by writ of fieri facias said Richard Watts did sell 100 acres, granted to John Johnston and conveyed to David Glyn deceased 13 Aug 1770, now sold for £2 s7 sterling. R. Watts (Seal), Wit: Fred Nance, William Satterwhite, William Johnston. Proved 27 July 1792 in Newberry County by the oath of William Johnston before David Ruff, J.P. Recorded 2 Jan 1793.

B, 241-244: Lease and release. 10 & 11 March 1786, David Martin, Preacher, of Newberry County, to James Caldwell of same, planter, for £200 sterling, 100 acres, part of 200 acres, the upper end of said tract called Williams' old mill, granted 9 June 1752 to Paul Williams & at his decease descended to his eldest son Jeremiah Williams, conveyed by Jeremiah Williams & wife Jane to Daniel Williams 7 April 1755 and said Daniel Williams, deceased, bequeathed the said land to his nephew John Pearson (decd) dated 9 Sept 1765, recorded in Secretaries Office in Book NN, page 226. David Martin (Seal), Wit: David Cannon, John Cannon, Augustus Williams. Proved in Newberry County by the oath of David Cannon 12 Sept 1792 before David Ruff, J.P.

B, 245-248: Lease and release. 17 & 18 Feb 1783, Ephraim Cannon, planter, of Ninety Six District, to David Cannon, his son of same, blacksmith, 100 acres, part of tract of 200 acres granted to said Ephraim Cannon 5 Aug 1769 in Craven County near Cannons Creek adj. land of Christopher White, John Cannon, recorded in Book DDD, page 346. Ephraim Cannon (Seal), Wit: Michael Dickert, George Martin, Adolph Laygroun. Proved in Newberry County by the oath of George Martin 12 Sept 1792 before David Ruff, J.P. Recorded 2 Jan 1793.

B, 249-254: Lease and release. 9 & 10 Sept 1779, George Neely of Ninety Six District, planter, to Gabriel Smithers of same, planter, for £1000 SC money, two tracts in the whole 350 acres, one of 150 acres in Berkley County on waters of Mudlick Creek adj. Mary Stedham, William Caldwell & Nathaniel Fooshe, granted to Oliver Towles 12 April 1771, conveyed by him to said George Neely 6 & 7 Sept 1771; the other tract of 200 acres on waters of Mudlick adj. William Caldwell, said Oliver Towles, John Robison, granted to John Robison 15 May 1771 and conveyed to George Neely 16 & 17 Jan 1772. George Neely (Seal), Wit: Nathaniel Norwood, Lewis Bunch (+), Mary Bunch (+). Proved 12 April 1785 in Charleston District by the oath of Lewis Bunch before John Bell, J.P. Recorded 3 Jan 1793.

B, 255-259: Lease and release. 23 & 24 Feb 1779, Henry Rugheley of Claremont County, Camden District, merchant, to John Coats of Scotch Creek in Ninety Six District, planter, for £2200 SC money, 357 in the fork between Broad & Saludy Rivers on Bush Creek. Henry Rugheley (Seal), Wit: James Coate, John Williamson. Proved in Ninety Six District 12 Aug 1779 by the oath of James Coate before Isaac Cook, J.P. Recorded 3 Jan 1793.

B, 260-264: Lease and release. 27 & 28 Feb 1776, Charles King of Kings Creek, Ninety Six District, planter, and Charity his wife, to Henry Rugheley, merchant of Charleston, for £100 SC money, 100 acres granted 10 April 1771 to Robert Bull, formerly surveyed for Terence Rayley on a small branch of Bush River, waters of Saludy River; 150 acres granted 18 May 1771 to Samuel Chapman on a small branch of Bush Creek adj. Hugh Crayton, Giles Chapman, Benjamin Adkins; 300 acres granted to Giles Chapman 17 Dec 1766 on Bush Creek, adj. Terrance Rayley, John Brooks, John Williamson, and said Robert Bull 1 May 1774 did convey to Charles King the first tract; Samuel Chapman conveyed to Robert Bull 9 July 1772 and then Robert Bull to Charles King 1 June 1774, the second tract; Giles Chapman conveyed 107 acres, part of 300 acres to said Robert Bull and Robert bull to Charles King 1 June 1774. Charles King (Seal), Charity King (Seal), Wit: Wm. H. Rughley, James Lindsey, Charles Chitty, William <u>Mealing</u>. Proved 12 Aug 1779 before Isaac Cook, J. P. for Ninety Six District, by the oath of William <u>Maldin</u>. Recorded 3 Jan 1793.

B, 265-266: 30 Nov 1792, Andrew Russell of Newberry County, to Jean Crooks of same, for £3 s10 sterling, tract of 7 acres in the fork between Broad& Saluda Rivers on a small branch of Williams Creek, granted to Edward Connally 30 February [sic] 1774. Andrew Russell (Seal), Wit: W. Malone Sr., John Davidson, Alexander Davidson. Proved 1 Dec 1792 by the oath of John Davidson before David Ruff, J.P. Recorded 4 Jan 1793.

B, 267: South Carolina, Newberry County, 27 May 1792. Personally appeared before J. R. Brown, Justice of County aforesaid, South Bradshaw and sayeth that on Thursday Morning being the 24th of this inst. May, he between daybreak and the rising of the sun saw William Andrew and Mary Andrew his sister driving two of Mr. John Younghusband's horses out of the woods to the Widow Andrew's house & attempting to catch them, whereupon the horses broke from them and he said the said persons make a second attempt on them and some others whereupon he (who had at first sight concealed himself discovered himself to them at which they desisted and appeared to be much alarmed but said nothing whereupon he drove the horses home) and he verily believes that the said Andrew and his sister had a falonous [sic] design under their conduct. South Bradshaw. Recorded 3 Jan 1793.

B, 268: South Carolina, Newberry County, 10 June 1792. William Collier came to be qualified concerning and oath and evil report which South Bradshaw had speared respecting of his having seen William Andrew & Mary his sister on Thursday morning 24 May last driving off two of Mr. Younghusband's horses up out of the woods to or near the widow Andrew's House, and sayeth That on the day aforesaid he was to go to the mill for Mrs. Andrews and when he came to her house she had to hunt for her horse to ride to the mill on but as she did not know her horses, Miss Polley Andrew went with him untill they heard a Bell which she said she believed was the right one whereupon she returned to the house and this deponant went and drove up two up near the house whereupon Polly came to the door & told him that they were Mr. Younghusband's horses and came out and went with him in search of her Mother's horses and before they had got far from the house they met South Bradshaw and Miss Polly asked him if he had seen anything of her Mother's hoses and his answer was No. Whereupon they went and four Mrs. Andrew's horses and brought him to the house and that it was he that drove up Mr. Young husband's horses through a mistake not knowing but they belonged to Mrs. Andrews until he was told better and that he knowed nor heard of no stranger being on the plantation nor does he believe William Andrew came out of his house at that time. William Andrew (mark), before J. R. Brown, J. N. C. Recorded 2 Jan 1793.

B, 268: Also Mary Andrew made oath that what William Collier has just made oath to is the just truth. Mary Andrew. J. R. Brown, J.N.C. Recorded 2 Jan 1793.

B, 269: South Carolina, Newberry County. Personally appeared before me, Robert Gilliam, Esquire, and being duly sworn sayeth that on the 24th of May last that William Andrew her husband was not out of her sight two minutes all the morning until after South Bradshaw drove Mr. Younghusbands horses from the Widows house... Martha Andrew (X). Robert Gilliam, J.P.

South Carolina, Newberry County. Personally appeared before me, Robert Gilliam, Esquire, Mrs. Jean Andrew and being duly sworn sayeth that on the 24th of May last that her son William Andrew was not over the branch from his house.... Jean Andrew (mark), Robert Gilliam, J. P. Recorded 3 Jan 1793.

B, 270-271: 31 Dec 1792, William Ragland and Elizabeth his wife of Newberry County to John James of same, for £150 Virginia money, 150 acres on both sides Kings Creek, a branch of Enoree River, tract granted to Abell Anderson 18 Jan 1765, recorded in the Aud'rs office in Book G No. 7, page 219, 26 Feb 1765. William Ragland (LS), Eliz'a Ragland (mark) (LS), Wit: Ballard Finch, Abra'm Lindsey, Edw'd Finch, J.P. Recorded 4 Jan 1793.

B, 271: Elizabeth James, the wife or called the wife of John James, rec'd my full dower which is £14, 15 Dec 1791. Test: Edward Finch, J.P., Pro: Williams, J.P. Recorded 4 Jan 1793.

B, 272: James Grayham of Newberry County to Alex'r Bookter of same place, for £5 sterling, one negro boy named Charles about 15 years old, 12 Dec 1792. James Grayham (Seal), Wit: Ephraim Liles Sen'r, Edward Kelley. Proved in Newberry County by the oath of Edward Kelley 12 Jan 1793 before Edward Finch, J.P. Recorded 16 Jan 1793.

B, 273: 31 Dec 1793, John James and Ann his wife of Newberry County to William Ragland of same, for £100 sterling, 56 acres, part of 100 acres granted to Robert Brown 9 Nov 1774 on Guilders Creek. John James (Seal), Ann James (+) (Seal), Wit: Edw'd Finch J. P., Abr: Lindsey, Ballard Finch.

B, 274: 31 Dec 1793, John James and Ann his wife of Newberry County to William Ragland of same, for £200 sterling, 100 acres granted to James Burnes 9 Sept 1774 and conveyed to John James, recorded in the Auditor's office in Book M. No. 13, page 385. John James (Seal), Ann James (+) (Seal), Wit: Edw'd Finch J. P., Abr: Lindsey, Ballard Finch. Recorded 16 Jan 1793.

B, 275: 31 Dec 1793, John James and Ann his wife of Newberry County to William Ragland of same, for £300 sterling, 184 acres on a branch of Indian Creek granted to John James 3 April 1786, recorded in Book IIII, page 347. John James (Seal), Ann James (+) (Seal), Wit: Edw'd Finch J. P., Abr: Lindsey, Ballard Finch. Recorded 16 Jan 1793.

B, 286: Isaac Campbell & Mary his wife of Newberry County appoint our trusty friend Joses Campbell, planter, of Culpeper County, Virginia, our attorney to receive from Usley Allen widow, & Abraham Colly who is now in an unlawful possession of a tract in Culpeper County on the Hazel River, 200 acres adj. land of Daniel Campbell, William Potter, and a tract adj. George Dych, 120 acres, dated 18 Jan 1793. Isaac Campbell (Seal), Mary Campbell (+) (Seal), Wit: Edw'd Finch, Richard Mansel, Abraham Campbell. Recorded 8 Jan 1793.

B, 277-280: Lease and release. 29 & 30 Aug 1792, John Robison Jun'r of Newberry County, planter, to James Davis and William Nelson of Fairfield County, Camden District, by grant dated 22 March 1769 to John Robison Sen'r, 350 acres in Berkley County on a small branch of Enoree River called the Beaverdam adj. James Stewart, Thomas Gibson, Isaac Pitchlin, and said John Robison & Elizabeth his wife did convey to Randolph Robison 26 Feb 1783 and said John Robison Sen'r by another deed dated 15 Sept 1786 to John Robison Jun'r, conveyed to John Robinson Junr 225 acres and said John Robison Jun'r did convey 100 acres to Thadeus Shirley in 1791, now for £100 sterling, said John Robison Jun'r conveys all the tract of 350 acres. John Robison Jun'r (Seal), Wit: Abner Nelson, C. D. Bradford, James Morgan (X). Proved in Fairfield County by the oath of Abner Nelson and James Morgan 14 Dec 1792 before Benj'a Boyd, JP. Recorded 1 Feb 1793.

B, 281-283: Lease and release. 18 & 19 Jan 1793. William Murray, planter, of Georgia, to Samuel Murray of Newberry County, SC, for £50 sterling, 80 acres on Enoree River adj. land of George Awberry, Thomas Gordon, Geo. Gordon. Wm Murray (Seal), Wit: Abel Anderson, James Murray, Robt Johnston. Proved in Newberry County by the oath of Robert Johnson 22 Jan 1793 before Edward Finch, J.P. Recorded 1 Feb 1793.

B, 284-290: Lease and release. 8 & 9 Jan 1793, Annamaria Miller of City of Charleston, SC, widow, and Jacob Williman of same place, gentleman & Mary his wife, to John Glymph of Newberry County, planter, for 50 guineas, tract granted to Ulrick Ener for 300 acres on Second Creek in Newberry County. Annamaria Miller (X) (Seal), Jacob Williman (Seal), Mary Williman (mark) (Seal), Wit: Ann Margratha Jaims (X), George Daugharty, James Daugharty. Proved in Newberry County by the oath of George Daugharty 22 Jan 1793 before Edw'd Finch, J. P. Mary, wife of James Williman, relinquished dower 11 Jan 1793 before Elihu Hall Bay, Judge of the Court of Common Pleas, Charleston District. Wit: Jas Nicholson. Recorded 4 Feb 1793.

B, 291-293: Lease and release. 29 & 30 July 1765, John Brooks and Lydda his wife of Berkley County, SC, Blacksmith, to Henry Coate of same, planter, for £70 SC money, 200 acres on Scotch Creek surveyed 26 Aug 1757 for said John Brooks. John Brooks (Seal), Wit: William Coate, Saml Kelly, James Coate. Proved by the oath of William Coate 2 Aug 1765 before Isaac Pitchlynn, J.P. for Colleton County. Recorded 8 Feb 1793.

B, 294-296: Lease and release. 14 & 15 Nov 1792, John Coate of Newberry County, to Peter Buffington of same, for £150 SC money, 200 acres on Scotch Creek granted 19 Sept 1758 to John Brooks. John Coate (Seal), Susanah Coate (mark) (Seal), Wit: George Latham, Benj. Long, Saml Kelly. Proved in Newberry County by the oath of Samuel Kelly Sen'r 5 Feb 1793 before Mercer Babb, J.P. Recorded 8 Feb 1793.

B, 297-299: Lease and release. 14 & 15 Jan 1793, Peter Buffington of Edgefield County, and Sarah his wife, to George Latham of Newberry County, for £140 SC money, 215 acres by resurvey on Scotch Creek granted 19 Sept 1758 to John Brooks, adj. Kelly, Rosanah Russel, John Coats, Pearson, John Barrot. Peter Buffington (Seal), Sarah Buffington (mark) (Seal), Wit: Saml Kelly Sen'r, Joseph Money, James Daugherty. Proved in Newberry County by the oath of Samuel Kelly Sen'r 6 Jan 1793 before Mercer Babb, J.P. Recorded 9 Feb 1793.

B, 300-303: Lease and release. 28 & 29 Nov 1773, James Jones & Hannah his wife of Ninety Six District, to George Gibson and Richard Gibson of same, by grant dated 20 Nov 1772 to James Jones, 200 acres in Berkley County, waters of Saluda adj. David Rees, John Richardson, now conveyed for £300 SC money. James Jones (X) (Seal), Hannah Jones (X) (Seal), Wit: Gilbert Gibson, Gibson Jones, Selthy Gibson. Proved in Ninety Six District by the oath of Gibson Jones 20 May 1773 before Jonathan Downs, J.P. Recorded 9 Feb 1793.

B, 304-305: Isaac Mitchel Jun'r of Newberry County to Thomas Wadsworth & William Turpin, merchants, by bond dated 9 Feb 1793, in the sum of £30 s6 d3 sterling, mortgage of negro fellow Tom about 30 years of age; six cows and calves, three beds and bedding, three breeding sows & all household furniture. Isaac Mitchel Jun'r (Seal), Wit: Dan Symnmes, John Gowin. Proved 11 Feb 1793 by the oath of Daniel Symmes before Elisha Ford, J. P. Recorded 11 Feb 1793.

B, 306-310: Lease and release. 26 & 27 Aug 1784, Richard Gibson of Ninety Six District, to Benjamin Wood of same, for £100 sterling, 100 acres, part of 200 acres granted 20 Nov 1772 to James Jones, on the Beaverdam, Berkley County, waters of Saluda adj. David Rees, John Richardson. Richard Gibson (Seal), Wit: James Johnston, William Burton Jun'r. Proved 23 March 1792 by the oath of James Johnston before Mercer Babb, J.P. Recorded 11 Feb 1793.

B, 311-314: Lease and release. 10 & 11 Feb 1793, Benjamin Wood, farmer, of Newberry County, and Judith his wife, to George Latham of same, merchant, for £100 sterling, 100 acres, part of 200 acres granted 20 Nov 1772 to James Jones, on the Beaverdam, Berkley County, waters of Saluda adj. David Rees, John Richardson. Benjamin Wood (X) (Seal), Judith Wood (X) (Seal), Wit: Titus Underdunk, Saml Kelley Sen'r. Proved in Newberry County 6 Feb 1793 by the oath of Samuel Kelley Sen'r before Mercer Babb, J.P. Recorded 11 Feb 1793.

B, 315-319: Lease and mortgage. 7 Feb 1793, William Irby of Newberry County, planter, to Thomas Wadsworth & William Turpin, merchants, bound in the penal sum of £100 sterling for the payment of £50 sterling, mortgage of tract on Saluda River adj. Thomas Brown, Joseph Goodman, James Tate, which said Irby purchased of William Tate, Esquire. William Irby (Seal), Wit: Daniel Symmes, John Garvis. Proved by the oath of Daniel Symmes 12 Feb 1793 before Mercer Babb, J.P. Recorded 13 Feb 1793.

B, 320-321: 11 Aug 1792, William Griffin of Ninety Six District to Thomas Wadsworth & William Turpin, merchants, for £30 SC money, 80 acres on waters of Carson Creek, part of 200 acres granted to Samuel Ford 19 Aug 1768 and conveyed by Samuel Ford to James Griffin 15 & 16 March 1773 and conveyed by James Griffin to William Griffin 23 Oct 1791. William Griffin (Seal), Wit: Wm. Young, James Young. Proved by the oath of James young 17 Nov 1792 before Wm. Hunter, J.P.

B, 322-324: Lease and release. 18 & 20 Aug 1792, Daniel Criswell & Pheby his wife of Wilks County, Georgia, to James Criswell of Newberry County, for £500 sterling, 100 acres granted to Wm Smith 1 Aug 1758 & one third of an undivided moiety of 200 acres granted to Robert Cunningham. David Criswell (Seal), Wit: Pat'k McDowal, William Mayson, Thos Talbot. Proved in Newberry County by the oath of William Mayson before J. R. Brown 3 Jan 1793. Recorded 15 Feb 1793.

B, 325: 24 Nov 1791, Abel Anderson of Newberry County to Stephen Shell of same, for £65 sterling, 100 acres on Kings Creek, a branch of Enoree River adj. Sims Brown, William Ragland, part of 300 acres granted to Thomas Morgan, recorded in Book AAA, page 399, in the auditor's office in Book H. No. 8, page 618, sold to said Abel Anderson by Thos Morgan. Abel Anderson (Seal), Wit: Jacob King, William Ragland, Edward Finch, J.P. Recorded 16 Feb 1793.

B, 326-327: 27 Dec 1792, Jean Dickey of Fairfield County, to James Caldwell of Newberry County, for £10 sterling, 100 acres in Ninety Six District on waters of Second Creek adj. Paul Williams, Daniel Horsey, granted to Jean Dickey in 1774, memorial entered in Book W No. 13, page 501, 8 June 1775. Jean Dickey (+) (Seal), Wit: Martha Hood (X), James Dickey, John Smith. Proved in Newberry County by the affirmation of John Smith 28 Dec 1792 before David Ruff, J.P. Recorded 16 Feb 1793.

B, 328-330: Lease and release. 8 & 9 Oct 1784, Ann & Bartholomew Johnson, exrs. of Daniel Johnson deceased, of Ninety Six District, to John Sparks of same, for £50 SC money, 32 acres, part of tract granted 12 Jan 1773 and memorial entered in Book M No. 12, page 115, 2 June 1774, to Daniel Johnston for 400 acres in the fork between Broad and Saluda Rivers in Berkley County on the draughts of Second Creek and Gossetts Creek adj. Samuel Wilson, John Souter, Melcom Key, now by the will of Daniel Johnston dated 8 Jan 1783, land between the line and the Waggon Road. Ann Johnson

(Seal), Bartholomew Johnson (Seal), Wit: John Hampton, Elizabeth Johnson (+), James Lindsey. Proved in Ninety Six District 9 Oct 1783 by the oath of John Hampton before W. Malone, J.P. Recorded 16 Feb 1793.

B, 331-332: 26 Dec 1792, Nathaniel Abney of Newberry County to James Tate Jun'r of Pendleton County, for £200 sterling, 150 acres on NE side Saluda River adj. land of Thomas Spearman, William Turner, being the same land bequeathed by William Turner deceased to his daughter Ann Abney's issue. Nathaniel Abney (X) (Seal), Wit: Wm Irby, William Stephens, Robt Tate. Proved in Newberry County by the oath of Wm Stephens 16 Feb 1793 before J. R. Brown, J. N. C. Recorded 23 Feb 1793.

B, 333-334: 13 Feb 1793, Michael Abney of Newberry County to James Tate of Pendleton County, for £25 sterling, a moiety of a tract laid out for Enoch Anderson and devised by William Turner deceased to his daughter Ann, also decd, the late wife of Michael Abney, on north side Saludy. Michael Abney (Seal), Wit: William Stephens, Robert Tate, William Irby. Proved in Newberry County by the oath of William Stephens before Jacob Roberts Brown, J.N.C., 16 Feb 1793. Recorded 23 Feb 1793.

B, 335-336: 15 Feb 1793, Nathaniel Abney Jun'r of Newberry County to James Tate Jun'r of Pendleton County, for £150 sterling, 250 acres on N side Saluda River, being the same land bequeathed by William Turner deceased to his daughter Ann Abney, mother of Nathaniel Abney. Nathaniel Abney (X) (Seal), Wit: Wm Irby, William Stephens, Robt Tate. Proved in Newberry County by the oath of Wm Stephens 16 Feb 1793 before J. R. Brown, J. N. C. Recorded 23 Feb 1793.

B, 337-338: 9 Feb 1793, Isaac Mitchell Junior of Newberry County, bound in the penal sum of £250 for the payment of £125 to Isaac Mitchell Senr, mortgage of negro fellow Tom about 30 years of age, six cows and calves, three breeding sows, three beds and bedding, all household furniture. Isaac Mitchel Jun'r (Seal), Wit: Dan Symmes, David Crews. Proved 18 Feb 1793 by the oath of Daniel Symmes before Robert Gilliam, J. P. Recorded 23 March 1793.

B, 339-340: 7 Feb 1793, William Irby of Newberry County, planter, to Thomas Wadsworth & William Turpin, merchants, bound in the penal sum of £102 sterling for the payment of £50 s12 sterling, mortgage of negro fellow Cesar about 30 years old, a negro wench named Chloe about 40 years of age, a fellow named Jack about 34 years of age, a negro wench Bett about 26 years of age a wench named Jenny about 50 years of age, a wench named Rhode about 15 years of age. William Irby (Seal), Wit: Daniel Symmes, John Garvis. Proved by the oath of Daniel Symmes 14 Feb 1793 before Mercer Babb, J.P. Recorded 25 March 1793.

B, 341-343: Lease and release. 22 & 23 Jan 1793, Philliman Waters of Newberry County to Joseph and Jacob Bulow of Charleston, SC, for £212 s10,

NEWBERRY COUNTY SC DEED ABSTRACTS

250 acres on Big Saludy at the mouth of Bush River. P. Waters (Seal), Wit: Daniel Parkins, John J. Bulow, Jno Cunningham. Proved 1 Feb 1793 by the oath of John J. Bulow before James Bentham, J. P. in Charleston District. Recorded 26 March 1793.

B, 344-345: 2 Dec 1790, William Irby, Planter, of Newberry County to John Symson, merchant, of Laurence County, mortgage for securing £96 s13 d4½, 200 acres, part of 400 acres granted to William Sinkfield 2 July 1752 and conveyed by William Tate to William Irby, adj. Thomas Brown and Saluda River. Wm Irby (Seal), Wit: Wm. Hunter, Wm Dunlap. Proved by the oath of Wm Dunlap 2 Dec 1791 before John Hunter, Esqr. Recorded 6 April 1793.

B, 346-347: 2 Dec 1791, William Irby, Planter, of Newberry County to John Symson, merchant, of Laurence County, mortgage for securing £84 s14 d4, negroes Jack, Sezar, Bett, Ginny, Chloe & Rhoda. Wm Irby (Seal), Wit: Wm. Hunter, Wm Dunlap. Proved by the oath of Wm Dunlap 2 Dec 1791 before John Hunter, Esqr. Recorded 6 April 1793.

B, 348-350: Lease and release. 2 & 3 Feb 1792, Nathaniel Abney to Thomas Spearman, both of Newberry County, for £100 sterling, 100 acres, part of tract granted to Enoch Anderson 3 Dec 1751 and conveyed to William Turner, then said William Turner deceased to his daughters Mary & Ann, Nathaniel Abney being the eldest son of Ann Abney, wife of Nathaniel Abney. Nathaniel Abney (X) (Seal), Wit: Joseph Towles, Edward Thweatt, John Atkison (X). Proved in Newberry County by the oath of Joseph Towles 1 March 1793 before Robert Gilliam, J. P. Recorded 8 April 1793.

B, 351-352: 21 Feb 1793, Michael Abney to Thomas Spearman, for £105 sterling, 200 acres of land part of 500 acres granted to Enoch Anderson and conveyed to William Turner, devised by William Turner deceased to his daughter Ann, also decd, the late wife of Michael Abney, on Saludy River. Michael Abney (Seal), Wit: John Spearman, Job Loftis (mark). Proved in Newberry County by the oath of John Spearman before Robert Gilliam, J. P., 1 March 1793. Recorded 8 April 1793.

B, 353-354: 17 Feb 1792, William Irby to Thomas Spearman, both of Newberry County, for £15 sterling, 30 acres of land part of 435 acres granted to William Irby 14 Oct 1784, recorded in Book FFFF, page 269. William Irby (Seal), Wit: Joseph Towles, Edward Thweatt, Michael Abney. Proved in Newberry County by the oath of Joseph Towles before Robert Gilliam, J. P., 1 March 1793. Recorded 8 April 1793.

B, 355-357: Lease and release. 14 & 15 Feb 1793, William Anderson to James Creswell, both of Newberry County, for £50 SC money, 200 acres on a small branch of Saludy River adj. Robert Cunningham, granted to Patrick Welch 23 Oct 1772 and conveyed to William Anderson 20 & 21 Nov 1772. William Anderson (Seal), Wit: J. Brown, R. Watts, Jas Mayson. Recorded 9 April 1793.

B, 358-359: 30 Nov 1785, Edmond Martin, Sheriff of Ninety Six District, to Thomas Brown, place, of same, for £81 SC money, 207 acres in Ninety Six District adj. William Turner, Saludy River, Gilliam, Abraham Turner, sold by sheriff by judgment at the suit of John Williams against Edmond Turner for £25. Edmond Martin (Seal), Wit: William Caldwell, Joseph Goodman. Proved in Newberry County by the oath of William Caldwell 9 March 1793 before Robert Gilliam, J.P. Recorded 10 April 1793.

B, 360: 18 Aug 1792, John Edwards and Mary his wife, Samuel Cotton & Elizabeth his wife, John Tune and Ruth his wife, Litisha Edwards, Rhoda Edwards & Margarett Edwards, daughters of John Edwards and Mary his wife of Newberry County, to Thomas Chappel of same, for £70 sterling, negro woman slave about 18 years old named Dinah, negro boy about 8 years old named Frank. John Edwards (Seal), Mary Edwards (mark) (Seal), Samuel Cotton (Seal), Elizabeth Cotton (X) (Seal), John Tune (Seal), Ruth Tune (mark) (Seal), Lititia Edwards (X) (Seal), Rhoda Edwards (X) (Seal), Margarett Edwards (Seal), Wit: William Satterwhite, Thomas Brown, Thomas McMahon (X). Proved in Newberry County by the oath of Thos McMahon 15 Feb 1793 before Robert Gilliam, J.P. Recorded 10 April 1793.

B, 361-363: Lease and release. 15 & 16 Dec 1785, John Hampton of Newberry County, to John Sparks of same, for £100 SC money, 65 acres granted to said John Hampton 6 June 1785 on waters of Enoree River adj. John Sparks, James Blair, recorded in Book DDDD, page 276. John Hampton (Seal), Joice Hampton (X) (Seal), Wit: John Malone, John Macoy, James Lindsey. Recorded 10 April 1793.

B, 364-366: Lease and release. 15 & 16 Dec 1785, John Hampton of Newberry County, to John Sparks of same, for £100 SC money, 39 acres granted to said John Hampton 6 June 1785 on waters of Broad River adj. William Darby, Souter, Ellewine, Roses & Widow Sparks, recorded in Book DDDD, page 277. John Hampton (Seal), Joice Hampton (X) (Seal), Wit: John Malone, John Macoy, James Lindsey. Recorded 11 April 1793.

B, 367-369: Lease and release. 23 & 24 March 1778, Abraham Anderson, now soldier, of SC, to John Sparks of the settlement of Enoree, for £100 SC money, 100 acres granted to said Anderson 3 April 1775 in Berkley County in the fork of Broad and Saludy Rivers on a branch of Enoree called Hoggs branch, adj. land of Daniel Johnson, recorded in Book WWW, page 472. Abraham Anderson (Seal), Wit: Robt Wilson, Williamson Liles, Thomas Johnson. Proved in Ninety Six District by the oath of Williamson Liles 3 Aug 1782 before George Ruff, J.P. Recorded 16 April 1793.

B, 370: Thorogood Chambers of Newberry County to Alexander Bookter, of same, for £50 sterling, including the execution levied on said Bookter by William Satterwhite, sheriff, one negro boy named Dick about 15 years of age, well grown, likely, and of a yellow complexion, dated 17 Jan 1793. Thorogood Chambers (Seal). Wit: Peter Stally, Andrew Crooks. Proved in Newberry

County by the oath of Peter Stally __ Jan 1793 before Edward Finch, J>P. Recorded 16 April 1793.

B, 371: 8 Jan 1793, Rachael Lark of Newberry County, to her son Cullen Lark of same, for love and good will, her dower in 190 acres of land as the widow of John Lark deceased. Rachael Lark (Seal), Wit: A. Robison, Daniel Parkins. Recorded 16 April 1793.

B, 371: Rec'd of Olleman Dodgen in full of all demands in my mother's estate, 7 Oct 1791. Elizabeth Toland (mark), Wit: Jane Brown (mark). Proved in Newberry County by the oath of Jane Brown 26 Feb 1793 before J. R. Brown, J. N. C. Recorded 16 April 1793.

B, 372: Ninety Six District, Newberry County. Suffias Robison of Newberry County to Robert Wilson of same, planter, for £50 sterling, two feather beds and furniture, one hunting saddle, cow and yearling, 12 hogs, 20 geese, all household and kitchen furniture. Suffias Robison (X) (Seal), Wit: Edward Kelly, John Stewart. Proved by the oath of Capt. Edward Kelley 16 Feb 1793 before Reuben Sims, J.P. Recorded 17 April 1793.

B, 373-375: Lease and release. 15 & 16 Feb 1793, Mark Love of Newberry County, and Sarah his wife, to Samuel Marshall of same, for £100 sterling, 135 acres, part of 271 acres granted 5 Oct 1783 to John Lindsey on waters of Indian Creek adj. Theodoras Feltman, Abraham Gray, John Pennington, recorded in Book AAAA, page 67. Mark Love (Seal), Sarah Love (Seal), Wit: John Bush, Hugh Marshal, John Johnson. Proved 1 March 1793 by the oath of Hugh Marshal before Providence Williams, J. P. Recorded 17 April 1793.

B, 376-377: South Carolina, Newberry County. Elizabeth Harden, late of Prince William County, Virginia, acknowledge the pretensions that I have hitherto made by claiming Col. Phillimon Waters as my lawful husband is false and evil and only a seducement of the Devil in order to extort from said Phillimon Waters a sum of money, that whatever pretentions I had in my proceedings against him is of 42 or 43 years back and that the ceremonial part of our pretended marriage was a mere pretence and performed by a minister when drunk, that our cohabitation did not last for more than 12 months when he left me & shortly afterwards went to the wars under Col. George Washington (now his Excellency) when said Waters went (as I was informed) to South Carolina with the Army. I had no manner of communication with him for at least 18 or 290 acres, about 5 or 6 years after said Waters left the State of Virginia, I the said Elizabeth Harden had a female child by one Robert Sanford, Christina Ailsey and in justice I do hereby forever quit all manner of claim, dated 5 Nov 1792. Elizabeth Harden (X) (Seal), Wit: William Musgrove, Elijah Calk, Smith Musgrove. Acknowledged in Newberry County before Peter Julin, J.P., 6 Nov 1792. Proved by the oath of William Musgrove 17 Nov 1792 before Peter Julin, J.P. Recorded 18 April 1793.

B, 377: South Carolina, Newberry County. Personally appeared Elizabeth Harden, late of Prince William County, Virginia, and made oath that P. Waters, Esqr., of Newberry County is justly indebted to her in the sum of £20 Virginia currency equal to £14 s5 d8 sterling. Elizabeth Harden (X), before Levi Manning, J. P. Rec'd of John Head £2 s3 d6 in part of the within account, 12 July 1786. Elizabeth Harden (X). Wit: John Summers, James Head. Recorded 18 April 1793.

B, 378-379: 29 June 1790, John Malone of Newberry County to Andrew Russell of same, for £70 sterling, 100 acres on a small branch of Broad River called Second Creek adj. Michael Ellewine, John Souter, Daniel Johnson, Samuel Wilson, Alexander Davidson, granted to said John Malone 30 Sept 1774, memorial recorded in Book M. No. 13, page 434. John Malone (Seal), Wit: John Liles, Ephraim liles, Josiah Goree (X). Proved 1 March 1793 by the oath of Josiah Gorree before Reuben Sims, J.P. Recorded 18 April 1793.

B, 380-381: 30 Dec 1790, Aron Cates of Newberry County to Andrew Russell of same, for £25 sterling, 20 acres on Second Creek, part of tract granted to Samuel Wilson 30 Aug 1762 and conveyed by him to John Hampton 22 Dec 1784, and since conveyed to A. Cates 20 Sept 1790. A. Cates (Seal), Wit: W. Malone Sen'r, Andrew Swan. Proved 1 March 1793 by the oath of W. Malone Sen'r before Reuben Sims, J.P. Recorded 28 April 1793.

B, 382-384: Lease and release. 29 & 30 March 1792, James Johnston & Sarah his wife of Ninety Six District, SC, to John Milligan of same, for £40 sterling, 150 acres on branches of Carsons Creek, waters of Little River, granted to said James Johnston 2 June 1788. James Johnston (Seal), Sarah Johnston (Seal), Wit: John Black, James Bryon, William Blake. Proved by the oath of John Black 3 July 1793 before John Hewster[?], J.P. Recorded 19 April 1793.

B, 385: Tobias Lagrone of Newberry County for love and affection to my son John Jacob Lagrone of same place, 125 acres on a branch of Cannons Creek adj. Nicholas Wise, Gray, granted to Laurence Lagrown in 1752 and became the property of Tobias Lagrone by the last will and testament of said Laurence Lagrown, dated 18 Sept 1786. Tobias Lagrone (Seal), Wit: Wm Houseal, John Lagrone (X). Proved in Newberry County by the oath of William Houseal 30 July 1792 before David Ruff, J.P. Recorded 26 April 1793.

B, 386-388: Lease and release. 23 & 24 Feb 1793, Peter Buffington of Edgefield County, Ninety Six District, and Sarah his wife, to John Barrott of Newberry County, carpenter, for £50 SC money, 100 acres, part of tract granted to John Brooks 19 Sept 1759 on a branch of Saluda River called Scotch Creek adj. land of Benjamin Pearson, Kelly, Rosanah Russell. Peter Buffington (Seal), Sarah Buffington (mark) (Seal), Wit: Ridgeway Elmore, William Morgan. Proved in Newberry County by the oath of Ridgeway Elmore 26 Feb 1793 before Mercer Babb, J.P. Recorded 26 April 1793.

B, 389-391: Lease and release. 28 March 1790, William Blair of Ninety Six District, planter, to Samuel McQuerns, blacksmith, of same, for £20 sterling, 108 acres on waters of Bush River granted to William Blair 1 June 1789, adj. land of Lester, Henry Dunn, William Blair, recorded in Book ZZZZ, page 411. William Blair (Seal), David Blair (X) (Seal), Wit: Miles Jennings, Patrick Carmichal, James McQuerns. Proved in Newberry County by the oath of James McQuerns 1 March 1793 before Mercer Babb, J.P. Recorded 26 April 1793.

B, 392-394: Lease and release. 21 July 1790, Thomas Willoughby Waters, Esquire of Ninety Six District, to Samuel McQuerns, Blacksmith of same, for £50 sterling, 88 acres on waters of Bush River, granted to Phillimon Waters, Esquire, 22 Apr 1786 and conveyed by him unto Thomas W. Waters, recorded in Book NNNN, page 11. Tho's W. Waters (Seal), Wit: John Wilson, Peter Kerr, Samuel Edwards (X). Proved 1 March 1793 by the oath of Peter Kerr before Mercer Babb, J.P. Recorded 29 April 1793.

B, 395: Simeon Ellis of Bush River, Ninety Six District, bound to Jacob Chandler of same, 23 March 1784, in the sum of £1000 sterling, title to tract of 100 acres granted to Isaac Williams and a tract of 150 acres granted to Henry Demory, and 250 acres granted to Benjamin Farrer, and 200 acres on Bush River. Simeon Ellis (Seal), Wit: Samuel Kelly, Hannah Kelly. Proved by the affirmation of Saml Kelley Sen'r 3 March 1793 before James Mayson, J.N.C. Recorded 29 April 1793.

B, 396-398: Lease and release. 7 Nov 1792, Reuben Flannagan, farmer, of Laurence County, farmer, to Samuel Law, late from Ireland, for £100 sterling, 200 acres consisting of three tracts: part of tract of 100 acres granted to said Flannegan 23 June 1774, part of tract of 320 acres granted to Robert Whitten 6 July 1789, and part of tract of 150 acres granted to said Flannegan 31 Aug 1774 on waters of Duncans Creek. Reuben Flannegan (Seal), Abilah Flannegan (A) (Seal), Wit: John Buoys, Samuel Law Jun'r, Robert McKee. Proved 1 March 1793 by the oath of John Buoys before Providence Williams, J.P. Recorded 30 April 1793.

B, 399-400: State of SC for £5 s19 sterling paid by Henry Herp, tract of 256 acres in Ninety Six District on north side Saluda River adj. land of Phillimon Waters, Oxner, dated 21 Jan 1785. Plat included dated 12 Oct 1783 by Ephraim Mitchell, D. S.

South Carolina, Edgefield County. Henry Harp for £10 SC money to Allen Robison, 256 acres, 30 Oct 1787. Henry Harp (mark) (Seal), Wit: James Young, James Williams, Sarah Harp (mark). Proved by the oath of James Williams 19 Nov 1792 before Wm. Anderson, J.E.C. Recorded 1 May 1793.

B, 401-403: Lease and release. 8 & 9 July 1791, Jonathan Motes of Laurence County, SC, planter, to John Younghusband, Esquire, of Newberry County, for £200 sterling, 200 acres on waters of Mudlick Creek, and 100 acres adj. it.

Jonathan Motes (I) (Seal), Audry Motes (A) (Seal), Wit: J. Brown, John Barlow, Timothy Goodman. Recorded 1 May 1793.

B, 404-406: Lease and release. 25 & 26 May 1787, George Ruff, Esquire, merchant, to George Buchanan, planter, for £100 sterling, 73 acres on Second Creek, recorded in Book RRR, page 199, 50 acres granted to George Ruff adj. Jacob Hufman, George Ellerwine and part of another tract granted to Jacob Hufman. George Ruff (Seal), Bary Ruff (mark) (Seal), Wit: James Daugherty, Benjamin Buchanan, Peter Julin. Proved by the oath of Benjamin Buchanan 2 Feb 1793 before David Ruff, J.P. Recorded 6 May 1793.

B, 407-410: Lease and release. 2 & 3 Nov 1792, George Ellewine, planter, of Newberry County, to George Buchanan, planter, for £50 sterling, 50 acres, part of 250 acres on Second Creek adj. land of Jacob Huffman, recorded in Book PP, page 92. George Ellewine (Seal), Catherine Ellewine (mark) (Seal), Wit: Benjamin Buchanan, Michael Dickert, John Ellewine (mark). Proved in Newberry County 2 Feb 1793 by the oath of Benjamin Buchanan before David Ruff, J.P. Recorded 6 May 1793.

B, 411-414: Lease and release. 21 & 22 Dec 1792, Christian Ruff, blacksmith, of Newberry County, to Benjamin Buchanan of same, for £ 20 sterling, 20 acres, part of 300 acres on Second Creek adj. Catherina Shearley granted to Jacob Huffman 20 June 1754 and conveyed by him to George Ruff 24 & 25 June 1765 and conveyed by him to Christian Ruff 2 May 1789. Christian Ruff (Seal), Wit: George Buchanan, Michael Dickert, John Ruff. Proved in Newberry County by the oath of George Buchanan 2 Feb 1793 before David Ruff, J.P. Recorded 9 May 1793.

B, 415-416: 12 Sept 1791, James Wilson & Jean his wife of Newberry County to Thomas Morgan of same, for £100 SC money, 200 acres granted to Jean Wilson & James Wilson as her bounty land 16 Feb 1773 on waters of Kings Creek, recorded in Book FFF, page 144. James Wilson (Seal), Wit: Samuel Ragland, William Guy, Jenet Mathis (+). Proved in Newberry County by the oath of Samuel Ragland 19 Jan 1792 before Edw'd Finch, J.P. Recorded 14 May 1793.

B, 417-418: 12 Sept 1791, Thomas Morgan of Newberry County to John & Melon Morgan, planters, of same, same, for £30 sterling, 100 acres granted to James Wilson's wife Jean Wilson as her bounty land 16 Feb 1773 on waters of Kings Creek, recorded in Book FFF, page 144, adj. John Brown. Thomas Morgan (Seal), Wit: Richard Tear, William Castle (X), Charity Gore (X). Proved in Newberry County by the oath of Charity Gore 19 Jan 1792 before Edw'd Finch, J.P. Recorded 14 May 1793.

B, 419: George Ruff of Newberry County to John Henry Ruff, his son, for love, god will & Affection, one negro fellow Daniel Bought in his name by my consent of J. & C. Liles, 130 acres of land of George Martin by consent, two colts, one bay mare, one negro Limas and also £300 sterling in goods now in my store. George Ruff (Seal), Wit: John Kinard, William Huffmaster. Proved in Newberry County by the oath of John Kinard 24 April 1793 before David Ruff, J.P. Recorded 15 May 1793.

B, 420: John A. Summers of Lexington County, SC, for love, good will, and affection to my son in law John Henry Ruff & my daughter Elizabeth, one tract of 250 acres which they are in possession of, called Mountz old mill place with the two mills & woods, two negroes: one child Peggy and one child Hager, one black horse, one spinet, dated 15 April 1793. John A. Summers (Seal), Mary Summers (MS) (Seal), Wit: Christian Algire, Henry Smith, William Hoffmaster. Proved in Newberry County by the oath of Christian Algire 29 April 1793 before David Ruff, J.P. Recorded 15 May 1793.

B, 421: 11 Feb 1786, George Neely of Ninety Six District, to James Daugherty, Deputy Surveyor, of same, for £50 sterling, 120 acres in Craven County, on waters of Second Creek granted 15 May 1775 and recorded in Book XXX, page 353, unto Samuel Neely & fell by heirship to said George Neely his son. George Neely (Seal), Wit: John Riley, Andrew Russell, John Boyd (mark). Recorded 17 May 1793.

B, 422-423: 25 April 1793, James Daugherty Jun'r of Charleston, to John Henry Ruff, merchant, for £18 sterling, 120 acres in Craven County, on waters of Second Creek granted 15 May 1775 and recorded in Book XXX, page 353, unto Samuel Neely & fell by heirship to said George Neely his son and sold by George Neely to James Daugherty Jun'r. James Daugherty. Wit: James Daugherty Senr (mark), Philip Croomer, John Houseal. Proved in Newberry County by the oath of Philip Cromer 26 April 1793 before David Ruff, J.P. Recorded 17 May 1793.

B, 424: 18 Aug 1792, George Martin & Sarah Martin to John Henry Ruff, all of Newberry County, for £50 sterling, 100 acres on Reedy Creek a branch of Cannons Creek granted to John Lum 23 June 1773, adj. Ephraim Cannon, Samuel Cannon, John Maypole, and made over to George Martin and Sarah his wife 1 Feb 1774 by said John Lum & Margret his wife, memorial recorded in Book M No. 12, page 260. George Martin (Seal), Sarah Martin (X) (Seal), Wit: David Ruff J. P., Philip Cromer, John Riley. Recorded 17 May 1793.

B, 424: 18 Aug 1792, George Martin & Sarah Martin to John Henry Ruff, all of Newberry County, for £10 sterling, 30 acres on Reedy Creek a branch of Cannons Creek granted to John Cannon from Conrad Myer by bonds in 1775 and made over to Ephraim Cannon in 1791 and from him to George Martin and Sarah Martin adj. Ephraim Cannon, said Martin. George Martin (Seal), Sarah Martin (X) (Seal), Wit: David Ruff J. P., Philip Cromer, John Riley. Recorded 17 May 1793.

B, 426-428: Lease and release. 15 & 16 Nov 1792, William Scott of Newberry County, farmer, to his daughter Mary Scott, of same, for £40, 100 acres, part of 450 acres granted to William Scott 13 May 1768. William Scott (X) (Seal),

Mary Scott (X) (Seal), Wit: John Housen Bush, Joseph Scott, William Sanders (X). Proved in Newberry County by the oath of John Housen Bush 18 May 1793 before John Speak, J.P. Recorded 17 May 1793.

B, 429-430: Katherine Thweatt of Newberry County, bound to Thomas Wadsworth and William Turpin, merchants, in the sum of £40, for the payment of £20, mortgage of negro Peter about 40 years of age, 18 March 1793. Kt: Thweatt (Seal), Wit: Dan Symmes. Proved by the oath of Daniel Symmes 15 April 1793 before Robert Gilliam, J.P. Recorded 28 May 1793.

B, 431-432: Bartlett Brooks of Newberry County, bound to Thomas Wadsworth and William Turpin, merchants, in the sum of £423 s16 d9, for the payment of £211 s18 d4, mortgage of negro Abram about 35 years of age, wench named Mary about 24 years of age, a wench name Jude about 45 years of age, Agg about 5 years, Old Suck about 4 years of age, David about 2 years of age, dated 13 April 1793. Bartlett Brooks (X) (Seal), Wit: Dan Symmes. Proved by the oath of Daniel Symmes 15 April 1793 before Robert Gilliam, J.P. Recorded 28 May 1793.

B, 433-436: Lease and mortgage. 29 & 30 March 1795, Bartlett Brooks of Newberry County, planter, to Thomas Wadsworth and William Turpin, merchants, bound in the sum of £423 s16 d9, for the payment of £211 s18 d4, mortgage of tracts of land on which said Bartlett Brooks now lives in Newberry County on both sides Mudlick Creek, a branch of Little River, two surveys: one granted to Henry Dukes 13 May 1768 and conveyed by said Dukes to Daniel McNeill in 1769 and from said Daniel McNeill to Bartlett Brooks 2 Feb 1793. Bartlett Brooks (X) (Seal), Wit: Dan Symmes, John Garvin. Proved by the oath of Daniel Symmes 15 April 1793 before Robert Gilliam, J.P. Recorded 29 May 1793.

B, 437: Thorogood Chambers of Newberry County to John Gorie, planter, for £22 s11 sterling, one negro girl named Jenney about 5 years of age. Thorogood Chambers (Seal), Wit: Mille Liles, Martha Grasty. Proved 1 Nov 1793 by the oath of Milly Liles before Reuben Sims, J.P. Recorded 30 May 1793.

B, 438: Whereas George Dawkins, late of Ninety Six District deceased, did give unto me, Joseph Dawkins, in his will the following negroes: Nell, Champ, Edenborough, Lewsy and Pegg, and by said will desire that his wife should be put to her thirds for which I the said Joseph Dawkins to give unto James Liles and his wife, one negro child named Phillis, dated 10 Dec 1785. Joseph Dawkins. Wit: Thomas Herbert, James Beard. Proved by the oath of Thomas Herbert 2 May 1785 before John Hampton, J. Quo. Recorded 31 May 1793.

B, 439-440: 9 Jan 1793, Samuel Burdine & Mary his wife of Newberry County to Rosanah Glynn of same, for £80 sterling, 100 acres on a branch of Kings Creek, part of tract granted 19 Sept 1770, recorded in Book FFF, page 232, memorial entered in Book K. No. 10, page 262, to Thomas Wadlington and conveyed by him to Joseph Thomas conveyed by Thomas to William Gray and by said Gray to Samuel Burdine. Samuel Burdine (Seal), Mary Burdine (+) (Seal), Wit: Edward Finch J. P., Charles Crenshaw, William Wilson Senr. Recorded 31 May 1793.

B, 441-442: 2 April 1793, Richard Bonds and Mary his wife of Newberry County to Joseph Lake of same for £60 sterling, 73 acres on Bailey's branch, waters of Enoree, adj. David Lake, Thomas Lake, William Towns[?] Leitz[?] line. Richard Bonds (R) (Seal), Mary Bonds (X) (Seal), Wit: Barber Hencock, Thomas Lake (X), James Vessells (J). Proved in Newberry County 19 April 1793 by the oath of Thomas Lake before Reuben Sims, J.P. Recorded 31 March [sic] 1793.

B, 443: 15 Nov 1792, George Montgomery of Newberry County to Maxamillion Hanie of same, for £5 sterling, 21 acres on a small branch of Second Creek, part of granted of 175 acres granted to George Montgomery. George Montgomery (GM) (Seal), Wit: W. Malone Sen'r, Joseph Caldwell, David Glenn. Proved 10 May 1793 by the oath of William Malone Sen'r before Edward Finch, J.P. Recorded 1 June 1793.

B, 444: 18 April 1793, Cary Gilbert to Thomas Haskett for £6 sterling, one cow and calf, one red heifer, etc. Cary Gilbert (Seal), Wit: James Wadlington, John Wright. Proved 17 May 1793 before Mercer Babb, J.P.

16 April 1793, Cary Gilbert to Thomas Haskett for £20 sterling, one bay mare about 14½ hands high, on sorrel mare colt. Cary Gilbert (Seal), Wit: James Wadlington, John Wright. Proved 17 May 1793 before Mercer Babb, J.P. Recorded 1 June 1793.

B, 445-446: 25 May 1793, Israel Gaunt of Newberry County to James Gaunt of same, for £100 sterling, 150 acres on waters of Bush River granted to said Israel Gaunt 19 Sept 1770 adj. land of John Kinard, Thomas Smith, Israel Gaunt, Patrick Dooly, Aaron Cates. Israel Gaunt (Seal), Wit: Thomas Atkins (X), Richard Clegg. Proved in Newberry County 29 May 1793 by the affirmation of Richard Clegg before Mercer Babb, J.P. Recorded 5 June 1793.

B, 447-448: 26 Sept 1789, Elijah Parrott of Hallifax County, Virginia, planter, to Abraham Larrowe, planter, of Fairfield County, SC, for £100 SC money, tract on north side Enoree River, part of tract laid out to William Nobles, and part laid out to John Anderson, 196 acres of tract to William Nobles & 119 acres of tract laid out to John Anderson, adj. John Gories, Williamson, Henry Mills. Elijah Parrott (Seal), Wit: Ed'wd Kelley, Thomas Lake, Henry Mills (X). Proved 10 Dec 1789 by the oath of Thomas Lake before W. Wadlington, J.P. Recorded 5 June 1793.

B, 449-450: 28 Feb 1793, William Mills, eldest son of Robert Mills who died intestate 5 February 1791), of Newberry County, to Robert Mills Junior of same, youngest son of said Robert Mills, for £100 sterling, 100 acres (Charity Mills', widow, one third excepted), part of grant to Thomas Hopkins for 200 acres, 24 Aug 1770, recorded in Book EEE, page 403, conveyed to said Robert Mills by Thomas Hopkins 30 Oct 1770. William Mills (Seal), Wit: Joseph Cook, Richard Clegg. Proved __ May 1793 in Newberry County by the affirmation of Richard Clegg before Mercer Babb, J.P. Recorded 6 June 1793.

B, 451-452: 12 Nov 1792, Thomas Parrott and wife Ceilah of Newberry County, Blacksmith, to John Gorie of same, planter, for £8 sterling, 100 acres on waters of Enoree called Kelly's Creek, recorded in Book SSS, page 391, granted to Michael Wingart 21 May 1772 who transferred the same to Stalem[?] Mack 15 Jan 1774 and transferred by him unto Mathias Wicker 15 Jan 1774, and Mathias Wicker did by will give to Simon Wicker, who transferred the same to Thomas Parrott 11 & 12 Aug 1790. Thomas Parrott (Seal), Cielah Parrott (mark) (Seal), Wit: James Kelley, Wm Fish (X), Edmund Kelly. Proved in Newberry County by the oath of James Kelly 13 May 1793 before Reuben Sims, J.P. Recorded 6 June 1793.

B, 453-456: Lease and release. 31 Oct & 1 Nov 1790, Phillimon Waters, Esquire, of Newberry County to William Taylor of same, for £100 SC money, 100 acres adj. John Waites land, granted to William Mazyck 14 Sept 1771 and by him devised to two of his sons William & Isaac Mazyck and by them conveyed to Colo. Philimon Waters 25 Oct 1791. P. Waters (Seal), Wit: John Waters, James Lester (mark). Proved in Newberry County by the oath of James Lester 1 May 1793 before Peter Julin, J.P.

B, 457: Samuel Morris of Newberry County appoints Benjamin Cobb of same, his attorney to recover of Jonathan Gilbert of Lexington County, all debts, etc., 27 May 1793. Samuel Morris (Seal), Wit: Jacob Frost, Robt Powell. Proved in Newberry County by the oath of Jacob Frost 10 June 1793 before Edw'd Finch, J.P.

B, 458: Thomas Busby of Newberry County puts himself apprentice to Aron Cates, hatter, of same place, for two years and one month, to learn the art of hatter. Thomas Busby (mark) (Seal), A. Cates (Seal), Wit: Robert Rutherford, W. Malone. Recorded 11 June 1793.

B, 459: 1 Jan 1793, William Malone Sen'r of Newberry County puts his nephew William Malone Jun'r apprentice to Aron Cates, hatter, of same place, for five years and six month, to learn the art of hatter. W Malone (Seal), A. Cates (Seal), Wit: Robert Rutherford, William Finch. Recorded 11 June 1793.

B, 460: South Carolina, Newberry County. Charles Patty of Newberry County for £70 sterling to James Patty of same, for £70 sterling, one bay mare, one black gelding, one waggon, two cows and calves, one runs at David Jay's, two feather beds and bedsteads & furniture, one rifle gun, spinning wheels and weaving looms, dated 14 May 1793. Charles Patty (Seal), Wit: Rob't Speer[?], Wm Spencer. Proved in Newberry County by the oath of William Spencer 15 June 1793 before Elisha Ford, J.P. Recorded 24 June 1793.

B, 461-464: Lease and release. 9 & 10 Jan 1793, William Ancrum & Aron Loocock of Charleston, SC, esquires, to John Kelly Sen'r, planter, of District of Ninety Six, for £80 sterling, 100 acres on a small branch of Bush River, granted to Joseph Stordy adj. John Brooks, John Stedham, conveyed by said Stordy to Samuel Kelly and John Furnass and conveyed by Samuel Kelly and John Furnas to William Ancrum and Aron Loocock; also 100 acres on a small branch of Bush River granted to John Furnas adj. John Brooks. Aron Loocock (Seal), Wm. Ancrum (Seal), Wit: George Logan, Will: Clarkson. Proved in Charleston District by the oath of William Clarkson 15 Jan 1793 before Peter Freneau, J.P. Recorded 24 June 1793.

B, 465: Rec'd 26 April 1793 of Mr. Gabriel Anderson full satisfaction against the estate of Captain Daniel Horsey (decd) and his widow Sarah Horsey. Daniel Horsey (H), Wit: James Lindsey, Geo Harbert. Proved in Newberry County by the oath of James Lindsey 16 June 1793 before Edward Finch, J.P. Recorded 26 June 1793.

B, 466: James Sims Sen'r of Union County, SC, for natural affection to my daughter Drucilla Brasilman, nine negroes: Phillis, Sarah, Ithea, Stephen, Benjamin, Abina, Braset[?], Susanah & Henry, 3 December 1792. James Sims (Seal), Wit: John Sims, S. Adams, John S. Sims. Proved 26 March 1793 by the oath of Sylvanus Adams before Edward Finch, J.P. Recorded 26 June 1793.

B, 467-469: 22 March 1793, James Sims Sen'r of Union County, SC, to Peter Brasilman of Newberry County, merchant, mortgage in the sum of £1070 to be paid by 22 March 1794, 600 acres in Union County on Tyger River; 150 acres on said Tyger River; another 100 acres, total 850 acres; also 36 negroes: Jack & Doll & their children Ambrose, Paul; Isaac & Tabby and their children Jack, Emille, Fanny, Robert; Molley and her children Charles, Edward, Delf, Abram, Sawny, Tom & Patience; Big Lucy and her children Mary, Henry, Peter; Delsey and her children Morning & Daniel, Isaac, Lucy, Amy Frank & Doll; ten horses, 30 head of Kine; 50 hoggs, five feather beds & furniture, plantation tools and a cart. James Sims Senr (Seal), Wit: James Sims Jun'r, Robt Powell. Proved 26 March 1793 by the oath of Robert Powell before Edward Finch, J.P. Recorded 29 June 1793.

B, 470: Thomas W. Waters of Newberry County for love, good will for Mary Davis, my wife's mother, one negro boy named George a child of a negro wench I bought of Henry & Frank Wilson, which said negro is to be her property during her natural life and not to be taken out of the state and after her death to revert to me, and I said, Waters, to pay said Negroes Tax, 6 Nov 1791. Thos W. Waters (Seal), Wit: Georg William ____ [German signature]. Proved in Newberry County by the oath of John Hays who states that said Thos W. Waters gave the deed of gift to Chesley Davis for his mother Mary Davis, 6 Nov 1791, before Peter Julin, J.P. Recorded 10 July 1793.

B, 471: State of South Carolina, Ninety Six District. John Wilson of District aforesaid for £60 sterling to Robert Neel of same, one chest of clothing of various kinds of wooling and linen and cotton and silk, stockings of various kinds and bed covers of different kinds with pillows and a medicine chest with various sorts of Doctors medicines and instruments, with all the books and book accounts. John Wilson (Seal), Wit: Charles Burton, Alex'r Taylor, John Swan. Proved in Newberry County by the oath of Charles Burton 4 July 1793 before David Ruff, J.P. Recorded 16 July 1793.

B, 472-473: 13 Dec 1790, William Finch and Elizabeth his wife of Newberry County, to Aron Cates of same, for £25 sterling, 20 acres on south side of Second Creek, part of tract granted to Robert Moore 1775, recorded in Book QQQ, page 211, and conveyed from said Moore to Right Resiner and from him to George Dawkins and willed by George Dawkins to his son Joseph and from Joseph Dawkins to Richard Speak and from said Speak to said William Finch. William Finch (Seal), Elizabeth Finch (X) (Seal), Wit: John Hampton, John Malone, Thomas Bauskett. Acknowledged in Newberry County by William Finch 17 June 1793 before David Ruff, J.P. Recorded 16 July 1793.

B, 474-476: Lease and release. 3 & 4 Feb 1793, Charles Crow Sen'r and Elizabeth his wife of Newberry County to Charles Crow Jun'r of same, for £100 SC money, 135 acres, part of 150 acres granted to said Charles Crow 15 Feb 1769, recorded in Book DDD, page 108, reserving to said Charles Crow Sen'r 15 acres, adj. Richard Level. Charles Crow Sen'r (C) (Seal), Elizabeth Crow (mark) (Seal), Wit: Mathew Brown, John Brown Jun'r. Proved in Laurence County by the oath of John Brown Jun'r 5 Feb 1793 before Roger Brown, Justice for said County. Recorded 17 July 1793.

B, 477-478: 20 Sept 1790, John Hampton and Joice Hampton his wife of Newberry County to Aron Cates of same, for £100 sterling, 200 acres granted 30 Aug 1762 to John Hampton on Second Creek adj. Edward Connerly, Daniel Johnston, Alexander Johnston, Joseph Hogg, recorded in Book WW, page 106. John Hampton (Seal), Joice Hampton (mark) (Seal), Wit: Robert Rutherford Jun'r, Thomas Bauskett. Joice Hampton relinquished dower 25 Sept 1790 before Robert Rutherford, J.P. Proved in Newberry County 21 June 1793 by the oath of Robert Rutherford before David Ruff, J.P. Recorded 18 July 1793.

B, 479-482: Lease and release. 17 & 18 May 1793, Phillimon Waters of Newberry County to Jacob Bieler and Joseph Bieler of Charleston, for £125 sterling, 300 acres below the fork of Bush and Saluda Creek in Newberry County adj. Jacob Smith, one Jones. Phillimon Waters (Seal), Wit: J. Algood, Danl Seiler. Proved 18 May 1793 by the oath of Daniel Seiler before Jas Bentham, J.P. Recorded 18 July 1793.

B, 483: 12 Feb 1791, Uriah Hardman of Newberry County to Peter Brasilman & Company of same, merchants, for £60 sterling, one negro boy named Dave, one negro wench named Hannah with her child Jude, a black mare, a bay horse, four cows, three feather beds and furniture with sundry household furniture, sixty hogs and sundry working tools. Uriah Hardman (Seal), Wit: Robt Powell. Recorded 22 July 1793.

B, 484-486: Lease and release. 14 & 15 May 1792, Jesse Anderson, planter, of Newberry County to Mathew Hall of same, planter, for £19 s10, 39 acres, part of 182 acres in Craven County on Second Creek adj. land of Jeremiah Williams, Abram Anderson, James Undin, Henry Anderson, Daniel Horsey, William Richardson, granted to Mathew Tully 31 Aug 1774 and conveyed to Henry Anderson 6 Sept 1778 but now by undoubted and lawful heirship, the undisputed property of Jesse Anderson, eldest son of said Henry, adj. Jesse Anderson, Abram Anderson, Mathew Hall, James Hall. Jesse Anderson (Seal), Ruth Anderson (Seal), R. Anderson (Seal), James Breading (X) (Seal), Wit: Levisea Anderson, Thomas Hall. A. Glazier. Proved by the oath of Thomas Hall 21 July 1793. Recorded 23 July 1793.

B, 487: South Carolina, Laurence County. Daniel Williams appoints friends Robert Gillam, Esqr., James Caldwell & James Goodman, his attorneys whereas a number of negroes on the plantation whereon I now live and whereas John Williams Jun'r has undertaken to set up claim unjust to part of them, and I am obliged to go to North Carolina on my lawfull business and suspecting that some John Williams or some person on his behalf in my absence may attempt to steal or inveigle the said negroes away, I appoint them to perform all manner of things necessary, dated 26 April 1793. Daniel Williams (Seal), Wit: J. R. Brown, Richard Williams. Recorded 5 Aug 1793.

B, 488: John Williams Jun'r of Laurence County. appoints John Wallace of Newberry County his attorney to settle his business, dated 18 May 1793. John Williams Jun'r (Seal), Wit: John Glover, James Dyson. Proved in Newberry County by the oath of James Dyson 27 July 1793 before Robert Gillam, J.P. Recorded 6 Aug 1793.

B, 489: State of South Carolina, Newberry County. William Finch of county aforesaid for £55 sterling to Aaron Cates of same, one negro girl named Tilles about ten years old, likely and well grown, 1 Feb 1793. William Finch (Seal), Wit: Alex'r Bookter, Peter Stalay. Proved in open court 29 July 1793 by the oath of Alexander Bookter. Recorded 6 Aug 1793.

B, 490: William Riddel of Parish of St. Thomas, Orange County, planter, for affection to my daughter Jennet Sheppard of province of South Carolina, a negro girl named Fellice, 22 Aug 1771. William Riddel (Seal), Acknowledged in a court held for Orange County, Thursday 22 Aug 1771 by said William Riddle. George Taylor, C.C. Recorded 6 Aug 1793. [While the province is not stated in this deed, St. Thomas Parish was in Orange County, Virginia.]

B, 491-492: South Carolina, Ninety Six District. 22 June 1793, John Eleman of Newberry County and Mary his wife to Aron Milles of same, for £30 sterling, 100 acres on waters of Saluda River, granted to said John Eleman 31 Aug 1774, recorded in Book M. No. 13, page 327. John Eleman (Seal), Mary

Eleman (mark) (Seal), Wit: John Harbert (H), Lydia Harbert (mark), Rebecah Mills. Proved in Newberry County 20 July 1793 by the oath of John Harbert before Mercer Babb, J.P. Recorded 8 Aug 1793.

B, 492-493: To whom it may Concern. Be it known that I, Judith Edmundson, have Received full & ample satisfaction for a Certain Annual Living allowed me by Caleb Edmonson (deceased) coming from the estate of Jacob Edmonson (decd) wherein Jacob Duckett is bound for the payment & do desire that the bond may be given to James Campbell as his right & property, 10 May 1791. Judith Edmonson (X). Proved by the oath of John Speak 30 July 1793 before Edw'd Finch, J.P. Recorded 20 Aug 1793.

B, 493-494: 18 Feb 1793, Godsend Ruff, planter, & Elizabeth his wife of Newberry County, to Walter Goodman of same, for £42 s10 sterling, 100 acres surveyed for Godsend Ruff 17 Sept 1771 (but by mistake of the Deputy Surveyor entered in the Surveyor Generals Office as Godsend Tufts) adj. Christian Ruff, Joseph Sellers, Adam Sellers. Godsend Ruff (R) (Seal), Elizabeth Ruff (8) (Seal), Wit: Alexander Glenn, John Morris, William Craige. Proved in Newberry County by the oath of William Craig 27 July 1793 before Reuben Sims, J.P. Recorded 21 Aug 1793.

B, 495-499: Lease and release. 12 & 13 June 1792, Isaiah Shirer of Ninety Six District, planter, to Simeon Elizer of Lexington County, for £150 sterling, 200 acres in two separate tracts, the first of 100 acres granted to John McClean on Broad River granted 19 Nov 1772, adj. Martin Shirer, John Peterman, John Gotsman, Mathias Wicker; the other tract of 200 acres above Saxegotha Township on SW of Broad River, granted 16 Oct 1752. Isaiah Shirer (Seal), Elizabeth Shirer (X) (Seal), Wit: John Vanlew, John Hutchison, Jesse Buchanan. Acknowledged in Newberry County by Isaiah Shirer before David Ruff, J.P. Recorded 20 Aug 1793.

B, 499-501: 27 July 1793, Ephram Liles Jun'r and Mildred his wife of Newberry County to Josiah Gorrey of same, for £150 sterling, 150 acres on south side of Enoree River in Ninety Six District, part of 550 acres granted to John Green Sen'r (decd) 10 Jan 1775 and recorded in Book GGG, page 167 and give by said Green to his son John Green Junr (decd) by will who in his lifetime disposed of said land to Ephraim Liles Junr, adj. Allin's line, James Kelly's land, William Wadlington's, except seven acres to James Kelly laid out at the upper end of said line). Ephram Liles (Seal), Mildred Liles (X) (Seal), Wit: Wm. Calmes, Johnson Fergason (X), John Gore. Proved in Newberry County by the oath of Johnson Ferguson 27 July 1793 before Reuben Sims, J.P. Recorded 21 Aug 1793.

B, 501-502: 14 Feb 1793, Robert Gilliam and Mary his wife of Ninety Six District, for £300 sterling to Capt. John Wallace of same, 200 acres, part of 350 acres granted to Henry Coats 19 Nov 1772 and conveyed by him to Robert Gilliam 10 Feb 1770 on a small creek of Saluda River called Goose Pond Creek adj. land of Joseph Freeman. Robert Gilliam (Seal), Mary Gilliam (mark) (Seal), Wit: Isham Mitchell, Randolph Robinson, Danl Dyson. Proved in Newberry County 29 July 1793 by the oath of Daniel Dyson before Mercer Babb, J.P. Plat included dated 17 June 1793 by William Caldwell, D. S., showing adjacent land owners David Caldwell, Henry Hasel, John Glover. Recorded 23 Aug 1793.

B, 503-504: 29 Oct 1792, Moses Embree of Washington County, Territories South of the River Ohio, planter, to Robert Gilliam of Newberry County, SC, planter, for £45 SC money, 100 acres on north side of Saluda River on waters of Mudlick Creek, adj. John Towls, granted to James McCool 31 Oct 1769 and conveyed by James McCool to Moses Embree 19 Sept 1771. Moses Embree (Seal), Margret Embree (Seal), Wit: John Embree, Samuel Duncan, Thomas Montgomery. Recorded 23 Aug 1793.

B, 504-507: Lease and release. 31 Aug & 1 Sept 1778, Henry Anderson of Ninety Six District, SC, planter, & Ruth his wife, to Mathew Hall, weaver for £500 SC money, 100 acres on a branch of Second Creek or Williams Creek called the mill branch, adj. land of James Murphy but afterwards granted to James Warden, Wm. Wadlington, Thomas Crossen, Abraham Anderson, tract was originally granted 2 May 1770 to Henry Anderson, recorded in Book EEE, page 322. Henry Anderson (Seal), Ruth Anderson (Seal), Wit: Jas Lindsey, Nathan Brown, John Baggs. Proved 7 Sept 1778 by the oath of James Lindsey before John Lindsey, J.P. Recorded 23 Aug 1793.

B, 508-509: 1 Oct 1792, Robert Kennady of Union County, SC, taylor, to Benjamin Hampton, planter, of Newberry County, for £20 sterling, 250 acres on waters of Enoree River granted to John Swint, on Foster Branch, adj. Isaac Pennington, Samuel Chandler. Robert Kennady (Seal), Wit: Edward Finch, Martha Finch (mark), Ballard Finch. Recorded 24 Aug 1793.

B, 509: Newberry County. Jacob Chandler for £1000 sterling to Israel Chamber, six head of horses, twelve horned cattle, two stills, a house clock, one waggon and harness, all farming articles and household furniture. Jacob Chandler (Seal), Wit: Onslow Barrott, Ruth Ellis. Proved in Newberry County by the oath of Onslow Barrott 22 Aug 1793 before Providence Williams. Recorded 27 Aug 1793.

B, 510-512: 17 May 1792, James Kennady, Esquire, Late Sheriff of Charleston District, to Robert Kennedy, whereas Lewis Ogier by his bond dated 20 July 1784 became bound to William Herriott, and said Herriott did implead in the court of common pleas, by a writ of fieri facias said Sheriff sells for £5 s4 d2 tract of 250 acres in Craven County on waters of Enoree River on Foster Branch adj. land of Samuel Chandler, Isaac Penington, Isaac Lindsey, granted to John Swint 4 May 1775. James Kennedy (Seal), Wit: Thomas Ogier, Jacob Strobel. Acknowledged in the City of Charleston by James Kennedy, Esquire, 17 May 1792 before John Sandford Dart, J.P., Q.U. Recorded 27 Aug 1793.

B, 513-515: Lease and release. 10 Aug 1792, John Satterwhite, planter, of Ninety Six District, to Alexander McKie of same, for £150 SC money, 200 acres on Mudlick Creek adj. land of Josiah Burton, Isaac Mitchell, John Satterwhite, part of 500 acres granted to John Satterwhite 2 April 1773. John Satterwhite (Seal), Wit: John Satterwhite Jun'r, Drury Satterwhite, Robert Gillam Sen'r. Recorded 28 Aug 1793.

B, 516-518: Lease and release. 7 & 8 Nov 1790, Robert Johnston & Elizabeth his wife, planter, to Alexander Chambers of same, for £100 sterling, 150 acres on a small draft of Enoree adj. land of Jacob Pennington, Zachariah Sparks. Robert Johnston (Seal), Elizabeth Johnston (X) (Seal), Wit: Robert Mars, William Chambers, Thomas McCracken, Edward Finch J.P. Acknowledged by Robert Johnston and wife before Edward Finch, J.P. Recorded 29 Aug 1793.

B, 519-520: 28 Jan 1793, Samuel Saxon, Esq., Sheriff of Ninety Six District, to Wm. Thomas Linton of Newberry County, whereas said wm Thomas Linton lately at the court of common pleas at Cambridge entered up a judgement against John Robison Sen'r, and by writ of fieri facias now sells for £10 s10 sterling, 397 acres on waters of Enoree River adj. Robert Wilson. S. Saxon Shff (Seal), Wit: William Jones, Joshua Downs, L. Wilson. Proved by the oath of William Jones 19 Jan 1793 before Edw'd Finch, J. P. Recorded 30 Aug 1793.

B, 521-523: Lease and release. 10 & 12 Apr 1785, John Johnston, planter, of Ninety Six District, to Robert Johnston of same, for £300 SC money, 150 acres on a small draft of Enoree adj. land of Jacob Pennington, Zachariah Sparks. John Johnston (II) (Seal), Wit: Saml Murray, James Murray, William Murray. Proved in Newberry County by the oath of Samuel Murray 3 June 1793 before Edward Finch, J.P. Recorded 3 Sept 1793.

B, 524-525: 4 April 1793, Robert Gilliam, Esqr., and Mary Gillam his wife of Ninety Six District, to John Glover, planter, of same, for £200 sterling, 363 acres in two tracts in Newberry County on Goose Pond Creek, waters of Saluda, adj. Robert Gillam, Daniel Clark, David Caldwell, John Wallace, John Towles, granted to Henry Coats 1772 and conveyed to said Gillam 10 Feb 1773 and part from a tract granted to Joseph Freeman, 250 acres conveyed by Freeman to said Gillam 18 May 1773. Robert Gillam Senr (Seal), Mary Gillam (X) (Seal), Wit: John Satterwhite Sen'r, John Caldwell Jun'r, John Wallace. Proved 29 July 1793 by the oath of John Satterwhite Sen'r before Mercer Babb, J.P. Recorded 4 Sept 1793.

B, 525-527: Lease and release. 30 Dec 1788, David Martin of Ninety Six District to John Worthington of same, for £10 sterling, 150 acres on Saluda River adj. David Martin, part of 300 acres granted to Henry Bradshaw 9 Jan 1755. David Martin (Seal), Martha Martin (X) (Seal), Wit: David Clary, Chesley Davis, E. Worthington. Proved in Newberry County by the oath of Chesley Davis 6 March 1790 before Thos. W. Waters, J.P. Recorded 5 Sept 1793.

B, 528-530: Lease and release. 5 & 6 Aug 1791, John Worthington of Newberry County to Benjamin Worthington of same, for £60 sterling, 78 acres, part of 300 acres granted to Henry Bradshaw 9 Jan 1755 adj. David Martin. John Worthington (Seal), Wit: Jacob Toland, Rhoda Babb, Phillip Sligh (mark). Proved in Newberry County by the oath of Jacob Toland 6 Aug 1791 before Thos. W. Waters, J.P. Recorded 6 Sept 1793.

B, 531-532: 13 Jan 1792, James Luster of Newberry County to Isaac Luster of same, for £50 sterling, 89 acres, part of 365 acres granted to James Luster 1 Feb 1787. James Luster (mark) (Seal), Wit: James Johnson, Abner Luster (X). Proved in Newberry County by the oath of James Johnson 19 Aug 1793 before Peter Julien, J.P. Recorded 9 Sept 1793.

B, 533-535: 3 & 4 May 1793, Col. Philimon Waters of Newberry County to James Lester Jun'r of same, for £60 sterling, 100 acres granted to James Morehead 12 Aug 1768, recorded in Book DDD, page 392, on Saluda River conveyed to said P. Waters from James Morehead, also 8½ acre, part of 500 acres granted to Wm Mazyck in 1772 and sold to said Phillimon Waters. P. Waters (Seal), Wit: James Lowery (O), William Auglar. Proved in Newberry County by the oath of William Taylor 16 Aug 1793 before Peter Julin, J.P. Recorded 15 Sept 1793.

B, 536-537: 22 Sept 1787, William Greenwood of Charleston, SC, merchant, to John Abernathy of Newberry County, planter, for £11 s10 sterling, 100 acres granted to Cathrine Pilckney on Bush River. William Greenwood (Seal), Wit: Edw'd Lowndes, William Turpin, Samuel Morris, James Abernathy. Proved by the oath of James Abernathy 6 April 1789 before Mercer Babb, J.P. Recorded 11 Sept 1793.

B, 537-539: 1 Dec 1787, John Abernathy of Newberry County, planter, to Isaac Toland of same, for £23 s2 d10 sterling, 100 acres granted to Cathrine Pilckney on Bush River 11 Jan 1759. John Abernathy (Seal), Rhoda Abernathy (X) (Seal), Wit: Mercer Babb, Samuel Pearson, Moses Lindsey. Proved by the oath of Mercer Babb before Providence Williams, J.P., 30 July ____. Recorded 12 Sept 1793.

B, 539-540: 15 Dec 1790, Isaac Toland of Newberry County to Stephen Williams of same, for £50 sterling, 100 acres granted to Cathrine Pilckney on Bush River 11 Jan 1759. Isaac Toland (Seal), Rachel Toland (Seal), Wit: John Levett, William Cole, James Cole. Proved 29 July 1791 by the oath of James Cole before Mercer Babb, J.P. Recorded 13 Sept 1793.

[there is no page numbered 541]

B, 542-544: 20 Dec 1790, Frederick Fraser of Charleston District to James Waldrop of Ninety Six District, for £57 sterling, 550 acres in Craven County on south side Enoree River adj. land of Joseph Waldrop, James Hall, Joseph Peterson, Luke Waldrop, granted 2 April 1772 to William Williamson deceased, formerly of the state afs'd, and conveyed by him to Frederick Fraser 20 & 21 Dec 1790. Fred'k Fraser (Seal), Wit: Ed'd Rutledge Jun'r, Solomon Waldrop, Samuel Waldrop. Proved in Newberry County by the oath of Samuel Waldrop 29 July 1793 before Mercer Babb, J.P. Recorded 17 Sept 1793.

B, 544-547: Lease and release. 1 & 2 April 1791, Joshua Teague, son and heir at law of Elijah Teague, deceased, of said county, to John Belton of same, for £15 sterling, 100 acres on a small branch called Bush Creek adj. Thomas Pearson, Marmaduke Coate, Elijah Teague, part of 200 acres granted to Elijah Teague deceased 22 Feb 1771. Joshua Teague (Seal), Wit: Thos Johnston, Wm Belton, Samuel Teague. Proved 14 Sept 1793 by the oath of William Belton before Providence Williams, J.P. Recorded 17 Sept 1793.

B, 548-549: Elizabeth Pearson, widdow of William Pearson, late of East Bradford Township in Chester County, Pennsylvania, deceased, Enoch Pearson, Phebe Pearson, Mary Pearson, Solomon Sylvester, William Pearson, Jane Pearson, Sarah Pearson & Elijah Pearson, children and heirs at law of said William Pearson deceased, to appoint George Powell of Newberry County, SC, our attorney to receive of Benjamin Pearson of South Carolina, formerly of Chester County, Pennsylvania, all sums of money due to us in right of our late father, said William Pearson, from said Benjamin Pearson, dated 23 July 1793. Jane Pearson (Seal), Elizabeth Pearson (mark) (Seal), Enoch Pearson (Seal), Phebe Pearson (Seal), William Pearson (Seal), Solomon Sylvester (Seal), Sarah Pearson (Seal), Elijah Pearson (Seal), Wit: Caleb Boldwin, Zeniah Wollerton. Certified that Caleb Boldwin who was administrator of the goods and chattels of William Pearson, late of East Bradford Township, Chester County, Pennsylvania, deceased at an orphans court 18 March 1793, made a final settlement. Benjamin Jacobs. Recorded 18 Sept 1793.

B, 550-552: Lease and release. 14 & 15 Feb 1772, John Sims of Craven County, SC, planter, to Henry Butler of same, for £100 SC money, 350 acres in Berkly County on waters of Little River adj. Robert Johnson, Charles Crow, Thomas Edghill, granted to John Sims 27 Sept 1769. John Sims (Seal), Wit: James Goggans, James Campbell, George Goggans. Proved by the oath of James Goggans before John Caldwell, J. P. for Ninety Six District, 23 Dec 1773. Proved in Newberry County by the oath of George Goggans 27 Sept 1793 before J. R. Brown, J. N. C. Recorded 1 Oct 1793.

B, 553-555: 29 Oct 1792, Moses Embree of Washington County, Territories South of the River Ohio, planter, to Robert Gilliam of Newberry County, SC, planter, for £45 SC money, 100 acres on north side of Saluda River on waters of Mudlick Creek, adj. John Towls, granted to James McCool 31 Oct 1769 and conveyed by James McCool to Moses Embree 19 Sept 1771. Moses Embree (Seal), Margret Embree (Seal), Wit: John Embree, Samuel Duncan, Thomas Montgomery. Proved by the oath of Samuel Dunkin before J. R. Brown, J. N. C., 20 July 1793. Recorded 15 Oct 1793. [This deed is also recorded in Deed Book B, pages 503-504.]

B, 555-556: State of South Carolina, Newberry County. Jonathan Neail for love and affection to my beloved sons Jonathan Neail & Lewis Neail, 230 acres in said county, Jonathan is to have the north side of the said land and Lewis is to have the south side, dated 30 Oct 1793. Jonothan Neail (Seal), Wit: Providence Williams, Isaac Taylor, John Williams. Proved 30 Oct 1793 by the oath of Isaac Taylor before Providence Williams, J.P. Recorded 2 Nov 1793.

B, 557: 26 Feb 1793, Newberry County. William Smith of Newberry County to William Crow of same, for £9 sterling, one gray horse, one brown mare, one dun cow and yearling marked on Joseph Kelly's mark, one feather bed and furniture, one kettle and pot, one half dozen of delf plates and one half dozen of pewter plates, two men's saddles, one shovel plow and two axes. William Smith (Seal), Wit: Thomas Richard, John Johnston. Proved 27 Feb 1793 by the oath of Thomas Richards before Providence Williams, J.P. Recorded 26 Nov 1793.

B, 558-560: Lease and release. 22 & 23 Oct 1792, Jacob Mourer, planter, of Newberry County, to Zetna[?] Reckana Mourer of same, for £20 sterling, 75 acres, half of 150 acres in Berkley County on a small branch of Hallmans Creek, granted 28 Jan 1771, recorded in Book EEE, page 461. Jacob Mourer (IM) (Seal), Wit: Michael Dickert Sen'r, Peter Dickert, George Dickert. Proved in Newberry County by the oath of Michael Dickert Sen'r 23 Oct 1792 before David Ruff, J.P.

B, 561-563: Lease and release. 22 & 23 Oct 1792, Jacob Mourer, planter, of Newberry County, to Elizabeth Catherina Mourer, spinster, of same, for £20 sterling, 75 acres, half of 150 acres in Berkley County on a small branch of Hallmans Creek, granted 28 Jan 1771, recorded in Book EEE, page 461. Jacob Mourer (IM) (Seal), Wit: Michael Dickert Sen'r, Peter Dickert, George Dickert. Proved in Newberry County by the oath of Michael Dickert Sen'r 23 Oct 1792 before David Ruff, J.P.

B, 564-565: 23 Oct 1792, Jacob Mourer, planter, of Newberry County, to loving daughters Zitna Reckana Mourer and Elizabeth Catherina Mourer, spinsters, of same, acknowledged that I have conveyed to them each 75 acres, half of 150 acres, now give to them all my goods, household stuff and furniture, implements, cattle, horses, etc. Jacob Mourer (IM) (Seal), Wit: Michael Dickert Sen'r, Peter Dickert, George Dickert. Proved in Newberry County by the oath of Michael Dickert Sen'r 23 Oct 1792 before David Ruff, J.P.

B, 565: 30 Sept 1793, William Morrow, planter, of Newberry County, and Elizabeth Austin of same, said Elizabeth Austin doth bind her daughter Delaney Austin to serve until she reaches age 18, and at the expiration of the term to give her a bed and furniture, and all decent apparel and produce, etc., bound in the penal sum of £100 sterling. William Morrow (Seal), Elizabeth Austin (X) (Seal), Wit: Robert Gillam, J.P. Recorded 29 Nov 1793.

B, 566-567: __ April 1793, Samuel Saxon, Sheriff of ninety Six District, Laurence County, to David Johnston, whereas Joachim Bulow entered upon a judgment against William Goggans, in the court of common pleas, and by a writ of fieri facias, said Sheriff sells for £16 sterling, 100 acres granted 1 May 1771 and 15½ acres part of 150 acres granted to Robert Johnston deceased, on Sandy Run, waters of Bush River & Saluda, sold by Joseph Smith and Elizabeth his wife to William Goggans 4 Dec 1777. S. Saxon, S 96 D (Seal), Wit: John Trotter, Thomas Pitts (X). Proved 28 Oct 1793 by the oath of Thomas Pitts before Providence Williams, J.P. Recorded 29 Nov 1793.

B, 568-569: 1 March 1775, Robert Stark, Sheriff of Ninety Six District, to Charles King of Kings Creek, whereas Joseph Davis was seized of a tract of 250 acres and whereas William Glenn the Elder and William Glen the younger, merchants in Charles Town, did in the court of common pleas at January Term 1774 obtain judgment against said Joseph Davis, now by writ of fieri facias, sells for £100 s14, 150 acres on a small spring branch of Kings Creek. Robert Stark, Sheriff (Seal), Wit: Phillip Singleton, John Munford. Proved by the oath of Phillip Singleton before Moses Kirkland, J.P., 6 March 1775. Recorded 30 Nov 1793.

B, 570-571: 30 March 1793, John McDaniel & Nelly his wife of Edgefield County, SC, for £30 sterling, to Beverly Courrum of same, 100 acres on north side Big Saluda River adj. Christopher Cains, Taits, and Crooks. John McDaniel (Seal), Elender McDaniel (X) (Seal), Wit: Jesse Wilson, Simon Beach (mark), Joshua Warren (X). Proved in Edgefield County 30 March 1793 by the oath of Simon Beach before Russell Wilson, J.P. Recorded 2 Dec 1793.

B, 572-574: Lease and release. 28 & 29 Aug 1790, Daniel Blackburn of Burk County, Georgia, to William Blackburn of Ninety Six District, Newberry County, for £50 sterling, 100 acres granted to William Blackburn deceased & fell to aid Daniel Blackburn, the surviving heir at law 2 Aug 1768, recorded in Book CCC, page 300, on a branch of Indian Creek called Long Branch, adj. land of James Bonds, John James. Daniel Blackburn (Seal), Wit: John Garriott (mark), Ignatius Garriott, John Garriott Jun'r (mark). Proved 10 Sept 1791 by the oath of John Garriott Jun'r before Providence Williams, J.P. Recorded 2 Dec 1793.

B, 575-577: Lease and release. 1 & 2 April 1789, William Irby and Henritter his wife of Newberry County to Joseph Towles of Edgefield County, for £50 sterling, 102 acres on north side of Saluda River on waters of Little River, part of tract granted 7 Nov 1785, recorded in Book 4F, page 469. William Irby (Seal), Henritter Irby (+) (Seal), Wit: Zach Smith Brooks, Thomas Eastland, John Adkinson (X). Proved in Newberry County 12 Oct 1793 by the oath of John Atkinson before Robert Gilliam, J.P. Recorded 4 Dec 1793.

B, 578: John Horning of Newberry County, weaver, for love, good will and affection to my loving step children John Brecht and Elizabeth Brecht, 150 acres on Bear Creek adj. land of John Hipp, part of 300 acres granted to Daniel Stagner 8 Oct 1775, dated 22 Nov 1793. John Horning (X) (Seal), Wit: William Houseal, Michael Kubler, John Kubler. Proved in Lexington County by the oath of William Houseal 3 Dec 1793 before John A. Summer, J.P. Recorded 11 Dec 1793.

B, 579: John Horning of Newberry County, weaver, for love, good will and affection to my loving wife Elizabeth Catherina and my loving child Catherina Horning, 150 acres adj. land of Henry Summer, granted to Fredrick Shefffer 5 Sept 1770, dated 22 Nov 1793. John Horning (X) (Seal), Wit: William Houseal, Michael Kubler, John Kubler. Proved in Lexington County by the oath of William Houseal 3 Dec 1793 before John A. Summer, J.P. Recorded 11 Dec 1793.

B, 580-581: Lease and mortgage. 16 & 17 Apr 1793, Benjamin Long & Priscilla Long his wife, planter, of Newberry County, to George Latham, merchant, for £129 s9 d11 SC money, mortgage of 250 acres on north side Saluda River, granted to William Turner 15 May 1751. Benj'a Long (Seal), Priscilla Long (+) (Seal), Wit: Samuel Kelly Sen'r, John Abernathy. Proved 19 Dec 1793 by the affirmation of Samuel Kelley before Mercer Babb, J.P. Recorded 24 Dec 1793.

B, 582-584: Lease and mortgage. 28 & 29 Apr 1793, John Turner of Newberry County, farmer, to George Latham, merchant, for £120 SC money, mortgage of 200 acres on north side Saluda River, granted to Richard Hampton 8 Aug 1753 and conveyed by him to William Turner and is the land where John Turner now lives. John Turner (I) (Seal), Francis Turner (mark) (Seal), Wit: Samuel Kelly Sen'r, John Kelly Sen'r. Proved 19 Dec 1793 by the affirmation of Samuel Kelly Sen'r before Mercer Babb, J.P. Recorded 24 Dec 1793.

B, 585-586: 6 July 1793, Mary Kelly, widow, of Charleston District, to John Loner of Newberry County, planter, for £50, 100 acres granted to Luesa Scheckem 19 Feb 1770 and recorded in Book EEE, page 333, on the big branch of south fork in Craven County adj. land of Johannes Andrews Mitchell, Jacob Webber. Mary Kelly (Seal), Wit: John Sebben, John Adam Summer. Proved in Orangeburgh District by the oath of Major John Adam Summer 23 Dec 1793 before John Hampton, J. Q. Recorded 26 Dec 1793.

B, 587: 23 Jan 1783 [sic], Henry Wilson of Newberry County to David Johnston of same, for £30 sterling, 32 acres surveyed for him 18 July 1787 on waters of Saluda adj. Hamilton Murdock, William Goggans, William Caldwell. Henry Wilson (Seal), Wit: Walter West, William Goggans, W. Swift. Proved in Newberry County 9 Oct 1793 by the oath of Walter West before Providence Williams, J.P. Recorded 26 Dec 1793.

B, 588-590: Lease and release. 1 & 2 Oct 1784, John Dominic Sen'r of Ninety Six District, Planter, to Elizabeth Dominic, his wife, spinster, for £50 sterling, tract granted to said John Dominic 30 Oct 1752 for 150 acres on a branch of

Broad River, adj. George Stoudemyer, George Eigleberger, Conrad Road. John Dominic (Seal), Wit: John Eiglebarger, William Houseal. Proved by the oath of John Eiglebarger 10 Oct 1784 before William Houseal, J.P. Recorded 27 Dec 1793.

B, 591-594: Lease and release. 9 Dec 1793, Daniel McNeel of State of Georgia to Bartlett Brooks of Newberry County, SC, for £200 sterling, 300 acres in three separate tracts: 150 acres on Mudlick Creek granted 13 May 1768 to Henry Dukes and conveyed by Henry Dukes to Daniel McNeel 22 & 23 Dec 1769; 100 acres adj. said 150 acres granted to Hamilton Murdock 12 Jan 1769 and conveyed by him to Daniel McNeel 22 & 23 Dec 1769; 50 acres granted to Henry Dukes and conveyed to Daniel McNeel at the time aforesaid adj. John Satterwhite, Benjamin Moore. Daniel McNeel (Seal), Sarah McNeel (+) (Seal), Wit: Daniel McNeel, James Marshall, Terrel Riley. Proved in Georgia by the oath of Daniel McNeel Jun'r 9 Dec 1793 before Waller Drans, J.P. Recorded 27 Dec 1793.

B, 595-597: Lease and release. 1 & 2 June 1775, Margarett Sligh of Ninety Six District, spinster, to Martin Livistone Jun'r of same, planter, for £100 SC money, 100 acres granted to Margarett Sligh 5 May 1774 on waters of Cannons Creek adj. Josiah Griffeth, Martin Liviston, Francis Witt, George Fouser. Margarett Sligh (X) (Seal), Wit: Phillip Sligh (X), Wm Houseal. Proved by the oath of Phillip Sligh 7 June 1775 before Wm. Houseal, J.P. Recorded 15 Jan 1794.

B, 598-599: 21 Dec 1793, Jariot Campbell and Sarah his wife of Newberry County to James Goggans of same, for £50 sterling, 25 acres, part of tract of 350 acres granted to Joseph Campbell deceased 2 May 1770, on the north side of s'd Jariot Campbell's spring branch adj. Daniel McKie, adj. Francis Davinport. Jariot Campbell (Seal), Sarah Campbell (mark) (Seal), Wit: George Goggans, Nimrod Goggans. Proved in Newberry County 23 Dec 1793 by the oath of Nimrod Goggans before Mercer Babb, J.P. Recorded 20 Jan 1794.

B, 600: John Price for £15 sterling to Samuel Muffet, a bay mare five years old. John Price (I) (Seal), Wit: George Brown, Adam Glazier. Proved in Newberry County by the oath of Adam Glazier 30 Dec 1793 before Edward Finch, J.P. Recorded 20 Jan 1794.

B, 601-603: 10 June 1791, William Summer of Lexington County, planter, to John Eiglebarger of Newberry County, planter, for £30 SC money, 100 acres in Newberry County on waters of Cannons Creek adj. Michael Kebler, Martin Leviston, granted to John Earnest Weaverlin 8 Dec 1774, recorded in Book GGG, page 227, and transferred 28 Jan 1777 to John Adam Menigh [Minnick] and from said John Adam Menigh to William Summer 1 & 2 June 1784. William Summer (Seal), Eva Margaretta Summer (X) (Seal), Wit: Johannes Kebler[?] [German signature], Andrew Thomas (A), Adam Lagrown (AL).

Proved in Newberry County by the oath of Andrew Thomas 19 Feb 1794 before David Ruff, J.P. Recorded 21 Jan 1794.

B, 604-607: Lease and release. 1 & 2 Sept 1786, William Houseal, planter, of Newberry County, for £25 SC money, 100 acres, part of 250 acres granted 4 July 1754 to Hans Peter Weyman, in the fork of Broad and Saluda Rivers, transferred to said William houseal 15 & 16 Sept 1774. William Houseal (Seal), Wit: Adam Lagrown (X), Mathias Reinhard (X). Proved in Newberry County by the oath of Adam Lagrown 19 Feb 1793 before David Ruff, J.P. Recorded 22 Jan 1794.

B, 608: Joseph Hampton to Robert Rutherford for £19 sterling, one half of tract granted to William Johnston for 182 acres in the District of Cambridge in Newberry County on a branch of Second Creek, dated 17 July 1793. Joseph Hampton (Seal), Wit: Stephen Kelly, Richard Darby (R), Benjamin Hampton. Proved in Newberry County by the oath of Richard Darby 11 Nov 1793 before Edward Finch, J.P. Recorded 27 Jan 1794.

B, 609: Thomas Wood of Newberry County for love, good will and affection to my son John Wood, 100 acres, part of 200 acres granted to Jacob Furger (alias Falker), and household furniture and plantation tools, dated 11 Dec 1793. Thos Wood (Seal), Wit: George Buchanan, Benjamin Buchanan, Jesse Buchanan. Proved in Newberry County by the oath of George Buchanan 21 Dec 1793 before David Ruff, J.P. Recorded 15 Feb 1794.

B, 610: Thomas Wood of Newberry County for love, good will and affection to my son Samuel Wood, 100 acres, part of 200 acres granted to Jacob Furger (alias Falker), dated 11 Dec 1793. Thos Wood (Seal), Wit: George Buchanan, Benjamin Buchanan, Jesse Buchanan. Proved in Newberry County by the oath of George Buchanan 21 Dec 1793 before David Ruff, J.P. Recorded 15 Feb 1794.

B, 611-614: South Carolina. 20 Nov 1765, Frederick Ennis of province aforesaid, and Cath'a his wife, to William Hamilton of same, tanner, for £80 SC money, 50 acres in the fork between Broad and Saluda Rivers on the south side of Enoree (otherwise Collens River) on a branch called Horse branch in Berkley County. Frederick Eheny (Seal), Catharine Eheny (X) (Seal), Wit: Daniel Stroble, Michael Doumar, Joseph Kelley (T). Proved 10 Feb 1767 by the oath of Joseph Kelly before Edward Musgrove, J.P. in Berkley County. Recorded 8 Feb 1794.

B, 615-617: Lease and release. 12 Aug 1793, Charles Patty of Newberry County to Wallis Jones of same, for £50 sterling, 100 acres granted to Charles Patty 18 May 1793 on waters of Big Creek, a branch of Saluda, adj. said Wallis Jones, Peter Hawkins, recorded in Book PPP, page 119. Charles Patty (Seal), Wit: Gray Jones (X), William Finch. Proved by the oath of Gray Jones before Peter Julien, J.P,. 22 Feb 1794. Recorded 11 March 1794.

B, 618-622: Lease and release. 27 & 28 Nov 1789, Col. Philimon Waters of Newberry County to Wallis Jones of same, for £21 s14 sterling, 70 acres on waters of Big Saluda adj. Peter Hawkins, Willis Jones, Philimon Waters, Isaac Elmore, Oratio Griffen, part of two tracts of land 54 acres being part of 150 acres granted to John Musgrove 19 June 1772 and conveyed to said Philimon Waters by John Musgrove 2 July 1775, the remainder part of tract granted to Woldrick Mires 4 Dec 1786, 530 acres. Philemon Waters (Seal), Wit: Peter Julien, Ellis Pugh. Proved in Newberry County by the oath of Ellis Pugh 10 Feb 1790 before Thos. W. Waters, J.P. Recorded 12 March 1794.

B, 622: 5 March 1795, Mr. Jacob Beiller maketh oath that his brand on all his stock of cattle is IB, Mark a Crop & Slit in one year and an upper keel in the other. Jacob Bieller (Seal), before John Hampton, J.Q. Recorded 12 March 1794.

B, 623-627: Lease and mortgage. 15 Feb 1794, Samuel Harris of Newberry County bound to James Creswell & Co., in the sum of £54 s5 d11 sterling, mortgage of 100 acres on waters of Pages Creek adj. land of Charles Gillum, Samuel Proctor. (Plat included by Patrick Cunningham, D. S.) Samuel Harris (Seal), Wit: Rich'd Watts, Elihu Creswell, L. B. [Littleberry] Harris. Proved by the oath of Rich'd Watts 4 March 1794 before J. R. Brown, J. N. C. Recorded 14 March 1794.

B, 628-629: William Hencock of Newberry County for £60 sterling to Alexander Bookter of same, a negro man named Harry about 21 years old, dated 22 March 1794. William Hencock (Seal), Wit: Peter Staley, D. Brummitt, John Mink. Proved in Newberry County by the oath of Peter Staley 22 March 1794 before Reuben Sims, J.P. Recorded 24 March 1794.

B, 629: Francis Davenport of Newberry County for £15 to James Davenport of same, one negro girl named Easther, dated 11 Dec 1792. Francis Davenport (Seal), Wit: George Goggans, Rich'd Henderson Waldrop. Proved by the oath of George Goggans 4 March 1794 before Rob't Gillam, J.P. Recorded 11 April 1794.

B, 630-631: 18 Jan 1793, John Lark died intestate and his widow Rachel Lark became the administratrix and purchaser of the whole estate, now Rachel Lark of Newberry County for £5 SC money does quit claim of all of the estate of said dec'd except one negro woman named Moll and her children Annica & Nance, two feather beds, one large trunk, one Loom & Giers, and the stock of geese, wholly unto Allen Robison, Daniel Parkins & Cullen Lark. Rach. Lark (Seal), Wit: Samuel Black, George King. Proved in Newberry County by the oath of Samuel Black before Peter Julien 3 March 1794. recorded 10 April 1794.

B, 631-632: Peter Conway of the Parish of X [Christ] Church and County of Lancaster, Virginia, to Edwin Conway of same, for £3000 gold or silver coin as current by law, the following negro slaves: Will, Dominy, Adam, Anthony,

Spencer, Isaac, Mark, Sam, Tom, Charles, Bond, Daniel, Sillah, Peter, Phill, Alie, Judy, a child unchristened, Edmund, Jesse, Siller, Polly, Jane, Weaver, Phill, Judy, Sarah, Letty, Fanny, Aron, Spencer & two children unchristened, Jeffrey, Hagan, Rachel, Nancy, Joe, Tabby, Molly, and Molly, dated 3 March 1783. Peter Conway (Seal), Wit: John Heath, Richard Selden. Proved in Ninety Six District, SC, by the oath of Richard Selden, Esqr., 30 Dec 1793 before James Mayson, J. N. C. Recorded 11 April 1794.

B, 633: Daniel McKie of Newberry County for £50 to Robert Spence, one negro man named Ben, between 28 and 30 years old, dated 2 Dec 1793. Daniel McKie (Seal), Wit: Wm Satterwhite, Samuel Lindsey, Caleb Lindsey. Proved in Newberry County by the oath of Samuel Lindsey 27 Feb 1794 before John Speake, J.P. Recorded 12 April 1794.

B, 634: Richard Selden of the State of Virginia to James Creswell of South Carolina for £36 sterling, two negro boys named Moses and Aron, dated 29 Nov 1790. Richard Selden (Seal), James Creswell (Seal), Wit: John Wallace, William Griffen. Proved in Newberry County by the oath of John Wallace 4 March 1794 before Robert Gillum, J.P. Recorded 15 April 1794.

B, 635-636: Samuel Martin of Newberry County to Daniel Dyson of same, for £60 sterling, one bay mare that I got from said Dyson branded ID, one bay mare that I got from Robertson, 15 years old known by the name of Nance, one bay horse that I got from Chiles, four years old named Starn, one pair of oxen named Buck & Berry, three cows and calves, three feather beds and furniture, two sows and 18 pigs, the wheat, rye, and spelt in the ground, dated 15 Feb 1794. Samuel Martin (Seal), Wit: Isaac Grant, Alexander McMullen. Proved in Newberry County by the oath of Alexander McMullen 20 Feb 1794 before Elisha Ford, J.P. Recorded 15 April 1794.

B, 636-637: Thomas Denson of Laurens County to John Cary Royston of same, for £15 sterling, one sorrel horse about sixteen years old, a black yearling, two sows and twenty pigs, two feather beds and furniture, one woman's saddle, and household furniture, dated 1 Feb 1794. Thomas Denson (X) (Seal), Wit: James Lindsey, William Gray, Nathan Anderson. Proved in Newberry County by the oath of Nathan Anderson 5 Feb 1794 before John Speake, J.P. Recorded 15 April 1794.

B, 638-639: Morris Fowler of Ninety Six District, for £10 sterling, to Thomas Chappell of same, one sorrel horse 12 years old, one black mare 12 years old, one red cow, heir and calf, one feather bed and furniture, one iron pot, one tea kettle, one iron kettle, etc., dated 24 Sept 1792. Maurice Fowler, Wit: Hump'y Wm Lindsey (mark), Wm Neel (X). Proved in Newberry County by the oath of William Neel 28 Feb 1794 before Robert Gillum, J.P. Recorded 15 April 1794.

B, 639-640: John Fincher of Union County bound to James Campbell of Newberry County in the penal sum of £500 SC money, 11 Sept 1790, to make deed to 125 acres known as the Edmonson place. John Fincher (X) (Seal), Wit: John Campbell, Jacob Duckett, Thomas Bishop. Recorded 15 April 1794.

B, 641-643: 22 April 1786, William Dixon of Newberry County, settlement of Gilders Creek, to Robert Dixon of same place, for £100 SC money, part of 400 acres granted to Nicholas Dixon (decd) on the head draughts of Gilders Creek, waters of Enoree, grant recorded in Book II No. 8, page 490, adj. Mary Reeder, Huffman, a line to divide the spring that is occupied by said William Dixon and Robert Dixon to include 150 acres. William Dixon (Seal), Wit: Robert Caldwell (X), James Lindsey. Proved 28 Feb 1794 by the oath of James Lindsey before Providence Williams, J.P. Recorded 16 April 1794.

B, 644-647: Whereas a marriage is intended to be shortly had between Phillimon Waters of Newberry County and Rachel Lark, widow, of same, 8 June 1793, marriage settlement, Daniel Parkins, trustee, all goods, chattels and effects of Rachel Lark for her use during the existence of said intermarriage, including one negro named Affrica. Philimon Waters (Seal), Rachel Lark (Seal), Daniel Parkins (Seal), Wit: A. Robison, Cullen Lark, Dennis Lark. Proved in Newberry County by the oath of Cullen Lark 4 March 1794 before Providence Williams, J.P. Recorded 16 April 1794.

B, 648-650: 6 Sept 1792, James Williams, planter, of Newberry County, to Thomas Gary of Laurens County, for £25 SC money, tract of land part in Newberry & part in Laurens County, granted to Providence Williams Senr 25 Oct 1772, which tract fell by heirship to James Williams, and from said James Williams Jun'r fell by heirship to present James Williams, land adj. Moses Kirkland, James Dalrymple, James Johnson, 150 acres. James Williams (Seal), Wit: John Johnson, John Williams. Proved 7 Nov 1792 by the oath of John Johnson before Providence Williams, J.P. Recorded 17 April 1794.

B, 650-652: 16 Jan 1794, William Crow, planter, of Newberry County to Thomas Gary Sen'r of same, for £75 sterling, 195 acres granted to said William Crow 6 March 1786 in Newberry County on waters of Dry branch, a branch of Bush River, recorded in Book HHHH, page 277. William Crow (Seal), Mary Crow (X), Wit: William Gary, Jonathan Reeder, Jesse Gary. Proved 27 Jan 1794 in Newberry County by the oath of William Gary before Providence Williams, J.P. Recorded 18 April 1794.

B, 652-654: 19 Feb 1793, John Caldwell Sen. & Susannah his wife of Ninety Six District to Capt. John Wallace of same, for £200 sterling, 150 acres on waters of Saluda River, part of a tract of 300 acres adj. James Dyson, Allen Cox, Richard Payne, Isaac Dyson, John Wallace, granted to Henry Hassell 9 Sept 1774 and conveyed 14 & 15 April 1785 to John Caldwell. John Caldwell Sen (Seal), Susanna Caldwell (X) (Seal), Wit: John Dyson, James Dyson, Benjamin Bunting. Proved in Newberry County by the oath of John Dyson 20 Feb 1794 before Robert Gillum, J.P. Recorded 18 April 1794.

B, 654-657: 4 March 1791, Henry Caloff of Charleston Neck, Inn Keeper, to Michael Paits [sic, for Bates?], of Ninety Six District, planter, for £20 SC money, tract at Champin Creek, adj. John Vink, 100 acres. Henry Caloff (Seal), Wit: Jos Tobias, John Kelly, Jos Tobias Jun. Proved 2 May 1793 by the oath of Joseph Tobias Jun. before Peter Bounetheau, J.Q.U. Recorded 23 April 1793.

B, 658-661: Lease and release. 1 & 2 May 1793, Hercules Daniel Bize of Charleston, to Michael Paits [sic, for Bates?], of Ninety Six District, planter, for £10 SC money, tract on Butsale and a branch of Camping Creek, adj. Michael Wingart, 500 acres in Craven County. Hercules Daniel Bize (Seal), Wit: Andrew Kreps, John Woddrop. Proved 2 May 1793 by the oath of Andrew Kreps before Peter Bounetheau, J.Q.U. Recorded 23 April 1793.

B, 661-665: Lease and release. 10 & 11 March 1791, William Hilburn Senr. of Newberry County to William Hilburn Jun'r of same, for £90 sterling, 100 acres, part of 350 acres granted to said William Hilburn Senr 25 Oct 1764 on waters of Bush River. William Hilburn (mark), Wit: David Pugh, John Summers, Robert Hilburn. Plat dated 24 Feb 1791 included showing land "laid off for William Hilburn Jun. off of the south side of his Father's old Survey." Proved in Newberry County by the oath of John Summers 17 Sept 1791 before Elisha Ford, JP. Recorded 24 April 1794.

B, 666-668: 9 April 1794, James Goggans Senr. of Newberry County to Thomas Goggans & Nancy Goggans and William Goggans & Rachel Goggans & Betty Goggans, James and Johnston Goggans & Mary Goggans & Abraham Goggans, for good & effection to his son Thomas Goggans, 150 acres of land on which I now live to be equally divided between them three, also to my son Thomas Goggans one bay mare, bridle & saddle one cow & one sow, one ewe, 100 bushels of corn on hand for £3 on William Blake; to my son William, one bay mare, bridle & Saddle, etc; to my two sons Johnson & Abraham one negro boy named Lewis to be sold when they come of age to be equally divided between the two; to my four daughters Nancy & Rachel & Betty & Mary, one feather bed & furniture apiece, also one cow & one sow and one ewe apiece, one sorrel mare to Nancy, the remainder of my household furniture to my daughter Mary. James Goggans (Seal), Wit: George Goggans, Richard Henderson Waldrop, Daniel Johnson. Proved in Newberry County by the oath of Daniel Johnson 11 April 1794 before Providence Williams, J.P. Recorded 24 April 1794.

B, 668-670: 13 March 1794. Josiah Gates, planter, of Newberry County to James Creswell & Co of same, for five shillings and for the debt of £24 s10½ dated 25 Jan 1794., mortgage of one roan mare six years old, one dark gelding, one bay filly, three head of cattle, three feather beds with homespun ticks and homemade furniture, one barr share plow, two shovels, etc. Josiah Gates (Seal), Wit: Richard Watts, William Andrew (X). Proved in Newberry County by the oath of Richard Watts 25 April 1794 before James Mayson, J. N. C. Recorded 29 April 1794.

B, 671-674: Lease and release. 16 & 17 April 1773, Frederick Glover of Ninety Six District to Thomas Eastland of same, for £300 SC money, 250 acres in Craven County adj. land of Joseph Davenport, Daniel Goggans, Johnson, John Davis, Rhodes, on Beaver Dam, a branch of Saluda River, granted to Frederick Glover 2 Feb 1773. Frederick Glover (Seal), Wit: John Beal (I), William Martin (M). Proved in Ninety Six District 16 April 1774 by the oath of William Martin before William Anderson, J.P. Recorded 29 April 1794.

B, 675-677: 4 Nov 1779, Thomas Eastland of Ninety Six District, to James Davenport of same, for £1000 SC currency, 250 acres in Craven County adj. land of Joseph Davenport, Daniel Goggans, Johnson, John Davis, Rhodes, on Beaver Dam, a branch of Saluda River, granted to Frederick Glover 2 Feb 1773. Thomas Eastland (Seal), Wit: Bartlett Satterwhite, Francis Davenport. Proved in Ninety Six District 22 March 1780 by the oath of Francis Davenport before Jo. Hays, J.P. Recorded 29 April 1794.

B, 679-680: 25 Dec 1788, Joseph Davenport & Margaret his wife of Newberry County, to James Davenport of same, planter, for £50, 100 acres adj. land of James Davenport, Joseph Davenport, part of 250 acres on waters of Little River granted to Daniel Goggans 7 April 1770 and by several conveyances became Francis Davenport and conveyed by Francis Davenport unto Joseph Davenport 14 & 15 Feb 1786. Joseph Davenport (Seal), Margret Davenport (mark) (Seal), Wit: William Caldwell, James Caldwell, Harris Gillam. Proved 6 Dec 1789 before William Caldwell, J.P., by the oath of Harris Gillam. Recorded 6 May 1794.

B, 681-683: 26 June 1777, Francis Davenport of Berkley County to James Davenport, planter, of same, for £50, 100 acres part of 250 acres on waters of Little River granted to Daniel Goggans 7 April 1770 and from him to Francis Davenport and conveyed by Francis Davenport unto Joseph Davenport 14 & 15 Feb 1786 [sic]. Francis Davenport (Seal), Wit: Bartlett Satterwhite, John Boyd. Proved 25 March 1779 by the oath of Bartlett Satterwhite before John Satterwhite, J.P. Recorded 6 May 1794.

B, 683: 31 Dec 1791, James Liles & Chloe Liles of SC to Jno H. Ruff of same, for £87 sterling, one negro fellow named Daniel. James Liles (T) (Seal), Chloe Liles (mark) (Seal), Wit: David Ruff. Recorded 6 May 1794.

B, 684-687: Lease and release. 22 & 23 Aug 1788, William Ancrum of Charleston, SC, to Jacob Ayres of said state, for £40, 100 acres, half of tract of 200 acres granted to Thomas Golden on Bush Creek adj. land of John Milhouse, William Coate, Samuel Kelly. William Ancrum (seal), wit: John Purvis, R. Lithgow. Proved 15 Feb 1791 by the oath of Robert Lithgow before Peter Freneau, J.P. Recorded 7 May 1794.

B, 687-688: 6 Nov 1793, Clement Davis Jun. of Newberry County, planter, to Jonathan Reeder of same, for £50 sterling, 100 acres on a branch called the Beaver Dam of Bush River, adj. William Mossaick, Wm. Winchester, granted

17 Aug 1772, recorded in Book LLL, page 268. Clement Davis (Seal), Wit: Onslow Barrett, Thomas Wood, Jonathan Chandler. Proved by the oath of Jonathan Chandler 13 Nov 1793 before Providence Williams, J.P. Recorded 7 May 1794.

B, 689-692: Lease and release. 23 & 24 April 1793, Jacob Ayres of Newberry County to Michael Gore of same, for £60 SC money, 100 acres, half of tract of 200 acres granted to Thomas Golden on Bush Creek adj. land of John Milhouse, William Coate, Samuel Kelly. Jacob Ayres (Seal), Jenesent Ayres (X) (Seal), Wit: James Riley, Edmund Lindsey Jun. Proved in Newberry County 5 May 1794 by the oath of Edmund Lindsey Jun. before John Speake, J.P. Recorded 7 May 1794.

B, 692-694: 1 Jan 1791, Anna Barbara Loner (alias Gromer or Groener) of Lexington County, SC, widow, to John Houseal, planter, for £60 sterling, 100 acres on south side Tyger River in Berkley County adj. land of John Pearson, granted to said Anna Barbara Groener or Gromer 14 June 1763 on the Bounty. Anna Barbara Loner (X), Wit: Benedict Mayer, J. A. Houseal. Proved in Orangeburgh District by the oath of John Adam Houseal 20 Jan 1794 before John Adam Summer, J.P. Recorded 8 May 1794.

B, 694-695: 15 Dec 1793, Clement Davis Jun. of Newberry County, planter, to Jonathan Reeder of same, for £20 sterling, 238 acres on Beaver Dam of Bush River, adj. William Reeder, William McMorris, Charles Crow, Clement Davis, Elizabeth Hunt, recorded in Book E No 5, page 405. Clement Davis (Seal), Wit: Andrew Fitts, John Coppock, Thomas Wood, Jonathan Chandler. Proved in Newberry County by the oath of Jonathan Chandler 19 April 1794 before Providence Williams, J.P. Recorded 8 May 1794.

B, 696-701: Lease and mortgage. 21 & 22 Feb 1794, John Glover of Newberry County to Thomas Wadsworth & William Turpin, merchants, bound in the penal sum of £153 sterling, mortgage of 363 acres on waters of Saluda River adj. land of Robert Gillam Senr, Daniel Clark, David Caldwell, John Wallace, John Towles part of tract granted to Joseph Freeman, conveyed by Freeman to Robert Gillam Sen'r 18 & 19 May 1773, including a tract granted to Henry Coates in 1772 conveyed by Coats to Robert Gillam Sen. John Glover (Seal), Wit: Dan: Symmes. Proved by the oath of Daniel Symmes 5 April 1794 before Robert Gillam, J.P. Recorded 10 May 1794.

B, 701-703: 1 Jan 1794, Bartlitt Brooks of Newberry County bound to Thomas Wadsworth and William Turpin, merchants, of same, negro fellow Abram about 35 years of age, a negro wench Mary about 25 years of age, Suck about five years of age, David three years of age & Sam, sold for the payment of £259 s6 d5 by bond dated 1 Jan 1794 in the penal sum of £518 s12 d10. Bartlitt Brooks (X), Wit: Dan: Symmes. Proved by the oath of Daniel Symmes 5 April 1794 before Robert Gillam, J.P. Recorded 12 May 1794.

B, 704-709: Lease and mortgage. 31 Dec 1793 & 1 Jan 1794, Bartlitt Brooks of Newberry County bound to Thomas Wadsworth and William Turpin, merchants, of same, by bond dated 1 Jan 1794 in the penal sum of £518 s12 d10, mortgage of 200 acres on Mudlick Creek, a branch of Little River, consisting of two surveys whereon said Bartlitt Brooks now lives: one granted to Henry Duke 13 May 1768, the other granted to Henry Duke 2 May 1770, and conveyed by Henry Duke to Daniel McNeil in 1769 and by said McNeil to Bartlitt Brooks. Bartlitt Brooks (X), Wit: Dan: Symmes, John Garvin. Proved by the oath of Daniel Symmes 5 April 1794 before Robert Gillam, J.P. Recorded 12 May 1794.

B, 709-710: 14 Dec 1793, James Campbell of Newberry County, SC, to John Hughs of same, for £16 sterling, 75 acres adj. land of James Hughes, Andrew Hipp, John Hipp, John Swinford. James Campbell (Seal), Wit: Edmond Lindsey, George Hughs (G), George White Hughs (O). Proved in Newberry County by the oath of George W. Hughs 16 May 1794 before John Speake, J.P. Recorded 28 May 1794.

B, 711-715: Lease and release. 9 & 10 Dec 1768, Francis Davis, planter, of Berkley County, SC, to John Adkins of same, planter, for £200 SC money, 300 acres in Berkley County on a branch of Enoree River called Kings Creek, granted to said Francis Davis 29 April 1768. Francis Davis (Seal), Margret Davis (Seal), Wit: Francis Adkins, William Adkins (H), Benjamin Adkins (B). Proved in Berkly County by the oath of Francis Adkins 27 Feb 1775 before Thomas Wadlington, J.P. Recorded 28 May 1794.

B, 716-717: Thomas Rowley, carpenter, of Newberry County to William Logan, planter, of same, for £30 sterling for two years work and some money, a certain sorrel horse about nine years old branded on the mounting shoulder S, a sorrel mare big with foal branded TW, with a new saddle and all the household furniture, dated 17 May 1794. Thomas Rowly (Seal), Wit: Michael Johnson, <u>Joseph</u> Elliot. Proved by the oath of <u>Josiah</u> Elliott 28 May 1794 before Providence Williams, J.P. Recorded 29 May 1794.

B, 717-722: Lease and release. 18 & 19 Aug 1775, John Adkins, planter, of Ninety Six District, and Sarah his wife, to Charles Wilson of same, planter, for £100 SC money, 300 acres in Berkley County on a branch of Enoree River called Kings Creek, granted to Francis Davis 29 April 1768, conveyed by Francis Davis and Margaret his wife to John Adkins 10 Dec 1768. John Adkins (X), Sarah Adkins (mark) (Seal), Wit: James Wilson, William Sims, John Armstrong. Proved 19 Feb 1775 by the oath of James Wilson before John Johnson, J.P. Recorded 29 May 1794.

B, 723-727: Lease and release. 10 & 11 Jan 1786, Charles Wilson of Kings Creek in Newberry County, weaver, to Richard Tear of same, for £50 sterling, 100 acres, part of 300 acres granted to Francis Davis 29 April 1768, conveyed by Francis Davis and Margaret his wife to John Adkins 10 Dec 1768, and by John Adkins and his wife Sarah to Charles Wilson 18 & 19 Aug 1775 on north side of Kings Creek adj. John Armstrong. Charles Wilson (Seal), Elizabeth Wilson (mark) (Seal), Wit: William Grey, Robert Brown, James Lindsey. Proved 5 ___ 1787 by the oath of James Lindsey before John Lindsey, J.P. Recorded 30 May 1794.

B, 728-730: 12 Sept 1792, Samuel Clowney of Union County, Pinckney District, SC, to Samuel Lindsey of Newberry County, Ninety Six District, SC, for £70 sterling, 100 acres granted to Samuel Clowney 6 April 1768 on a small branch of Kings Creek, adj. Gabriel Anderson, John Lindsey, recorded in Book DDD, page 42. Samuel Clowney (Seal), Wit: James Campbell, James Lindsey, John Anderson. Proved 19 May 1794 in Newberry County by the oath of James Campbell before John Speake, J.P. Recorded 30 May 1794.

B, 730-733: Lease and mortgage. 6 & 7 April 1794, Benjamin Cobb of Ninety Six District, Newberry County, to Mercer Babb, Esqr., of same, bound in the sum of £32 for the payment of £16, mortgage of 400 acres below the line on the north side of Saluda River, granted 7 Nov 1785. Benjamin Cobb (Seal), Wit: Jude Stidman, Catharine Eutes, Mercer Wadlington. Proved by the oath of Catharine Eutes 2 May 1794 before Peter Julien, J.P. Recorded 3 May 1794.

B, 734-739: Lease and release. 26 & 27 Nov 1774, John Baptist Tear of Province of SC, to John Renwick of same, for £300 SC money, 250 acres on Gilders Creek, a small branch of Indian Creek, waters of Enoree, adj. land of Anthony Park, Francis Shearer, William Cannon, Andrew McMahan, recorded in Book RRR, page 654, and in the Auditors office in Book M No. 13, page 254. John Baptist Tear (I) (Seal), Cloe Tear (mark) (Seal), Wit: James Lindsey, William Wilson, Abraham Wright. Proved in Ninety Six District by the oath of James Lindsey 8 March 1784 before Robert McCrery, J.P. Recorded 3 June 1794.

B, 739-741: 10 Dec 1793, Andrew Russel & Jane his wife of Newberry County, planter, to John Crooks of same, for £30 sterling, 60 acres on south west side of Broad River granted to Henry Oxner 25 May 1774 and conveyed by him to John Pearson, then to Randolph Buzzard, and then to Andrew Russel adj. land of Jacob Falter, Randolph Buzzard. Andrew Russel (Seal), Jane Russel (X) (Seal), Wit: Ephraim Liles, Alex'r Glenn, Ephraim Liles Sen. Proved 24 Dec 1793 by the oath of Alex'r Glenn before Reuben Sims, J.P. Recorded 4 June 1794.

B, 742-744: 10 Dec 1793, Andrew Russel & Jane his wife of Newberry County, planter, to John Crooks of same, for £80 sterling, 60 acres on a branch of Broad River granted to Randolph Buzzard 2 April 1773, and conveyed by Randolph Buzzard Jun'r, heir at law to Randolph Buzzard Sen'r, to Andrew Russel. Andrew Russel (Seal), Jane Russel (X) (Seal), Wit: Ephraim Liles, Alex'r Glenn, Ephraim Lies Sen. Proved 24 Dec 1793 by the oath of Alex'r Glenn before Reuben Sims, J.P. Recorded 4 June 1794.

B, 745-746: 28 Jan 1794, John Buzart, planter, of Newberry County, to Elisha Anderson of same, for £30 sterling, 50 acres on waters of Cannons Creek adj. land of Peter Hare, John Buzart, part of 250 acres granted to John Buzart. John Buzart (B) (Seal), Wit: David Ruff J. P., Frederick Davis, Peter Hare Jun (X). "I, David Ruff, do certify that out of a mistake I wrote Elisha instead of Elijah." Recorded 4 June 1794.

B, 746-747: We the under named Persons, Legatees of the late Jacob Kippleman [Cappleman] decd, do bind in the just sum of £300 sterling by any who doth not agree to the division & determination of Jacob Buzart, Martin Hollowback & John Lattiner Volentine, freeholders of Newberry County, in dividing the estate of Jacob Kippleman, 6 Jan 1794. _____ [German signature], John Cappleman, George Petter ___ [German signature], Maria Elisabeth Taylor (mark), Martin Taylor, Catherina Slike widow (X), Margret Yone (X), Johan Jacob ium [German signature], Lovey Tar (X), Frederick Tar (X), Eva Feltman (X), George Feltman (O), Elisabeth Hogg (mark), John Hogg, Wit: Adolf Legrone [German signature], Johann Boland [German signature], Nicholas Lathinger (L). Proved in Newberry County by the oath of Nicholas Lathinger 20 May 1794 before Peter Julien, J.P. Recorded 4 June 1794.

B, 748-751: 15 Jan 1767, Benjamin Eple of Province of SC, planter, to Martin Hauk of Berkly County, Province of SC, weaver, for £100 SC money, 50 acres on a branch of Kings Creek in Berkley County adj. land of John Shely. Benjamin Epple [German signature], Wit: John Hips, John Furnas, Michael Mintz. Proved by the oath of Michael Mintz 15 March 17-- before Thomas Fletchall, J.P. for Craven County. Recorded 5 June 1794.

B, 752-757: Lease and release. 25 & 268 Aug 1769, John Windle Sheley of Berkly County, SC, planter, to Martin Hauk of same, for £48 SC money, 50 acres, part of 400 acres adj. Martin Hauk, granted to John Shely and devolved on John Windel Shealy, eldest son of the aforesaid John Sheley. John Windle Shely (X) (Seal), Wit: Moses Kirkland, Philip Pearson J. P. Proved 1 Sept 1769 by the oath of Philip Pearson before John Hamilton, J.P. Recorded 5 June 1794.

B, 758-761: Lease and release. 10 & 11 Dec 1793, Samuel Murray, planter, of Newberry County, to Thomas Johnston, planter, for £50 sterling, 80 acres on Enoree River in Newberry County adj. land of George Awberry, Thomas Gordon, George Gordon, Jacob Penington. Samuel Murray (Seal), Wit: William Wilson, Robert Johnston, Robert Elliott. Proved in Newberry County by the oath of Robert Johnston __ June 1794 before John Speak, J.P. Recorded 10 June 1794.

B, 761-765: Lease and release. 23 & 24 March 1784, John Johnston, cordwiner of Ninety Six District, to Thomas Johnston Sen'r, planter, for £20 sterling, 200 acres, part of tract granted to said John Johnston, on Enoree River. John Johnston (II) (Seal), Wit: William Wilson, Samuel Murry, James Murray.

Proved in Newberry County by the oath of Samuel Murray 7 June 1794 before John Speak, J.P. Recorded 10 June 1794.

B, 765-770: Lease and release. 26 & 27 Oct 1789, John Lenard Harman and wife Mary of Newberry County, planter, to Michael Kinard, farmer, of same, for £350 old currency, 150 acres granted to said Harmon 25 May 1772 on Buffaloe Creek, waters of Saluda, recorded in Book LLL, page 44, in the auditor's office in Book I No. 11, page 287. John Larance Harman (Seal), Mary Harman (X) (Seal), Wit: George Stoddemire (X), Peter Couns (mark), Frank Pope (X). Proved in Newberry County by the oath of George Stoudemire 28 Dec 1791 before Geo. Ruff, J. N. C. Recorded 11 June 1794.

B, 770-775: Lease and release. South Carolina, Ninety Six District. 21 & 22 Oct 1791, James Griffen, planter, of said district to William Griffin, late overseer for Francis Davenport, of same, for £30 SC money, 80 acres on waters of Carsons Creek, part of 200 acres granted to Samuel Ford 19 Aug 1768 and conveyed by him unto James Griffin 15 & 16 March 1773, between two small branches of Carsons Creek adj. Charles Pitts. James Griffen (X) (Seal), Merah[?] Griffen (Seal), Wit: Charles Griffen, William Burton, Rosamond Burton (X). Proved by the oath of William Burton 22 Feb 1794. Recorded 16 June 1794.

B, 775: James Campbell, planter, of Newberry County, to Henry Crick, a negro woman slave named Judy, 17 June 1794. Wit: John Speake, J.P. Recorded 17 June 1794.

B, 776-780: Lease and release. 19 & 20 Feb 1790, Henry Kountz Sen of Newberry County, planter, and Mary Elizabeth his wife, to John Fellow of same, carpenter, for £14 s6 sterling, 50 acres, part of a tract of 150 acres granted to Herman Noulfer 9 Jan 1775 [sic] adj. Daniel Ebb, recorded in Book PP, page 288, conveyed for £100 by Noulfer to Martin Single, 4 & 5 Aug 1761, and by Martin Singley for £150 to Henry Countz. Henry Countz (mark) (Seal), Mare Elizabeth Counts (X) (Seal), Wit: Jacob Single (X), Henry Warts (HW), Je. McDaniel. Proved in Newberry County by the oath of Jeremiah McDonald 30 Jan 1791 before Thos. W. Waters, J.P. Recorded 17 June 1794.

B, 781-785: Lease and release. 16 July 1793, John Ellmore of Charleston District, Carpenter, & Stephen Ellmore of Orangeburgh District, planter, to David Reid, planter, of Newberry County, for £100 SC money, 200 acres on a branch of Broad River called Cannons Creek, adj. Coppleman, granted to William Ellmore 15 July 1768, and by the will of William Ellmore bequeathed to John & Stephen Ellmore, his sons. John Ellmore (Seal), Stephen Ellmore (Seal), Rachel Ellmore (X), Wit: Patrick Carmichel, Samuel Morras (X), Mary Lomanick (X). Proved in Newberry County by the oath of Patrick Carmichel 13 July 1793 before Mercer Babb, J.P. Recorded 17 June 1794.

B, 785-790: Lease and release. 8 & 9 Nov 1792, Daniel Ohara and Peter Bounetheau, gentlemen, administrators of the estate of William Downes, late of SC, land surveyor, deceased, of Charleston, SC, to John Simpson of Ninety Six District, for £43 s15 sterling, 350 acres in the District of Ninety Six on the wets side of Bush River on a ranch thereof, granted to James Wright 15 Sept 1774 and conveyed by James Wright and Rebecca his wife to William Downes 21 Sept 1775. Daniel Ohara as admr (Seal), Peter Bounetheau as admr (Seal), Wit: John Diamond, Charles Griffen, William Graham. Receipt witnessed by Andrew Smith, John Diamond, Charles Griffin, William Grayham. Proved in Charleston District 30 Nov 1793 by the oath of John Diamond before Ger. Hall, J.P. Recorded 18 June 1794.

B, 790-793: Lease and release. 6 & 7 March 1794, Philemon Waters Senr to Daniel Parkins, both of Newberry County, for £27 s3 d9 sterling, 50 acres, part of tract granted to William Turner Senr deceased but now by purchase the property of said Philemon Waters Senr, upon Bush River adj. James Patty. P. Waters (Seal), Wit: John Abney, Cullen Lark. Recorded 18 June 1794.

B, 794-795: South Carolina, Newberry County. Saml Kelly, Abijah O'Neal, John Kelly and Robert Kelly, of county aforesaid, planters, heirs in the estate of John Kelly deceased which estates consists of some slaves, which slaves by will of said deceased were to be divided amongst his heirs, and we having come into possession f our part thereof, namely Jeffrey a yellow man of about 40 years of age with his wife Judith a black woman, about that age, and their son Ben a yellow man about 23 years old, one other negro man about 60 years of age and his wife, Jack & Dina, and their son bill a black man 20 years old, also Cloe daughter of said Jack and Dinah, a black woman about 28 years of age with three of her children Lucy, a yellow girl 9 years old past since the 8th of month last, & Dick a black boy three years old & also ben the youngest child of said Cloe, and we believing that liberty is the natural right of all mankind, 27th day of the six month 1793, have manumised from the bonds of Slavery forever, those that have arrived to the number of years that is commonly call'd of age, and the three children of Cloe above mentioned to remain in the service of care of their Masters until they are of age. (Agreed to that the girl should be free at eighteen years old and the boys at twenty-on.) Samuel Kelly (Seal), Abijah Oneal (Seal), John Kelly (Seal), Robert Kelly (Seal), Wit: Jehue Inman, Henry Steddom, Saml Miles. Proved by the statement of Jehue Inman 12 May 1794 before Mercer Babb, J.P. Recorded 18 June 1794.

B, 796-799: 28 March 1792, Doct'r John Caldwell of Newberry County to Richard Payne of same, for £90 sterling, 308 acres, part of tract granted to Henry Hasell 9 Sept 1774 adj. Eveleigh, James Mayson, Allen Cox, John Caldwell, Isaac Dyson. John Caldwell Senr (Seal), Susanah Caldwell (X) (Seal), Wit: Robert Gillam Sen'r, John Wallace, Benj. Bunting. Recorded 29 June 1794.

B, 800-803: Lease and release. 9 June 1794, Michael Gore of Newberry County to Isaiah Pemberton of same, for £100 sterling, 100 acres on Bush Creek, half of a tract granted to Thomas Golden adj. land of Samuel Kelly.

Michael Gore (Seal), Catharine Gore (X) (Seal), Wit: Wm Satterwhite, Saml Kelly Sen., John Kelly Sen. Proved in Newberry County by the affirmation of Samuel Kelly Senr before Mercer Babb, J.P. Recorded 19 June 1794.

B, 804-808: Lease and release. 6 & 7 Jan 1792, Isaac Davenport to Jesse Kerby, both of Newberry County, for £50 sterling, 50 acres, part of 300 acres granted to said Isaac Davenport 15 May 1773 in Berkley County (now Newberry) on waters of Little River, adj. William Stephens, John Newton but now James Thomas. Isaac Davenport (Seal), Elizabeth Davenport (mark) (Seal), Wit: Thomas Peterson, William Davenport. Proved by the oath of Thomas Peterson 19 May 1794 before Mercer Babb, J.P. Recorded 20 June 1794.

B, 809-811: 28 Aug 1793, Jesse Kerby of Ninety Six District to John Griffin of same, for £30 sterling, 50 acres, part of 300 acres granted to Isaac Davenport 15 May 1773 and conveyed by said Davenport to Jesse Kerby 6 & 7 Jan 1792 in Berkley County (now Newberry) on waters of Little River. Jesse Kerby (Seal), Mary Kerby (X) (Seal), Wit: Charles Griffin, William Davenport, Isaac Davenport. Proved by the oath of Charles Griffin 19 May 1794 before Mercer Babb, J.P. Recorded 20 June 1794.

B, 812-814: 17 Jan 1793, Isaac Davenport of Newberry County to John Griffin of same, for £47 sterling, 116 acres, part of tract granted to said Isaac Davenport 5 May 1773 adj. said Isaac Davenport, William Davenport, Jesse Kerby, John Newton. Isaac Davenport (Seal), Elizabeth Davenport (mark) (Seal), Wit: Charles Griffin, Susannah Davenport (mark), Elisabeth Davenport (mark). Proved by the oath of Charles Griffin 19 May 1794 before Mercer Babb, J.P. Recorded 21 June 1794.

B, 815-819: Lease and release. 12 & 13 May 1794, John Newton of Edgefield County, SC, to Martin Chester of Newberry County, SC, for £55 sterling, 80 acres, part of 300 acres granted to John Abney 3 Dec 1787 on Beaver Dam a branch of Saluda River, adj. Stiddam, Bartlitt, Polly Taylor. John Newton (Seal), Noami Newton (X) (Seal), Wit: John Thomas S. M., Robert Longshore, Thomas Peterson. Proved by the oath of Robert Longshore 19 May 1794 before Mercer Babb, J.P. Recorded 25 June 1794.

B, 820-825: Lease and release. 3 & 4 April 1783, Dederick Utts of Ninety Six District, weaver, to Johannes Flick, planter, of same, for £350 SC money, 200 acres granted 2 March 1768 to said Dederick Utts on a branch of Cannons Creek, recorded in Book CCC, page 226. Dederick Utts (Seal), Wit: Aberham Taylor (AT), Michael Dickert, George Feltman (G). Proved in Ninety Six District by the oath of Aberham Taylor 19 April 1783 before George Ruff, J.P. Recorded 25 June 1794.

B, 826: 3 April 1794, Robert Elliott of Newberry County for £15 sterling to Robert Spence, a sorrel horse colt. Robert Elliott (Seal), Wit: George Wells,

Nathan Anderson. Proved in Newberry County by the oath of Nathan Anderson 31 May 1794 before John Speake, J.P.

B, 827-829: 8 Oct 1793, Richard Watts, Esquire, Sheriff of Newberry County, to George Latham of same, for £13 s10 sterling, 42 acres on waters of Bush River, sold by sheriff by judgment obtained by George Latham against Charles Rowan in the amount of £15 s13 d8½. Richard Watts (Seal), Wit: Wm Satterwhite, John Satterwhite. Proved in Newberry County by the oath of William Satterwhite 26 June 1794 before J. R. Brown, J. N. C. Recorded 27 June 1794.

B, 829-833: Lease and mortgage. 8 & 10 April 1794, William Stuart of Newberry County, to George Latham of same, bound in the penal sum of £51 s10 sterling, mortgage of 150 acres granted to said Stuart 10 Jan 1774 adj. Jennet Stuart, John Glenn. William Stuart (Seal), Wit: David Pugh, John Kelly Sen'r, Saml Kelly Senr. Proved in Newberry County 5 June 1794 by the statement of Saml Kelly before Mercer Babb, J.P. Recorded 27 June 1794.

B, 834-837: 25 Nov 1789, William Blair of Ninety Six District, weaver, to Patrick Carmichael of same, planter, for £50 sterling or a plantation containing 294 acres, tract of 135 acres on Campen Creek adj. Bulow, Tidmore, granted to James McMaster 3 July 1786. William Blair (Seal), David Blair (X) (Seal), Wit: Miles Jennings, Samuel McQuerns, William Aspenell (O). Proved in Newberry County by the oath of William Aspenell 10 Jan 1792 before Peter Julien, J.P. Recorded 30 June 1794.

B, 837-840: 25 Nov 1789, William Blair of Ninety Six District, weaver, to Patrick Carmichael of same, planter, for £50 sterling or a plantation containing 235 acres, tract of 120 acres on north side of Saluda River on waters of Bush River, recorded in Book WWWW, page 130, granted to said William Blair 2 Jan 1788. William Blair (Seal), David Blair (X) (Seal), Wit: Miles Jennings, Samuel McQuerns, William Aspenell (O). Proved in Newberry County by the oath of William Aspenell 10 Jan 1792 before Peter Julien, J.P. Recorded 30 June 1794.

B, 841-846: Lease and release. 2 & 3 June 1788, William Johnson, sole admr. of the estate of Robert Johnson deceased, of Newberry County to Thomas Peterson of same, for £187 s10 SC money, 100 acres on waters of Little River adj. land of Samuel Neilson, granted to said Robert Johnson 25 Aug 1769. William Johnson (Seal), Wit: Robert Speer, Matthew Brooks, Joseph Stuart (X). Proved in Newberry County by the oath of Robert Speer 31 Dec 1789 before Thos. W. Waters, J.P. Recorded 1 July 1794.

B, 847-851: Lease and release. 7 & 8 March 1794, Bartlitt Brooks of Newberry County, to William Pool of same, for £100 sterling, 100 acres on Mudlick Creek adj. John Stewart, Thomas Turner, Robert Gordy, part of 350 acres granted to Hamilton Murdock and conveyed by him to Daniel McNeel and by said McNeel to Bartlitt Brooks. Bartlitt Brooks (X) (Seal), Wit: Drury

Satterwhite, Ann Pool, Dudly Brooks. Proved in Newberry County by the oath of Drury Satterwhite 10 June 1794 before J. R. Brown, J. N. C. Recorded 2 July 1794.

B, 852-856: Lease and release. 22 & 23 Sept 1790, Philimon Bozman of Newberry County to Joseph Williamson of same, for £100 sterling, 138 acres, part of 500 acres granted to John Sansom 3 Nov 1770 adj. Isaac Mitchell, Hopkin Williams. Philemon Bozman (Seal), Susannah Bozman (X) (Seal), Wit: Isaac Mitchell Jun, Thomas Mitchell, David Bozman. Proved in Newberry County by the oath of David Bozman 31 May 1794 before Robert Gillam, J. P. Recorded 4 July 1794.

B, 857-861: Lease and release. 21 & 22 Feb 1787, Philimon Bozman of Newberry County to David Bozman of same, for £50, 120 acres, part of 500 acres granted to John Sansom 3 Nov 1770 adj. Mrs. Dyson, Mr. Burgess, Lewis Bozman. Philemon Bozman (Seal), Susannah Bozman (X) (Seal), Wit: Isaac Mitchell, Wm Griffin, sadler. Proved in Newberry County by the oath of Isaac Mitchell Jun 31 May 1794 before Robert Gillam, J. P. Recorded 5 July 1794.

B, 862-867: Lease and release. 10 & 11 March 1791, William Hilburn Sen. of Newberry County to Levi Hilburn of same, for £90 sterling, 100 acres on waters of Bush River, part of 350 acres granted to said William Hilburn Senr 25 Oct 1764. William Hilburn (mark) (Seal), Wit: David Pugh, Wm. Hilburn Jun., John Summers. Proved 9 May 1794 in Newberry County by the oath of John Summers before Mercer Babb, J.P. Recorded 10 July 1794.

B, 868-871: Lease and release. 22 & 23 Jan 1794, William Hilburn Sen. of Newberry County to Levi Hilburn of same, for £90 sterling, 100 acres on waters of Bush River, part of 350 acres granted to said William Hilburn Senr 25 Oct 1764. William Hilburn (mark) (Seal), Wit: Richard Thompson, Robert Hilburn, John Hilburn (I). Proved 9 May 1794 in Newberry County by the oath of Robert Hilburn before Mercer Babb, J.P. Recorded 10 July 1794.

B, 873: At a court held for Granville County [North Carolina] 5th March 1754 on Motion of Robert Gillam his Ear Mark was Recorded a crop & slit in the left ear and a half crop in the right. Danl Weldon, C. Ct. Recorded 14 Aug 1794.

B, 872-876: Lease and release. 10 & 11 March 1791, William Hilburn Sen. of Newberry County to Robert Hilburn of same, for £90 sterling, 50 acres on both sides of Bush River, part of 350 acres granted to said William Hilburn Senr 25 Oct 1764. William Hilburn (mark) (Seal), Wit: David Pugh, Wm. Hilburn Jun., John Summers. Proved 9 May 1794 in Newberry County by the oath of John Summers before Mercer Babb, J.P. Recorded 10 July 1794.

B, 877: Nicholas Corry, David Smith, and Frances Harrington of Union County, exrs. & extx. of John Harrington deceased, to Robert Rutherford of

Newberry County, a negroe woman named Suck about 27 years old, 3 June 1794. Frances Harrington (mark) (Seal), Nicholas Corry (Seal), David Smith (Seal), Wit: Sephthah Harrington, Jeremiah Leary. Proved 3 June 1794 in Union County by the oath of Nicholas Corry, J.P. Recorded 14 June 1794.

B, 878-880: 2 June 1794, Robert Rutherford of Newberry County, Esqr., and Fanny Harrington, of Union County, widow of John Harrington deceased, John Rutherford and Thomas Mathews, trustees, marriage settlement, whereas a marriage is intended to be had and solemnized between said Robert Rutherford and Fanny Harrington. Robert Rutherford (Seal), Frances Harrington (mark), David Smith (Seal), Nicholas Corry (Seal). Certified by Nicholas Corry, J.P., 3 June 1794. Recorded 18 Aug 1794.

B, 880-881: 8 July 1794, Philip Proctor of Ninety Six District, to James Creswell & Co. of same, for £13 s10 d5, one dark bay mare, one roan gelding, one yearling horse, one brindle cow, one pale red cow, one white faced heifer, one yearling steer, two feather beds with homespun ticks and their furniture, one loom and its geers, one dozen pewter plats, three pewter dishes, four pewter basons, two dutch ovens, four irons pott,s one flax wheel, one cotton wheel, one desk, two chests, and one case, half dozen chairs, and about 4 acres of standing corn and one rifle gun. Philip Proctor (Seal), Wit: Richard Watts, Saml Martin. Proved in Newberry County by the oath of Richard Watts 30 July 1794 before J. R. Brown, J. N. C. Recorded 20 Aug 1794.

B, 882-883: 15 Feb 1794, Robert Whitten of Newberry County, and waters of Dunkins Creek, to Samuel Law Sen. of same county, for £12 s10 sterling, 112 acres, part of 320 acres granted to Robert Whitten 6 July 1789, recorded in Book YYYY, page 533. Robt Whitten (Seal), Wit: Patk Lowry, John Whitten. Proved in Newberry County by the oath of Patrick Lowry 21 __ 1794 before John Speake, J.P. Recorded 20 Aug 1794.

B, 884-888: Lease and release. 1 & 2 Jan 1790, John Waits of Newberry County, to Henry Criek of same, for £40, 50 acres on north side Saluda River on waters of Hawlick Creek, part of 230 acres granted to said John Waits 6 March 1786. John Waits (Seal), Wit: Horatio Griffin, Isaiah Quartemus, John Criek. Proved in Newberry County by the oath of John Criek 12 July 1794 before Peter Julien, J.P. Recorded 22 Sept 1794.

B, 889-892: Lease and release. 4 & 5 Oct 1791, Samuel Etherdige of Edgefield County to Henry Criek of Newberry County, for £50 sterling, 150 acres in the county of Edgefield on the south side of Saluda River adj. land of Mary McDougal, granted to Dougal McDougal 13 May 1768 and conveyed by him to Samuel Etheridge 11 & 12 Sept 1789. Samuel Etheridge (X) (Seal), Wit: Jno Criek, W. W. Waters, William Ham. Proved in Newberry County by the oath of John Criek 12 July 1794 before Peter Julien, J.P. Recorded 23 Sept 1794.

B, 893-896: Lease and release. 28 & 29 Dec 1790, James Harp, planter, of Newberry County to Henry Criek, merchant, for £20 sterling, 19 acres, part of tract granted to Nehemiah Roden[?] 5 March 1787, on waters of Hawlick Creek on north side Saluda, adj. McDogan, Philimon Waters, John Waits. James Harp (H) (Seal), Wit: A. Robison, John Criek, George Baldwin, Isaiah Quartemus. Proved in Newberry County by the oath of John Criek 12 July 1794 before Peter Julien, J.P. Recorded 23 Sept 1794.

B, 897-899: Lease and release. 22 & 23 July 1794, Samuel Gaunt of Newberry County to Nebo Gaunt of same, for £50, 158 acres, part of 500 acres granted to Jacob Brooks adj. Samuel Gaunt, Thomas Brooks, Wadlington, Sarah Gaunt. Samuel Gaunt (Seal), Abigail Gaunt (Seal), Wit: Joseph Cook, Henry Corll. Recorded 24 Sept 1794.

B, 900-902: 12 June 1794, John Palmer of Newberry County to Nehemiah Thomas of same, for £8 sterling, 20 acres on Bush River granted to David Linch and conveyed by him to John Palmer 16 Aug 1787. John Palmer (Seal), Hannah Palmer (mark) (Seal), Wit: Daniel Parkins, John Jay, Thomas Mils (T). Proved by the statement of Thomas Mills 28 July 1794 before Elisha Ford, J.P. Recorded 24 Sept 1794.

B, 903-906: 21 & 22 Feb 1794, David Pugh to John Wilkerson Senr., both of Newberry County, for £20 sterling, 148 acres, part of 200 acres granted to John Wilkerson and conveyed to David Pugh 30 Aug 1788, on Scotts Creek, a branch of Bush River. David Pugh (Seal), Wit: Edward Benbow, David Downs (mark), William Shaw. Proved in Newberry County 24 July 1794 by the affirmation of Edw'd Benbow before Mercer Babb, J.P. Recorded 24 Sept 1794.

B, 906-908: 12 Aug 1792, Jacob Chandler of Newberry County, admr. of the estate of William Gilleland, to Mathew Brooks of same, by bond of performance of William Gilleland to Mathew Brooks, hath sold 150 acres, part of 250 acres adj. land of John Coppock, David Miles, granted to Jeremiah Lewis 27 Nov 1770 and conveyed by him to William Gilliland 20 & 21 Dec 1771, grant recorded in Book 3D, page 15. Jacob Chandler (Seal), Wit: Radmul Smith, Robert Longshore. Proved in Newberry County 10 Aug 1792 by the oath of Radmul Smith before Mercer Babb, J.P. Recorded 25 Sept 1794.

B, 908-912: Lease and release. 22 & 23 March 1784, John Johnson, planter, of Ninety Six District, to Robert Johnson of same, for £500 SC money, 250 acres on a small branch of Broad River called Collins River. John Johnson (II) (Seal), Wit: William Wilson, Saml Murray, James Murray. Proved by the oath of James Murray 25 May 1784 before Robert Rutherford, J.P. Recorded 26 Sept 1794.

B, 912-916: Lease and release. 19 July 1794, Robert Gillam of Newberry County to William Andrew of same, for £45 SC money, 100 acres on waters of Mudlick Creek adj. Land of John Towles, granted to James McCool 31 Oct

1759 and conveyed by him to Moses Embree 19 Sept 1774, and by said Embree to Robert Gillam 29 Oct 1792. Robert Gillam Sen. (Seal), Mary Gillam (X) (Seal), Wit: Daniel Williams Jun., Martha Gillam, Joshua Gillam. Proved in Newberry County by the oath of Daniel Williams Jun. 26 July 1794 before Jacob R. Brown, J. N. C. Recorded 1 Oct 1794.

B, 917-921: Lease and release. 28 & 29 Oct 1787, John Coate of Newberry County, planter, to John Maxwell of same, planter, for £72 SC money, 150 acres in Craven County otherwise Newberry County adj. Charles Nix, on Beaver Dam, a small branch of Saluda River, granted to said Coates 4 July 1769. John Coate (I) (Seal), Rachel Coate (mark), Wit: Robert Speer, Thomas Haskit, James Rushton. Proved in Newberry County by the affirmation of Thomas Haskit 28 July 1794 before Elisha Ford, J.P. Recorded 6 Oct 1794.

B, 921-925: Lease and release. 31 Jan & 1 Feb 1794, Asa Garrett of Newberry County to James Bonds of same, for £70 sterling, tract granted 5 May 1773, recorded in Book O, page 521, memorial entered in Book M. No. 12, page 382, 18 Aug 1773, adj. David Spence, James Kenady, Henry Middleton, on waters of Indian Creek, the said Asa Garrett, the heir at law to the said Thomas Garrett decd, to the said 100 acres of land, conveyed by him the said Asa Garrett, his mother namely Ann Garrett, the widow of the decd. Thomas Garrett, doth acknowledge all right of dower. Asa Garrett (Seal), Ann Garrett (mark) (Seal), Wit: John Lofton, Thomas Lofton, James Lindsey. Proved 2 Feb 1794 by the oath of James Lindsey before Providence Williams, J. P. Recorded 7 Oct 1794.

B, 926-929: Lease and release. 2 & 3 July 1794, Elizabeth Robinson & Margret Price Robinson of Charleston, to James Creswell of Newberry County, for £100 SC money, 250 acres on a small branch of Saluda River adj. Robert Cunningham, Joseph White, granted to Margret Robinson (the mother of said Elizabeth and Margret Price Robinson) 3 June 1769 now deceased and descended to them as heirs at law to said Margret Robinson who died intestate. Elizabeth Robinson (Seal), Margret P. Robinson (Seal), Wit: James Spears, Peter Freneau. Recorded 8 Oct 1794.

B, 929-933: Lease and release. 23 & 24 June 1786, Ingle Stockman of Newberry County, surgeon, to John Kinard of same, for £60 sterling, 133 acres granted 4 April 1786 to Ingle Stockman on waters of Cannons Creek, recorded in Book KKK, page 136. Ingle Stockman (mark) (Seal), Katherine Stockman (X) (Seal), Wit: Adam Glazier, John Riley, Michl Currl [Charles]. Proved in Newberry County by the oath of John Riley 6 Sept 1794 before David Ruff, J.P. Recorded 9 Oct 1794.

B, 934-937: Lease and release. 20 & 21 Feb 1787, Frederick Gray, planter, of Newberry County, to John Kiner of same, planter, for £28 d10 sterling, tract of 137 acres granted to Frederick Gray 6 June 1785, recorded in Book DDDD, page 314, on waters of Broad River adj. Marpole, Ricord, David Edwards. Frederick Gray (Seal), Cloye Gray (X) (Seal), Wit: Jacob Hubern

[German signature], John Riley, Jeremiah Williams. Proved in Newberry County by the oath of John Riley 6 Sept 1794 before David Ruff, J.P. Recorded 9 Oct 1794.

B, 938: Frederick Nance, Clerk of Newberry County. Please to enter full satisfaction for Mortgage. William Stewart to George Latham, And you'll oblige yours &C. October the 2d 1794. George Latham. Recorded 16 Nov 1794.

END OF DEED BOOK B

Baker, R'd Bohun 76
Baldre, George 98
Baldwin, George 159
Balinger, John 101
Ballinger, James 43, 62
  Liddia/Lydia 43
Barlow, John 126
Barnes, Barnett 41
  Barney 41
  G. 64, 67
  George 61, 63, 67, 105
Barns, Barbery 41
  Barnet 41
  Elizabeth 41
  George 63
  James 41
Barrett, Arthur 39
  Jacob 39, 49, 66
  James 39
  Onslow 149
Barrott, Arthur 39
  Beth [Elizabeth] 41
  James 39
  John 118, 124
  Onslow 135
  Sarah 39
Bartlitt, 155
Bartram, George 70
Bates, John 35, 44
  Michael 147
Bauskett, Thomas 132
Bay, Elihu Hall 117
Beach, Abraham 102
  Simon 140
Beaks, Samuel 48, 89
Beal, John 148
Bean, William 11
Beard, James 80, 128
  John 104
  Thomas 11
  William 11
Bearden, Ansel 39, 48, 65
  John 54
  William 44, 54
Beardin, Ansel 44
Bee, Thos 76
Beem, Daniel 34
Beiller, Jacob 144
Bell, John 114
Belton, John 138
  William 138
Benbow, Edward 159
Bennet/t, Jno. B. 89
  Micajah 24, 89
Bentham, James 121, 132
Benton, William 63
Berry, Benjamin 61, 81, 85, 89
  Sarah 61
Beuford, Jas 22

Biddy, John 92
Bieler, Jacob 132
  Joseph 132
Bieller, Joseph 107
Bill, Silvester 110
Binnicker, Charles 101
Bishop, Thomas 146
Bize, Hercules Daniel 147
Black, Adam 27, 30
  James 102
  John 124
  Rosena (Kraud[?]) 30
  Samuel 144
Blackburn, Daniel 44, 48, 103, 140
  William 3, 57, 140
Blair, David 125, 156
  James 8, 59, 122
  William 2, 125, 156
Blake, William 124, 147
Blalock, 12
  John 10, 16, 19, 21, 35, 66
Blandon, William 5
  John 49
Blewer, John 67
Bocquet, Peter 74
Boland, Johann 152
Boldwin, Caleb 138
Bond 32
  Deadly 56
  Fanny 78
  Noah 78
  Richard 78
Bondrake, Charles 80
Bonds, Dudly 57
  Fanney 78
  James 61, 87, 140, 160
  Mary 129
  Menoah 23
  Noah 78, 96
  Richard 78, 129
  Sarah 74
Bookter, Alexander 64, 90, 91, 96, 111,
    116, 122, 133, 144
Booth, Christiana 52
Bossart, Anna[?] 74
  Felix 74
Boszart, Jacob 29
Boulware, George 26
Bounetheau, Peter 147, 153, 154
Bousard, Felix 74, 83
  Rudolph 74, 83
Boushard, Anna Mary (Heir) 87
Bowers, Andrew 10
  William 9
Bowl, George 16
Boyd, Benj'a 117
  David 85
  Hugh 16, 19, 47, 107

Bulow 156
  Aemelia 6
  Amelia 21
  Jacob 120
  Joachim 2, 4, 6, 20, 96, 101, 140
  John J. 121
  Joseph 120
Bunch, Lewis 114
  Mary 114
Bundrick, 4
  Nicholas 5
Bunting, Benjamin 146, 154
Buoys, John 125
Burden, Thomas 107, 108
Burdine, Mary 128, 129
  Nathaniel 85
  Samuel 107, 128, 129
Burgess, 157
Burk, Aedanus 76
Burnes, James 116
Burney, John 97
Burns, James 2
Burrows, Francis 89
Burton, Benjamin 106
  Charles 86, 132
  Gibeon 36, 106
  James 106
  Josiah 136
  Phebe 35
  Rosamond 153
  Sintha 36
  Thomas 55
  William 35, 36, 63, 66, 106, 118, 153
Burtz, Frederick 37
  Michael 37
Busby, Benjamin 5, 6, 34, 39
  Nathan 30
  Thomas 130
Bush, John 123
  John Housen 128
Bushard, Felix 72
  Marian 72
  Rudolph 68, 70, 72
Bushart, Rudolph 72
Butler, Benjamin 52
  Catrine 77
  Elizabeth 52
  Henry 77, 95, 138
  Mary 77
  Moses 95, 96
  Nicholas 109
Buyer, Peter 72, 73, 83
Buzard, Jacob 92
  Robert 46, 47
Buzart, John 152
Buzbee, Benjamin 36
Buzzard, John 83
  Randolph 151
  Robert 1, 47, 57

  Rudolph 24, 25
Byerly, Casper Philip 74
Cabler, Elizabeth 8
Cade[?], Charles 77
Cains, Christopher 140
Caldwell, Daniel 113
  David 135, 136, 149
  James 10, 37, 43, 61, 88, 113, 119, 133, 148
  Jean 44, 98
  Jno 27
  John 6, 31, 33, 42, 44, 55, 58, 63, 73, 107, 108, 110, 113, 136, 138, 146, 154
  Joseph 6, 17, 40, 48, 68, 85, 93, 110, 113, 129
  Paul 56
  Robert 146
  Susanna/h 146, 154
  William 17, 37, 40, 43, 54, 60, 61, 63, 65, 71, 77, 81, 85, 87, 90, 91, 98, 103, 114, 122, 135, 141, 148
  Wm. Thos 44
Calhoun, Pat 60
Calk, Elijah 123
Callaway, William 63
Callerson[?], Michael 38
Callman, Henry 99
Calmes, Betsy 12
Calmes, William 12, 61, 97, 110, 134
Caloff, Henry 147
Calwell, John 1
Cambell, Diana 33
Campbell, Abraham 117
  Daniel 117
  Elizabeth 16, 17, 22
  George 14, 87, 91
  Isaac 117
  James 32, 46, 92, 134, 138, 145, 150, 151, 153
  Jariot 142
  John 146
  Joseph 142
  Joses 117
  Mary 117
  Robert 16, 22
  Sarah 142
  Thomas 14
  William 14, 81
Campfield, Joseph 74
Camron, Robert 64
Cannon, David 18, 112, 114
  Elenor 113
  Elizabeth 28, 111
  Ephraim 15, 16, 48, 66, 109, 111, 113, 114, 127
  John 38, 66, 100, 106, 107, 111, 112, 114, 127
  Joseph 28
  Keziah 39

(Cannon) Lidda 111
  Rosanah 28
  Samuel 39, 90, 106, 111, 127
  William 14, 55, 111, 151
Cappleman, Jacob 152
  John 152
Cargill, Cornelius 12
  John 12
  Rachel 12
  Thomas 3
Carmichael, Patrick 156
Carmichal, Elizabeth 97
  Patrick 97, 125
Carmichel, Patrick 153
Carr, Jean 106
Carradine, Abraham 111
Carson, Charles 60
  John 102
Carter, Shadrack 100
Carthlin, Moses 71
Casey, Abner 52
  Levi 13, 26, 43, 46-48, 52, 53, 58, 60, 64,
    71, 85, 92
Cashaw, 55
Cassells, James 45
Castle, William 126
Catarna 4
Cates, A. 4, 10
  Aaron 47, 57, 90, 129, 133
  Aron 1, 2, 16, 124, 130, 132
  Robt 2
  Thos 2
Cato, James 52
Catter, Jas 55
Cauldwell, Wm. 8
Caymet, Martin 98
Chamber, Israel 135
Chambers, Adam 106
  Alexander 136
  Thorogood 122, 128
  Thoroughgood 31
  William 136
Chandler 87
  Abednego 22
  Bailey 67, 105
  Haggeth 41
  Jacob 125, 135, 159
  James 24
  Jeremiah 13, 31
  Joe 41
  Joel 30, 31, 41, 48
  John 22, 61, 78, 112
  Jonathan 149
  Mecheck 11
  Rachel 61
  Samuel 63, 135
  Susannah 31
  William 112
Chapman, Abraham 52

Giles 55, 97, 114
  Joseph 26, 44
  Samuel 86, 90, 114
  William 86
Chappel/l, Thomas 69, 122, 145
Charles, Michl 160
Chatman, Joseph 16
Chester, Levi 45
  Martin 39, 155
Chiles, 145
  Francis 111
  Reuben 105
Chitty, Benjamin 10
  Charles 115
Churn, Charlotte 73
Clagg, Richard 55
Clark, 22, 41
  Charles 69
  Daniel 53, 136, 149
  George 70
  Henry 43
  John 13, 30-32, 42, 48, 63, 79, 95, 112
  Mary 13, 42
  Richard 24, 25
  Stephen 32
  Thomas 54, 55, 69, 97
Clarkson, William 131
Clary, D. 51
  Daniel 10, 30
  David 136
  Mary (Brooks) 91
  Vachael 91
  Wm. 87
Clear, James 8
Clegg, Richard 80, 98, 129, 130
Cleland, James 36, 39, 42
Clemmons, Hosea 49
Clemons, Gabriel 35
Clitherall, 76
Cloud 78
  Valentine 62
Clowny/ey, Samuel 102, 151
Coast, William 74
Coate, Henry 117, 149
  James 114, 117
  John 64, 65, 77, 118, 160
  Marmaduke 138
  Rachel 160
  Susanah 118
  Susanna 77
  William 117, 148, 149
Coats 74
  Ann 110
  Barton 90
  Charles 34, 73, 110
  Henry 39, 81, 134, 136
  John 39, 77, 90, 107, 114, 118
  Netty 90
  Susannah 77, 90

(Coats), William 90
Cobb, Ann 43
  Benjamin 43, 65, 130, 151
  James 65
  John 57
Cobbs, John 33
  Judith 33
Cochran, Thomas 76
Cock, 24
Cockerill, Sanford 14
Cockin, "Ann Brigitta hard" 15
Cockran, Cornelius 25, 43
Cockrill, Sanford 42
Cocks, John 4
Coffee, Salathel 68
Colcock, 76
Cole, James 137
  William 137
Coleman, Conrad 92
  Henry 92
  Herman 92
Collier, William 115, 116
Collingsworth, William 99
Collins 2
  Charles 101
  Peter 44
Colly, Abraham 117
Colvin, Job/e 97, 98
  John 97, 98
  Mary 97
Colyon, Michal 111, 112
Connally, Edward 1, 8, 115
  Mary 1
Connell, John 9
Conner, Uriah 20
  William 20
Connerly, Edward 90, 132
Conway, Agatha 88
  Edwin 88, 144
  Peter 144, 145
Conwill, Benjamin 102
Cook, Charity 107
  Isaac 18, 19, 114, 115
  James 46, 80
  John 17
  Joseph 130, 159
Cooner, Jacob 7
  Sarah 7
Cooper, Rob't 76
  Thomas 91
  Timothy 55
Cooter, Andrew 69
Copack, John 30
Coppleman, 153
Coppock, John 25, 149, 159
  Joseph 27, 67
  Martha 62
Cordes, John 86
Corll, Henry 159

Corry, Nicholas 157, 158
Cote, John 18
Cotton, Elizabeth 56, 122
  Samuel 122
Coudey, Valentine 86
Couns, Peter 153
Counts, Mare Elizabeth 153
Countz, Henry 153
Courfauld, 76
Courrum, Beverly 140
Coursey, Levi 82
  Lewis 33
Cox, Allen 55, 146, 154
  John 29
Craig, James 27
  William 134
Craige, William 134
Craton, Hugh 46
Crawford, Daniel 111
Crawls[?], 53
Crayton, Hugh 114
Creek, Henry 103, 108
Creighton, Hugh 66, 109, 113
Crenshaw, Charles 44, 53, 67, 85, 87, 104,
  129
  Robert 69, 70
  Unice 67
Creswell, Elihu 144
  James 2, 88, 121, 144, 145, 147, 158, 160
Crews, David 120
  Joseph 58
Crick, Henry 153, 158, 159
  John 158, 159
Crim, Georg 44
  Peter 4, 17, 18, 34, 74
Criser, Christopher 67
Criswell, Daniel 119
  James 119
  Pheby 119
Croll, 37
  James 84
Cromer, 17
  Frederick 20
  George 12, 103
  Jacob 36, 103
  Michal 14
  Philip 127
Crommer, Michael 15
Crooks, 140
  Andrew 122
  Jean 115
  John 64, 73, 90, 151
Croomer, Philip 127
Cross, Alexander 14
  John 81
  Thomas 103, 104
Crossan, Thomas 14
Crossen, Jenn 15
  Thomas 15, 135

(Dickey), Ann 23
  James 119
  Jane 23
  Jean 23, 119
  John 17, 23
Dickson, David 84
  William 85
Dillard, James 73
Dillon, Robert 55, 69, 102
Dinkins, Joshua 49
Diton, Robert 54
Dixon, Nicholas 146
  Robert 146
  William 146
Dobbs, Arthur 53
Dodgen, James 84, 88
  Oliman 84
  Olleman 88, 123
  Olleyman 66, 73
  Olney Mann 60
  William 60, 66, 108
Dogeon, William 35
Doherty, James 71
Dominic, Elizabeth 141
  John 141, 142
Domney, John 111
Donnavan, James 63
Donovan, James 60
Dooly, Jno 81
  Patrick 129
  Thos 81
Dormer, Michael 62
Dougharty, James 49, 113
Douglas, James 102
Doumar, Michael 143
Dowber, Frederick 12
Downes, William 153, 154
Downs, David 159
  Jonathan 25, 44, 118
  Joshua 136
Drans, Waller 142
Dry, Coln. 76
Dubber, Frederick 4, 92
  Jos Frederick 92
Dubbert, Fredrick 4, 5
  John Frederick 4, 5
Dubert, Fredrick 4
  Jacob 38, 60
Duckett, Jacob 106, 107, 134, 146
  Thomas 89, 92, 95
Dudgeon, Elizabeth 66
  William 17, 65, 66
Dugan, Robert 11, 38, 60
  Thomas 10, 38, 56
Duglass, John 100
Duke/s, Henry 128, 142, 150
Dukesson, William 8
Duncan, Elizabeth 46
  James 31

Jean 31
John 31, 42, 46, 62, 80
Miles 46
Moses 31
Nealson 62
Rebeca 62
Robert 78
Samuel 27, 62, 105, 135, 138
Dunkin, Samuel 138
Dunlap, Wm 121
Dunn, David 97
  Henry 87, 125
Dunnon, Robert 81
Dunrymple, 57
Durr, Jacob 101
  Nicholas 3, 18
Dych, George 117
Dye, Martin 34
Dyson, 157
  Daniel 69, 135, 145
  Isaac 69, 146, 154
  James 1, 54, 69, 133, 146
  John 146
  Margaret 69
Eagner, Mathias 24
Eakins, George 89
Ealy, John 62
Earle, John 83
Earlybush, Michael 29
Earnest, George 9
East, Isham 98
  Thomas 1
Eastland, Thomas 1, 5, 140, 148
Eatcherson, Susanah 46
Eaton, John 113
Eaynes, Uldraugh 2
Ebb, Daniel 153
Eddins, Abraham 61
Edgehill, Thomas 72
Edghill, Thomas 111, 138
Edmonson, 146
  Caleb 134
  Jacob 134
  Judith 134
Edmundson, Judith 134
Edrington, Christopher 96
  James 96
Edson, C. R. 105
Edwards, Cateren (Brustill) 109
  Catharene 8
  David 3, 22, 25, 30, 160
  Edward 75
  Jane 22
  John 27, 41, 55, 56, 103, 122
  Josiah 25
  Litisha 122
  Lititia 122
  Margarett 122
  Mary 122

(Edwards), Obadiah 46
  Rhoda 122
  Samuel 125
Eheny, Catharine 143
  Frederick 143
Eigelberger, George 78
  John 142
Eigleberger, George 101, 142
  John 29
Ekins, George 19
Eleman, John 133
  Mary 133, 134
Elivine, Michael 1
Elizer, Simeon 134
Elleman, Enos 5, 6, 39, 69, 90
  John 5
Ellett, George 26
  Rebecah 26
  William 26
Ellewine, 122
  Catherine 126
  George 126
  John 126
  Michael 124
Ellimon, Enos 42
Elliot, Joseph 30, 150
Elliott, Isiah 43
  Josiah 31, 43, 66, 107, 150
  Robert 152, 155
Ellis, Ruth 135
  Simeon 125
Ellit, Rebeccah 26
  William 26
Ellmore, John 153
  Rachel 153
  Stephen 91, 153
  William 153
Elmore, Elizabeth 66
  Isaac 50, 144
  John 28
  Mathias 87
  Matthias 2, 6, 21, 66
  Ridgeway 124
  Sarah 18
  Stephen 5, 6, 18, 25, 45, 66, 87
  William 2, 16, 28
Elton, Anthony 10, 17
Embree, Evan 37
  Jesse 6
  John 2, 5, 6, 90, 135, 138
  Margaret 5
  Margret 37, 135, 138
  Mary 5, 6
  Moses 5, 6, 36, 37, 39, 42, 90, 135, 138,
    160
Emery, David 35
Emick, Conrad 90
Emory, David 66
Ener, Ulrick 117

Ennis, Cath'a 143
  Frederick 143
Eple/Epple, Benjamin 152
Erwin, Andrew 58
Estes, Bartlett 50
Etherdige, Samuel 158
Eutes, Catharine 151
Evance, Rebeca 76
Evans, 89
  Isaac 89
  John 2, 14
Eveleigh 154
  Mary 75
  Nicholas 4, 75, 76
  Thomas 75, 76
Eveliegh, Mary 74
  Nicholas 74
Ewing, Saml 75
Fagans, Philip 32
Fairchild, John 73
Falker, Barbara 23
  Jacob 2, 23-25, 143
Falter, Jacob 151
Farguson, 41
Farington, Jacob 55
Farquhar, Thomas 55
Farr, Nicholas 3
Farrar, Benjamin 107, 108, 125
Farrow, S[aml] 45
Fayssoux, Doctor 76
Felker, Jacob 1, 14, 46, 47, 57
Fellow, John 153
Feltman, Eva 152
  George 152, 155
  Theodoras 123
  Thodorous 56
Feltmat, Theodurus 92
Feltmet, Doris 29
  Dorus 95
  Theodorus 89
Felton, Harrel 96
Felts, Andrew 77
Ferdrees, Cathrine 29
  John 29
Ferdress, Catherine 29
  John 29
Ferguson/Fergason, Johnson 134
Few, Benjamin 113
Fickling, Samuel 62
Fike, Nathan 6
Filpot, Thomas 111
Finch, Ballard 116, 135
  Edward 12, 21, 26, 33, 50, 52, 63, 82, 87,
    88, 90, 92, 97, 99, 102, 104, 105, 110,
    111, 113, 116, 117, 119, 123, 126,
    129-131, 134-136, 142, 143
  Elizabeth 132
  Martha 135

(Finch), William 44, 53, 90, 92, 111, 130, 132, 133, 143
Fincher, John 145, 146
Fish, Ann 34
  John 34
  Joseph 2, 34, 73
  Josiah 23
  Wm 130
Fisher, Ferdinand 11
  Joseph 67, 68
Fither, Ferdinand 11
Fitts, Andrew 149
Flanagan, Bartholomew 37
Flannagan, Reuben 58, 125
Flannegan, Abilah 125
Flannigan, Reuben 95
Fletchall, Thomas 152
Flick, Johannes 155
Floyd, John 58
Folk, John 100
Follmer, John 8, 35
Follmore, John 35
Folmar, John 4
Folmer, Jcaob 83
Fooshe/e, Nathaniel 17, 43, 114
Foote, John 73
Ford, Elisha 48, 89, 91, 99, 101, 103, 108, 113, 118, 130, 145, 147, 159, 160
  James 13
  John 97
  Samuel 119, 153
Foshee, Nathaniel 37, 65
Foster, 98
Fouser, George 142
Fowler, Maurice 145
  Morris 145
Fraer, Alexander 76
Fraser, Frederick 137, 138
Frayser, Alexr 75
Frederick, Jacob 71
Freeman, Joseph 4, 53, 58, 81, 134, 136, 149
  Wm 4
Freneau, Peter 86, 131, 148, 160
Freshley, George 17
Frew, Charles 11
Frick, Martin 78
Frost, Jacob 105, 130
  Mary 28, 113
Fulehener, Benjamin 109
Fulk, Conrad 29
  Jacob 83
Fullerton, Jeane 69
Furger, Jacob 2, 23, 143
Furlow, William 4, 75
Furman, Thomas W. 113
Furnace, Mary 109
Furnas, John 28, 69, 131, 152
  Joseph 69, 113

  Sally 113
Furnis, Esther 63
  Joseph 63
  Thos W. 69
Gaillard, Tacitus 107
Gallman, Casper 12
  Conrad 4, 5
  Gosper 4, 12
  Henry 4, 5, 12
  Herman 5
  John 4
  John Conrad 4
Gambill, Alexander 57
Gant, John 3, 70
Ganter, Michael 91
Garratt, John 48
Garrett, Ann 160
  Asa 160
  John 53, 65, 89
  Thomas 160
Garriott, Ignatius 140
  John 140
Garrot, John 20
  Susannah 20
Gartman, Cateran 7, 21
  Daniel 7, 21
  George 10
Garvin, John 128, 150
Garvis, John 119, 120
Gary, Charles 28, 57, 99, 104
  Hannah 104
  Jesse 146
  John 18, 28, 31, 34, 57, 89, 104
  Thomas 31, 104, 146
  William 28, 57, 72, 104, 146
Gates, Josiah 147
Gaunt, Abigail 159
  Abijah 103
  Hannah 78
  Israel 21, 40, 62, 78, 97, 129
  James 129
  Joseph 97
  Mary 91
  Nebo 74, 91, 159
  Samuel 74, 91, 159
  Sarah 159
  Zebulon 91
  Zimri 91
Gaurtman, Bartholomew 51
  Daniel 7
Geary, William 33
Geiger, Herman 7, 15, 21
  Hermand 7
  Hermond 7, 21
George, David 51
  Sarah 51
Geril, Mary 13, 14
  Thomas 13
Gervais, J. L. 76

Gibbs, Howell 49
  John 49
Gibson, Ann 38
  Feby 106
  George 16, 118
  Gilbert 118
  Jane 16
  Richard 118
  Selthy 118
  Thomas 13, 14, 38, 104
Gilbert, Caleb 44, 49, 55, 63
  Cary 63, 129
  Hanamell 63
  Jonathan 39, 49, 82, 95, 130
  Jonothan 63
Gilder, Gilbert 27, 50, 103, 104
  Isaac 104
  Jacob 10, 50, 58
  Lucrease/Lucresa 50
  Reubin 31
Gill, Hanah/Hannah 60, 61
  Thomas 60, 61
Gillam, Harris 17, 22, 40, 148
  Joshua 160
  Martha 160
  Mary 136, 160
  Robert 21, 26, 53, 54, 56, 58, 64, 133,
    136, 139, 144, 149, 150, 154, 157, 159,
    160
Gilleland, William 159
Gillem, William 7
Gilliam, 122
  Charles 40
  Harris 88
  Mary 134
  Robert 81, 87, 88, 92, 97, 103, 108, 110,
    116, 120-122, 128, 134-136, 138, 140
  William 91
Gilliland 78
  William 22, 44, 159
Gillum, Charles 144
  Robert 145, 145
  William 6, 7
Gilreath, William 53
Glasgow, John 19
  Robert 19
Glass, Henry 109
Glassgow, Robt 65
Glazier, A. 133
  Adam 15, 40, 97, 111, 142, 160
  M. 1, 25
Glen, David 109
Glenn, Alexander 134, 151
  David 129
  John 156
  Rosannah 8
  William 140
Glover, Frederick 148
  John 133, 135, 136, 149

Glymph, John 117
Glyn/n, 70
  Daniel 109
  David 8, 110, 113
  George 12
  Jacob 67
  John 82
  Rosanah 20, 84, 128
  Rose 28
Godfrey, Hannah 14
  John 14, 97
  Margaret 14
  Mary 14
  Sarah 14
Goggans, Abraham 147
  Betty 147
  Daniel 45, 148
  George 5, 36, 41, 42, 45, 58, 72, 96-98,
    138, 142, 144, 147
  James 34, 36, 58, 72, 96, 99, 138, 142,
    147
  Johnston 147
  Mary 99, 147
  Nancy 147
  Nimrod 142
  Rachel 72, 106, 147
  Thomas 147
  William 72, 101, 102, 106, 140, 141, 147
Goggins, George 99
Gold, William 102
Golden, James 109
  Thomas 148, 149, 154
  William 16
Golding, John 54, 108
  Reuben 22
  Richard 54
Goodin, Abraham 45
  John 45
Goodman, James 31, 55, 65, 81, 133
  Joseph 32, 56, 71, 72, 97, 103, 108, 119,
    122
  Samuel 17, 81
  Timothy 63, 126
  Walter 110, 134
Goodwin, John 34
Gordan, Eli 69, 70
  Jessee 69, 70
Gordon, 41
  Benjamin 12, 109
  Elizabeth 22, 37, 69, 70, 111
  George 70, 111, 117, 152
  Govin 10
  Jesse 32, 53
  John 16, 70, 109
  Mary 53
  Thomas 5, 8, 10, 16, 22, 25, 32, 37, 53,
    64, 69, 70, 77, 78, 84, 92, 97, 109, 111,
    117, 152
  William 31

Gordy, Robert 156
Gore, Catharine 155
  Charity 126
  Clement 39, 45, 93
  Daniel 9
  Edward 25
  John 134
  Michael 149, 154, 155
Goree, Daniel 17
  Josiah 124
Gorie, John 128-130
Gorre, Daniel 9
Gorree, Claudes 22
  John 91
Gorrey, Josiah 134
Gotsman, John 134
Goudey/Goudy, Robert 35, 66
Gould, William 102
Gow, John 110
Gowin, John 118
Graff, Henry 24
Graham -- see also Grayham 43, 76
  George 12, 79
  James 41, 79
  Joseph 59
  Mary 79
  William 154
Grant, Isaac 21, 43, 145
Grasty, John 23, 24, 32, 78, 110
  Marshall 24
  Martha 128
  Sarshel 32
  Thomas 32, 78
Gray, 124
  Abraham 25, 52, 53, 56, 58, 89, 123
  Ann 89
  Casper 23, 37
  Cloye 160
  Frederick 16, 41, 160
  George 20, 27, 37, 84
  Mary (Pennington) 58
  Mary 29
  William 19, 27, 53, 64, 65, 87, 106, 107,
    128, 129, 145
Grayham 88
  George 97, 104
  James 7, 111, 113, 116
  John 23, 82
  Joseph 59
  William 154
Green, Edward 8, 9
  John 8, 9, 15, 17, 73, 110, 134
  Miltret (Liles) 8, 9
  Sarah 17
  Thomas 17, 35, 66, 9, 108
  William 8, 9, 108
Greenwood, William 137
Gregg, Elizabeth 30
  Hugh 30

Gregory, Benjamin 3
Greh[?], George 37
Grey 15
  William 151
Griffen-- see also Griffin
Griffen, Charles 153, 154
  James 153
  Merah[?] 153
  Oratio 144
(Griffen), William 145
Griffeth, Josiah 142

Griffin, Charles 28, 77, 155
  Horatio 35, 100, 158
  James 73, 119
  John 35, 63, 70, 155
  Jones 35
  Joseph 63
  Mary 63
  Patsey 100
  Timothy 26
  William 119, 153, 157
Griggs, John 89
Grim, Peter 3
Grober, Philip 7
Groener, Anna Barbara 149
Gromer, Anna Barbara 149
  Michal 2
Grown, Robert 88
Gruber, Philip 8
Guerard, Benj'a 76
Guilder, Jacob 106, 107
Guinger[?], Adam 83
Gullen, Daniel 38
Gullick, Daniel 38, 60
Guy, William 46, 126
Habold, Henry 83
Hair, John 2
  Mathias 87
Hall, Doctor 66
  Ger. 154
  James 133, 137
  Mathew 68, 133, 135
  Thomas 133
  W. 113
Hallor, John 14
Halman, Jacob 96
Ham, Avarilla 61
  James 61
  Jeremiah 10, 21, 61
  William 21, 61, 158
Hambleton, William 82
Hamilton 33
  James 23
  John 51, 152
  Thomas 11, 23, 41, 51
  William 11, 21, 23, 41, 87, 102, 143
Hamiter, Ann Mary 100
  George Simon 100

(Hamiter), Michael 99, 100
  Thomas 67, 100
Hammer, John 78
Hammilton, Thomas 12
Hampton 35
  Ann 80
  Benjamin 1, 11, 12, 64, 80, 96, 97, 135,
    143
  John 8, 13, 18, 35, 36, 42, 83, 84, 88, 98,
    120, 122, 124, 128, 132, 141, 144
  Joice 122, 132
  Joseph 12, 33, 34, 50, 63, 67, 82, 105,
    143
  Rachel 63, 105
  Richard 141
  Thomas 63
Hamton, Benj'n 1
  Thomas 73
Hancock, 51, 89
  Barber 24, 51
  Barbery 37
  Betsey 31
  Elizabeth 21
  Richard 31, 51
  W. 7
  William 21, 31, 65
Hanes, Samuel 17
Hanie, Maxamillion 129
Hannah, Robert 86
Harbert, Geo. 112, 131
  John 134
  Lydia 134
  Thomas 45
  Walter 43
Harbison, Margaret 60
Harden, Elizabeth 123, 124
Hardman, Ulrick 70
  Uriah 132, 133
Hardwick, W. 5
Hardy, Christopher 26
  Freeman 110
  James 110
  Jean 26
  Thomas 22, 110
Hare, Peter 152
Harleston, John 75
Harman, John Larance 153
  John Lenard 153
  Mary 153
Harp, Henry 125
  James 159
  Sarah 125
Harper, Robert G. 101
Harr, Peter 20
Harrell, Jacob 61
Harrington, Fanny 158
  Frances 157, 158
  John 157, 158
  Sephthah 158

Harris, Berry 22
  Little B. 43
  Little Berry 40
  Littleberry B. 144
  Nathaniel 59, 88, 107
  Natt 59
  Samuel 22, 40, 65, 144
  William 7
Harrison, Micajah 82
Harvey, Charles 81
Hasel/l, Henry 135, 154
Haskett, Thomas 39, 129
Haskit, Thomas 160
Hassell, Henry 146
Hatcher, Linney 102
  Seth 30, 102
Hauberd, Jacob 88
Hauk, Martin 152
Havard, Henry 18, 19
Hawkins, Peter 33, 143, 144
  Susanah 17
Hayes, Robert 34
Haygood, Johnson 101
Haynie, Charles Maximilian 30
  Maximilian 11, 30
  Nancy (Rutherford) 30
Hays, Jo. 148
  John 131
  Joseph 22, 81
Hayworth, Nathaniel 37
Hazlehurst, Rob't 76
Head, James 124
  John 124
Heath, John 145
Heaton, Benjamin 48, 49
Heer, Mathias 87
Heir, Anna Mary (Boushard) 87
  Mathias 87
  Peter 87
Hemeter, 78
Hencock, Barber 110, 129
  Clemmon 73
  William 65, 72, 144
Henderson, John 71
  Nathaniel 78
Hendricks, Henry 79
  Jabesh 74
  William 46
Hendrickson, Henry 14
Hendrix, William 94, 104
Henning, D. 67
  Daniel 61, 105
Henry, Hugh 4
Henson, William 31, 32
Herbert, Thomas 128
  Walter 30
Herbison, Margaret 38
Herndon, Benjamin 92
  Joseph 85, 92

Herp, Henry 125
Herring, Delilah 11
  William 11
Herriott, William 135
Hertel, George 101
Hewster[?], John 124
Hewston, John 106
  William 106
Heyet[?], Franz 73
Heyward, Hannah 76
Hicks, Tobias 109
Hidle, Martin 88
  Mary Ann (Seaman) 88
Hilburn, John 157
  Levi 157
  Robert 147, 157
  William 147, 157
Hill, Henry 94
  John 41, 45, 51, 110
  Thomas 22, 29, 37, 41, 45, 51, 110
  William 9, 41
Hillburn, William 69
Hiller?, Adam George 15
Hillin, James 38, 39
  Kesiah/Keziah 38
  Nathaniel 38, 39
Hiot, Francis 72
Hipp, Andrew 150
  John 141, 150, 152
Hoffman, Jacob 40
Hoffmaster, William 127
Hogg, Elisabeth 152
  James 39, 70
  John 8, 13, 48, 58, 73, 110, 152
  Joseph 8, 13, 132
  Lewis 18, 50, 61, 80
  Mary (Horsey) 93
  Sarah 56, 59, 73
Holcomb, Jonathan 23
Holliday, William 9
Hollingsworth, Susanah 105-107
Hollowback, Martin 152
Holman, Christian 5
  John 5
Holmes, John Bee 74
Holson, Stephen 18, 19
Holt, Beveley 43
Holtz, Leonard/Leanard 72
Hood, Jane 23
  Martha 119
Hoofman, 69
Hooper, George 76
Hope, John 11
Hopkins, Thomas 129, 130
Hopton, William 111, 112
Hord, James 5, 23
Horning, Catherina 141
  Elizabeth Catherina 141
  John 140, 141

Horsey, Abel Jones 93
  Daniel 10, 34, 41, 50, 58, 62, 82, 93, 94,
    119, 131, 133
  Isaac 34
  Mary (Hogg) 93
  Sarah 56, 58, 59, 82, 93, 131
  Thomas 15
Houber, Jacob 88
Houbert, Jacob 88
Houseal, John 127, 149
  John Adam 149
  John William 7
  Willia 101
  William 14, 41, 62, 87, 94, 101, 124,
    141-143
Hovacre, Jacob 29
Howell, Francis 96
  John 16
  William 16
Hubern, Jacob 160
Hudgens, John 71
Hudgins, John 55
Hudson, Tabitha 71
Huet, Francis 24
Huffman, 146
  Jacob 73, 81, 126
Huffmaster, William 127
Huger, B. 76
  Daniel 76
  Genl 84
Hughes, George 4, 79
  James 150
Hughins, Richard 90
Hughs, George 150
  George White 150
  John 150
Huiet, Cristena (Shoemaker) 83
  Jacob 84
Huit, Christine (Shoemaker) 84
  Francis 74, 83
  Jacob 83, 84
Humphries-- see Umphries
Hunt, Elizabeth 149
  Ralph 42, 43
Hunter, Andrew 49, 98, 109
  George 112
  John 33, 60, 69, 77, 121
  Susana 69
  Wm. 119, 121
Hushington, Joseph 61
Huston, John 39, 42
  Margaret 106, 107
Hutchison, John 134
  Joseph 61
  William 5, 17, 29, 42
Ihly, John 62
Imick[?], Conrad 6
Imunick[sic], Conrad 90
Infinger, John George 7, 15, 21

Inman, Benjamin 7
  Jehu/e 37, 45, 67, 154
  Jemima 7
  Joshua 6, 7, 39, 45, 37
Insco, Abel 91, 113
  James 113
Ioor, George 75
Irby, Henritter 140
  William 5, 46, 79, 85-87, 97, 99, 102,
    119-121, 140
Isaacks, Samuel 50
Ium, Johan Jacob 152
Izard, Ralph 75
Jackson, John 1
  William 21, 32, 87
Jacobs, Benjamin 138
Jacobson, Geo 83
Jaims, Ann Margratha 117
James, Ann 116
  Elizabeth 87, 116
  John 87, 88, 116, 140
  Philip 78
Jay, David 130
  John 159
Jenkins, David 25, 43, 90
  Isaac 30
  Thos 40
  William 45
Jennings, Miles 79, 125, 156
Jinkins, Isaac 78, 79, 95
  Wm. 25
Johnson, 148
  Alexander 8
  Ann 24, 119
  Bartholomew 12, 18, 24, 99, 119, 120
  Cynthia 16
  Daniel 1, 8, 27, 44, 48, 59, 72, 119, 122,
    124, 147
  Elizabeth 24, 120
  George 8, 12, 18, 24, 52, 112
  James 16, 43, 45, 55, 137, 146
  Jane 18
  Jean/e 12, 99
  Jessee 71
  John 28, 67, 123, 146, 150, 159
  Levi 12, 18
  Michael 28, 150
  Peggy 43
  Rachel 45
  Robert 1, 72, 73, 99, 117, 138, 156, 159
  Thomas 122
  William 33, 34, 99, 156
Johnston, Alexander 8, 17, 36, 64, 65, 70,
    132
  Andrew 98
  Anne 1
  Bartholomew 1, 80, 99, 112
  Burr 6
  Daniel 1, 34, 80, 99, 101, 102, 119, 132

  David 140, 141
  David 36
  Elizabeth 22, 77, 81, 136
  James 19, 28, 36, 57, 86, 98, 101, 102,
    118, 124
  Jehu/e 34, 101
  Jenett 70
  John 17, 20, 31, 36, 52, 64, 70, 73, 89,
    94, 98, 101, 102, 108, 109, 113, 136,
    139, 152
  Levi 18
  Margret 31
  Mary 1
  Michael 20, 28, 42
  Rob't 61
  Robert 1, 45, 58, 63, 70, 107, 136, 140,
    152
  Sarah 124
  Thomas 1, 11, 34, 36, 77, 101, 102, 138,
    152
  William 1, 17, 31, 33, 34, 36, 52, 57, 63,
    70, 73, 109, 113, 143
Jones 4, 132
  Catharine 29, 36
  Charles 31
  Elizabeth 4
  Gibeon 35, 36, 42
  Gibson 36, 118
  Gideon 35
  Gray 143
  Hannah 118
  Jacob 26
  James 118
  John 36, 42, 53
  John Little 29
  Joseph 29
  Martha 31
  Marthy 78
  Mary 31, 42
  Reuben 17, 78
  Reubin 78
  Susannah 53
  Thomas 29, 34, 101
  Walles 35
  Wallice 100, 108
  Wallis 143, 144
  William 100, 113, 136
  Willis 144
Julian, Peter 32
Julien, Peter 85, 98, 103, 137, 143, 144,
    151, 152, 156, 158, 159
Julin, Peter 50, 96, 99, 100-102, 108, 123,
    126, 130, 131, 137
Kaller 23
Kallor, Wm[?] 2
Kapperman, Jacob 96
Karr, Peter 2, 6
Keary, Simon 16
Keating 76

176

Kebler, Johannes 142
  Michael 142
Kelch, Henry 82, 83
Keller, Adam 66, 67
  Adam George 7, 15, 21
  George Adam 21
  Johannes 5
Kelley, Edward 24, 109, 116, 123, 129
  James 17, 26, 130
  John 17
  Joseph 143
  Mary 109
  Richard 17
  Samuel 38, 118, 125
Kelly 124
  Edmund 130
  Edward 92, 98, 123
  H. 97
  Hannah 125
  Jacob 100
  James 15, 31, 73, 130, 134
  John 103, 131, 141, 147, 154-156
  Joseph 139
  Mary 141
  N. 53, 98
  Rich'd 21
  Robert 154
  Samuel 91, 101, 103, 109, 117, 118, 125,
    131, 141, 148, 149, 154-156
  Stephen 143
  William 69, 70, 104
Kenady, James 65, 80, 160
Kenemore, Mich'l 25
Kennada 44
Kennady, James 135
Kennamore, Michal 3
Kennedy, 48
  James 135
  Robert 109, 135
Kennerly, Joseph 4, 92, 93
Kerby, Jesse 155
  Mary 155
Kerr, Peter 125
Kershaw, John 91
Kessissen, Eva Cathrine 60
Ketchener, Benjamin 8
Ketinger, Fight 4
Keuhn[?], Hans Jacob 70
Key, Melcom 119
Keysirin, Eve Catherine 38
Kibler-- see also Kebler
Kibler, Michael 101
Killard, Joseph 11
Killer, Adam 67
  Mary 67
Killpatrick 87
  Jane 19
  Marthew 19
  William 19

Kilpatrick, Marthew 19
  William 19, 89
Kinard, John 83, 127, 129, 160
  Matthias 15
  Michael 153
Kiner, John 160
King, Charity (Pennington) 12, 35, 85
  Charity 12, 114, 115
  Charles 12, 25, 26, 31-33, 35, 50, 52, 55,
    63, 77, 82, 85, 89, 95, 105, 114, 115,
    140
  Elizabeth 44, 88
  George 144
  Isaac 68
  Jacob 88, 93, 98, 119
  Joseph 44, 51, 55, 101
  Penington 32, 88, 93, 98
Kippleman, Jacob 152
Kirkland, Moses 31, 56, 57, 95, 140, 146,
  152
Knox, John 1, 17
Koon, Henry 100
  Ulrick 83
Koone, Benedick 52, 100
  Christiana 100
  George 100
Kounts, John 88
Kountz, Henry 153
  Mary Elizabeth 153
Krand[?], John 30
  Rosena (Black) 30
Krausse, Christopher 28
Kreps, Andrew 147
Kriser, Christopher 67
Kroomer, Christiana Barbara (Priester) 96
Krouse, Francis 96
Kubler, John 141
  Michael 141
Kuhn, Johann 98
  Ulrich 83
Lagrone, John 124
  John Jacob 124
  Tobias 124
Lagrown, Adam 142, 143
  Laurence 124
Lake, Absolom 93
  Daniel 10
  David 10, 129
  John 84, 110
  Joseph 129
  Thomas 11, 24, 31, 84, 129
Lane, Edw'd 62
  Long 102
  Maryann 34
Lang, John 1
  Maria Cathrina/ena 2
  Robert 107
Langford, Eli 31
  Jacob 100

Livingston, Barnard 37
  John 37
  Michael 94
  William 75
Liviston/e, Martin 142
  Michael 7
  Rosina 7
Lockey 76
Loften, John 18, 39
  William 44
Loftin, Thomas 56
Loftis, Job 121
Lofton, John 57, 160
  Thomas 160
  Wm 48
Logan, George 131
  William 150
Lomanick, Mary 153
  Michael 66, 67
Lonam, Samuel 27, 50, 58
Loner, Anna Barbara 149
  John 141
Long, Benjamin 72, 77, 85, 86, 99, 103,
    118, 141
  Catherine 98
  Elizabeth 99
  George 14, 98, 100
  Jacob 14
  Michal 14
  Precilla 99
  Priscilla 141
  William Henry 99
Longen[?], Catherina 98
Longshear, Euclidus 49
Longshore, Euclidus 45
  Robert 155, 159
Loocock, Aron 131
Loston, Joseph 71
Love, Isaac 49
  Mark 56, 89, 92, 123
  Sarah 123
Lowery, James 137
Lowndes, Edw'd 137
  Rawlins 76
Lowry, Charles 55
  John 55
  Patrick 19, 20, 31, 43, 88, 106-108, 158
  Pt 65
Lucas, John 58
  Samuel 79
Lum, John 23, 127
  Margret 127
Luster, Abner 137
  Isaac 137
  James 137
Mabin, Mathew 83
Mabry, Joel 74
Mack, Adam 11, 81
  Mary 11

Stalem[?] 130
Mackey, Daniel 35
Mackleduff, Daniel 5
  Fenter 5
  John 5
  William 5
MaclDuff, Daniel 79
  Ruth (Lewallen) 79
Macoy, John 122
Maffit, James 106
  William 106
Majors, Sarah 54
Maldin, William 115
Malone, John 1, 90, 122, 124, 132
  Sarah 80
  W. 8, 11, 12, 18, 34, 35, 52, 63, 90, 94,
    99, 115, 120, 124
  William 1, 24, 27, 61, 68, 80, 81, 91, 107,
    110, 129, 130
Mangrum, John 81
Mangum/Mangrum, William 77
Manning, Adam 50
  Levi 38, 62, 124
  Rosanah 62
Mansel, Richard 117
Mantz, Barnard 72, 83, 101
  George 83
Marpole, 160
Marr, Ambrus 76
Mars, Robert 1, 111, 136
Marshal, Hugh 123
Marshall, James 142
  Samuel 123
Marshell, Hugh 89
Martin, Ann 62
  David 20, 27, 62, 113, 114, 136, 137
  Edmond/Edmund 2, 4, 92, 110, 111, 122
  George 114, 126, 127
  James 37, 75
  John 37, 75, 110, 111
  Martha 136
  Samuel 145, 158
  Sarah 127
  William 148
Maskill, Richard 60
Mason, Cha's 47
  James 4
Mathews, Thomas 158
Mathis, Jenet 126
  Thomas 10, 27, 30, 53
Matts, Charles 15
  Henry 15
Maty, Charles 7
Maverick, S. 69
Maxedon, John 98
Maxidon, John 41
Maxwell, John 40, 160
Mayer--see also Meyer, Miers, Myers,
    and Moyer

179

(Mills), Isaac 21, 35, 85
  John 10, 20, 21, 55, 109
  Mary 10, 21
  Rebecah/ca 10, 134
  Robert 21, 129, 130
  Thomas 21, 159
  William 10, 21, 61, 129, 130
Minck, John 41
Mink, John 144
Minnick, John Adam 142
Mintz, Michael 30, 152
Mires, Woldrick 144
Mitchel/l, Ephraim 125
  Isaac 87, 118, 120, 136, 157
  Isham 135
  Johannes Andrews 141
  John 16, 22, 37, 53
  John B. 86, 87
  Thomas 157
Mitsher, Henry 74
Mitsker, Henry 83
Mobbley, Eliz'r 9
Mobley, Eleazir/Elizer 9
Mock, Adam 15
Money, Joseph 118
Monk, John 22
Montgomeries, John 68
Montgomery, Ann 1
  Elizabeth 70, 110
  George 1, 11, 13, 14, 17, 97, 110, 129
  George S[?] 11
  Thomas 135, 138
Mooney, Joseph 55
Moore, Benjamin 107, 108, 142
  John 60
  Robert 20, 32, 84, 132
  Robert William 84
  William 27, 59, 106
Moorhead, James 62
More, Robert 20, 25, 27, 44
  William 20
Morehead, James 86, 96, 98, 137
Morff, Hans Jacob 7, 21
Morgan, Ann 9, 10
  Diana/na 64, 98
  Isaac 9, 10, 41, 47, 74, 82, 101
  Isobel 13
  James 117
  John 126
  Joshua 64
  Melon 126
  Thomas 13, 119, 126
  William 124
Morgin, Isabell 13
  Reuben 84
  Thomas 13
Morras, Samuel 153
Morrel, Jurdon 84
Morris, John 17, 134

Nimrod 7
  Richard 54
  Samuel 130, 137
Morriss, Mary 43
  Samuel 68
Morrow, William 139
Mossaick, William 148
Mote, David 18, 19, 90
Motes, Audry 126
  Jonathan 125, 126
Mounts, George 84
Mountz, 127
  Barnet/t 20, 27
Mourer, Elizabeth Catherina 139
  Jacob 139
  Zetna[?] Reckana 139
  Zitna Reckana 139
Mouro, Daniel 64
Mouzon, Henry 75
Moyer, Benedick 83, 84
  Conrad/e 111, 112
  John 83, 84
Muffet, Samuel 142
Munford, John 140
Murdock, Hamilton 35, 60, 66, 141, 142, 156
  William 105, 106
Murfey, James 22, 30
Murff, Johannas 4
  John 7, 21
Murphey, James 82
Murphy, Edward 82
  James 53, 74, 82, 135
  Sarah 82
Murray, James 1, 117, 136, 152, 159
  John 36
  Samuel 1, 117, 136, 152, 153, 159
  William 1, 28, 117, 136
Murry, Samuel 152
Musgrove, Carolina 38
  Edward 143
  John 35, 38, 49, 50, 100, 144
  Mary 38
  Smith 123
  William 38, 108, 123
Myer, Conrad 127
  Ulrick 78
Myers, Andreas 100
Nance, Frederick 74, 90, 113, 161
Neail, James 16
  Jonathan 139
  Lewis 139
Neal, Charles 34
Neece, Boltus 86
  Doroty 86
Neel, Robert 131
  William 145
Neelly, John 36
  see also Neely

189

(Wilson), James 3, 18, 57, 59, 80, 126, 150
  Jane 67
  Jean 126
  Jehu 17
  Jesse 96, 140
  John 27, 40, 66, 67, 96, 103, 104, 125,
    131, 132
  L. 136
  Mary 107
  Mathew 80
  Robert 112, 122, 123, 136
  Russell 140
  Samuel 1, 8, 119, 124
  T. 88
  William 14, 43, 63, 67, 86, 88, 102, 105,
    112, 129, 151, 152, 159
  Wilmoth 95
Win, John 1
Winchester, Comfort (Stephens) (Polson)
  54
  Daniel 44, 54, 81, 102, 103
  Joseph 103
  Willeby 81
  William 54, 64, 77, 81, 97, 102, 148
Windel, John 107
  Susanna (Dewalt) 37
Windle, John 27, 107
  Susanna 37
Wingard, Michael 11
Wingart, Mary 81
  Michael 81, 130, 147
Winn -- see Win
Wiott, Elender 40
  Isum 40
  Nelly 40
  Solomon 40
Wise, Nicholas 37, 124
Wiseman, Agness 15
  Hugh 15, 36
  Nancy 15
  Robert 14
Witt, Francis 142
Woddrop, John 147
Wollerton, Zeniah 138
Wood, Benjamin 118
  John 143
  Jonathan 69
  Judith 118
  Samuel 143
  Thomas 2, 23, 143, 149
Woodall, John 51, 89
  Joseph 51
  William 19, 51, 52, 88
Worthington, Benjamin 66, 137
  E. 136
  John 136, 137
  Rachel 69
Wright-- see also Right
  Abraham 14, 151

Charity 84
James 99, 154
Jemima 102
John 18, 85, 99, 102, 129
Joseph 18, 19, 84, 85
Rebecca 154
William 18
Wyly 66
Yancey, James 77
Yates, Thos 39
Yeargain, Andrew 25, 52
Yone, Margret 152
Youn, Georg Adam 67
Young, Elizabeth 29
  Henry 93
  James 2, 14, 61, 119, 125
  William 16, 29, 41, 61, 119
Younghusband 116
  John 115, 125
Zeigler, Nicholas 83
Zigler, Hans Adam 83
Zuber, Conrad 25
  Leonard 47
  Michael 47

(Slave), Abina 131
  Abraham 62
  Abram 128, 131, 149
  Adam 144
  Affrica 146
  Agg 128
  Alie 145
  Ambrose 131
  Amey 71
  Amy Frank 131
  Annaky 57
  Annica 144
  Anthony 144
  Aron 145
  Arther 110
  Bash 13
  Beckah 99
  Ben 145, 154
  Benjamin 131
  Bett 13,,38, 93, 120, 121
  Betty 13, 14, 56, 88
  Big Lucy 131
  Bill 154
  Bond 145
  Braset[?] 131
  Buck 13
  Carolina 4, 62, 71
  Cate 77
  Catoe[?] 88
  Cesar 120
  Champ 64, 90, 128
  Charles 78, 116, 131, 145
  Charlotte 85
  Chloe 120, 121, 154

Heritage Books by Brent H. Holcomb:

Ancestors and Descendants of Charles Humphries (d. 1837)
of Union District, South Carolina, 1677–1984

Bute County, North Carolina, Land Grant Plats and Land Entries

CD: Early Records of Fishing Creek Presbyterian Church,
Chester County, South Carolina, 1799–1859

CD: Kershaw County, South Carolina, Minutes of the County Court, 1791–1799

CD: Marriage and Death Notices from The Charleston [S.C.] Observer, *1827–1845*

CD: South Carolina, Volume 1

CD: Winton (Barnwell) County, South Carolina Minutes of
County Court and Will Book 1, 1785–1791

Chester County, South Carolina, Deed Abstracts,
Volume I: 1785–1799 [1768–1799] Deed Book A-F

Chester County, South Carolina, Will Abstracts: 1787–1838 [1776–1838]

Death and Marriage Notices from the Watchman *and* Observer, *1845–1855*

Early Records of Fishing Creek Presbyterian Church, Chester County,
South Carolina, 1799–1859, with Appendices of the Visitation List of
Rev. John Simpson, 1774–1776 and the Cemetery Roster, 1762–1979
Brent H. Holcomb and Elmer O. Parker

Guide to South Carolina Genealogical Research and Records, Revised

Jackson of North Pacolet: Descendants of Samuel Jackson, Sr.

Kershaw County, South Carolina, Minutes of the County Court, 1791–1799

Laurens County, South Carolina, Minutes of the County Court, 1786–1789

Marriage and Death Notices from Columbia, South Carolina Newspapers, 1838–1860;
Including Legal Notices from Burnt Counties

Marriage and Death Notices from Baptist Newspapers of South Carolina, 1835–1865

Marriage and Death Notices from The Charleston Observer, *1827–1845*

Marriage and Death Notices from the
Charleston, South Carolina, Mercury, *1822–1832*

Marriage and Death Notices from the Southern Presbyterian:
Volume I: 1847–1865
Volume II: 1865–1879
Volume III: 1880–1891
Volume IV: 1892–1908

Marriage and Death Notices from the Up-Country of South Carolina
as Taken from Greenville Newspapers, 1826–1863

Memorialized Records of Lexington District, South Carolina, 1814–1825

Newberry County, South Carolina Deed Abstracts,
Volume I: Deed Books A-B, 1785–1794 [1751–1794]

Newberry County, South Carolina Deed Abstracts,
Volume II: Deed Books C, D-2, and D, 1794–1800 [1765–1800]

Newberry County, South Carolina Deed Abstracts,
Volume III: Deed Books E Through H, 1786–1787

www.ingramcontent.com/pod-product-compliance
Lightning Source LLC
Chambersburg PA
CBHW061735270326
41928CB00011B/2243